TEN

SERMONS OF RELIGION,

BY

THEODORE PARKER,

MINISTER OF THE TWENTY-EIGHTH CONGREGATIONAL CHURCH, IN BOSTON.

SECOND EDITION.

BOSTON:
TICKNOR AND FIELDS.
M DCCC LXI.

Entered according to Act of Congress, in the year 1852, by

THEODORE PARKER,

in the Clerk's Office of the District Court of the District of Massachusetts.

TO

RALPH WALDO EMERSON,

WITH ADMIRATION FOR HIS GENIUS,

AND WITH KINDLY AFFECTION FOR WHAT IN HIM IS FAR NOBLER THAN GENIUS,

THIS VOLUME IS DEDICATED

BY HIS FRIEND,

THEODORE PARKER.

PREFACE.

I HAVE often been asked by personal friends to publish a little volume of Sermons of Religion, which might come home to their business and bosoms in the joys and sorrows of their daily life. And nothing loth to do so without prompting, I have selected these which were originally part of a much longer course, and send them out, wishing that they may be serviceable in promoting the religious welfare of mankind on both sides of the ocean. They are not Occasional Sermons, like most of those I have lately published, which heavy emergencies pressed out of me; but they have all, perhaps, caught a tinge from the events of the day when they were preached at first. For as a country girl makes her festal wreath of such blossoms as the fields offer at the time, — of violets and wind-flowers in the spring, of roses and water-lilies in summer, and in autumn of the fringed gentian and the aster, — so must it be with the sermons which a minister gathers up under serene or stormy skies. This local coloring from time and circumstances I am not desirous to wipe off; so the sad or joyous aspect of the day will be found still tinging these printed

Sermons, as indeed it colored the faces and tinged the prayers of such as heard them first.

Sometimes the reader will find the same fundamental idea reappearing under various forms, in several places of this book; and may perhaps also see the reason thereof in the fact, that it is the primeval Rock on which the whole thing rests, and of necessity touches the heavens in the highest mountains, and, receiving thence, gives water to the deepest wells which bottom thereon.

I believe there are great Truths in this book, — both those of a purely intellectual character, and those, much more important, which belong to other faculties nobler than the mere intellect; truths, also, which men need, and, as I think, at this time greatly need. But I fear that I have not the artistic skill so to present these needful truths that a large body of men shall speedily welcome them; perhaps not the attractive voice which can win its way through the commercial, political, and ecclesiastical noises of the time, and reach the ears of any multitude.

Errors there must be also in this book. I wish they might be flailed out and blown away; and shall not complain if it be done even by a rough wind, so that the precious Truths be left unbroke and clean after this winnowing, as bread-stuff for to-day, or as seed-corn for seasons yet to come.

August 24th, 1852.

CONTENTS.

SERMONS.

I.

OF PIETY, AND THE RELATION THEREOF TO MANLY LIFE.

THOU SHALT LOVE THE LORD THY GOD WITH ALL THY HEART, AND WITH ALL THY SOUL, AND WITH ALL THY MIND. — Matt. xxii. 37.

THERE are two things requisite for complete and perfect religion, — the love of God and the love of man; one I will call Piety, the other Goodness. In their natural development they are not so sharply separated as this language would seem to imply; for piety and goodness run into one another, so that you cannot tell where one begins and the other ends. But I will distinguish the two by their centre, where they are most unlike; not by their circumference, where they meet and mingle.

The part of man which is not body I will call the Spirit; under that term including all the faculties not sensual. Let me, for convenience' sake, distribute these faculties of the human spirit into four classes: the intellectual,—including the æsthetic,—moral, affectional, and religious. Let Mind be the name of the intellectual faculty,—including the threefold mental powers, reason, imagination, and understanding; Conscience shall be the short name for the moral, Heart for the affectional, and Soul for the religious faculties.

I shall take it for granted that the great work of mankind on earth is to live a manly life, to use, discipline, develop, and enjoy every limb of the body, every faculty of the spirit, each in its just proportion, all in their proper place, duly coördinating what is merely personal, and for the present time, with what is universal, and for ever. This being so, what place ought piety, the love of God, to hold in a manly life?

It seems to me, that piety lies at the basis of all manly excellence. It represents the universal action of man according to his nature. This universal action, the bent of the whole man in his normal direction, is the logical condition of any special action of man in a right direction, of any particular bent that way. If I have a universal idea of universal causality in my mind, I can then understand a special cause; but without that universal idea of causality in my mind, patent or latent, I could not understand any particular cause whatever. My eye might see the fact of a man cutting down a tree, but my mind would comprehend only the conjunction in time and space, not their connection in causality. If you have not a universal idea of beauty, you do not know that this is a handsome and that a homely dress; you notice only the form and color, the texture and the fit, but see no relation to an ideal loveliness. If you have not a universal idea of the true, the just, the holy, you do not comprehend the odds betwixt a correct statement and a lie, between the deed of the priest and that of the good Samaritan, between the fidelity of Jesus and the falseness of Iscariot. This rule runs through all human nature. The universal is the logical condition of the generic, the special, and the particular. So the love of God, the universal object of the human spirit, is the logical condition of all manly life.

This is clear, if you look at man acting in each of the four modes just spoken of, — intellectual, moral, affectional, and religious.

The Mind contemplates God as manifested in truth; for truth — in the wide meaning of the word including also a comprehension of the useful and the beautiful — is the universal category of intellectual cognition. To love God with the mind, is to love him as manifesting himself in the truth, or to the mind; it is to love truth, not for its uses, but for itself, because it is true, absolutely beautiful and lovely to the mind. In finite things we read the infinite truth, the absolute object of the mind.

Love of truth is a great intellectual excellence; but it is plain you must have the universal love of universal truth before you can have any special love for any particular truth whatsoever; for in all intellectual affairs the universal is the logical condition of the special.

Love of truth in general is the intellectual part of piety. We see at once that this lies at the basis of all intellectual excellence, — at love of truth in art, in science, in law, in common life. Without it you may love the convenience of truth in its various forms, useful or beautiful; but that is quite different from loving truth itself. You often find men who love the uses of truth, but not truth; they wish to have truth on their side, but not to be on the side of truth. When it does not serve their special and selfish turn, they are offended, and Peter breaks out with his "I know not the man," and "the wisest, brightest" proves also the "meanest of mankind."

The Conscience contemplates God as manifested in right, in justice; for right or justice is the universal category of moral cognition. To love God with the conscience, is to love him as manifested in right and justice; is to love right or justice, not for its convenience, its specific uses, but for itself, because it is absolutely beautiful and lovely to the conscience. In changeable things we read the unchanging and eternal right, which is the absolute object of conscience.

To love right is a great moral excellence; but it is plain you must have a universal love of universal right before you can have any special love of a particular right; for, in all moral affairs, the universal is the logical condition of the special.

The love of right is the moral part of piety. This lies at the basis of all moral excellence whatever. Without this you may love right for its uses; but if only so, it is not right you love, but only the convenience it may bring to you in your selfish schemes. None was so ready to draw the sword for Jesus, or look after the money spent upon him, as the disciple who straightway denied and betrayed him. Many wish right on their side, who take small heed to be on the side of right. You shall find men enough who seem to love right in general, because they clamor for a specific, particular right; but erelong it becomes plain they only love some limited or even personal convenience they hope therefrom. The people of the United States claim to love the unalienable right of man to life, liberty, and the pursuit of happiness. But the long-continued cry of three million slaves, groaning under the American yoke, shows beyond question or cavil that it is not the universal and unalienable right which they love, but only the selfish advantage it affords them. If you love the right as right, for itself, because it is absolutely just and beautiful to your conscience, then you will no more deprive another of it than submit yourself to be deprived thereof. Even the robber will fight for his own. The man who knows no better rests in the selfish love of the private use of a special right.

The Heart contemplates God as manifested in love, for love is the universal category of affectional cognition. To love God with the heart, is to love him as manifested in love; it is to love Love, not for its convenience, but for itself, because it is absolutely beautiful and lovely to the heart.

Here I need not reiterate what has already been twice said, of mind and of conscience.

Love of God as love, then, is the affectional part of piety, and lies at the basis of all affectional excellence. The mind and the conscience are content with ideas, with the true and the right, while the heart demands not ideas, but Beings, Persons; and loves them. It is one thing to desire the love of a person for your own use and convenience, and quite different to have your personal delight in him, and desire him to have his personal delight in you. From the nature of the case, as persons are concrete and finite, man never finds the complete satisfaction of his affectional nature in them, for no person is absolutely lovely, none the absolute object of the affections. But as the mind and conscience use the finite things to help learn infinite truth and infinite right, and ultimately rest in that as their absolute object, so our heart uses the finite persons whom we reciprocally love as golden letters in the book of life, whereby we learn the absolutely lovely, the infinite object of the heart. As the philosopher has the stars of heaven, each lovely in itself, whereby to learn the absolute truth of science, — as the moralist has the events of human history, each of great moment to mankind, whereby to learn the absolute right of ethics, — so the philanthropist has the special persons of his acquaintance, each one a joy to him, as the rounds of his Jacob's ladder whereby he goes journeying up to the absolutely lovely, the infinite object of the affections.

The Soul contemplates God as a being who unites all these various modes of action, as manifested in truth, in right, and in love. It apprehends him, not merely as absolute truth, absolute right, and absolute love alone, but as all these unified into one complete and perfect Being, the Infinite God. He is the absolute object of the soul, and corresponds thereto, as truth to the mind, as justice to the conscience, as love to the heart. He is to the soul absolutely true, just, and lovely, the altogether beautiful. To him the soul turns instinctively at first; then also, at length, with conscious and distinctive will.

The love of God in this fourfold way is the totality of piety, which comes from the normal use of all the faculties named before. Hence it appears that piety of this character lies at the basis of all manly excellence whatever, and is necessary to a complete and well-proportioned development of the faculties themselves.

There may be an unconscious piety: the man does not know that he loves universal truth, justice, love; loves God. He only thinks of the special truth, justice, and love, which he prizes. He does not reflect upon it; does not aim to love God in this way, yet does it, nevertheless. Many a philosopher has seemed without religion even to a careful observer; sometimes has passed for an atheist. Some of them have to themselves seemed without any religion, and have denied that there was any God. But all the while their nature was truer than their will; their instincts kept their personal wholeness better than they were aware. These men loved absolute truth, not for its uses, but for itself; they laid down their lives for it, rather than violate the integrity of their intellect. They had the intellectual love of God, though they knew it not; though they denied it. No man ever has a complete and perfect intellectual consciousness of all his active nature; something instinctive germinates in us, and grows under ground, as it were, before it bursts the sod and shoots into the light of self-consciousness. Sheathed in unconsciousness lies the bud, erelong to open a bright, consummate flower. These philosophers, with a real love of truth, and yet a scorn of the name of God, understand many things, perhaps, not known to common men, but this portion of their being has yet escaped their eye; they have not made an exact and exhaustive inventory of the facts of their own nature. Such men have unconsciously much of the intellectual part of piety.

Other men have loved justice, not for the personal convenience it offered to them, but for its own sake, because it married itself to their conscience, — have loved it with a disinterested, even a self-denying love, — who yet scorned religion, denied all consciousness of God, denied his providence, perhaps his existence, and would have resolved God into matter, and no more. Yet all the while in these men, dim and unconscious, there lay the religious element; neglected, unknown, it gave the man the very love of special justice which made him strong. He knew the absolutely just, but did not know it as God.

I have known philanthropists who undervalued piety; they liked it not, — they said it was moonlight, not broad day; it gave flashes of lightning, all of which would not make light. They professed no love of God, no knowledge thereof, while they had the strongest love of love; loved persons, not with a selfish, but a self-denying affection, ready to sacrifice themselves for the completeness of another man's delight. Yet underneath this philanthropy there lay the absolute and disinterested love of other men. They knew only the special form, not the universal substance thereof, — the particular love of Thomas or of Jane, not the universal love of the Infinite. They had the affectional form of piety, though they knew it not.

I have known a man full of admiration and of love for the universe, yet lacking consciousness of its Author. He loved the truth and beauty of the world, reverenced the justice of the universe, and was himself delighted at the love he saw pervading all and blessing all; yet he recognized no God, saw only a cosmic force, which was a power of truth and beauty to his mind, a power of justice to his conscience, and a power of love to his heart. He had not a philosophic consciousness of the deeper, nobler action which went on within him, building greater than he knew. But in him also there were the several parts of piety, only not joined into one total and integral act, and not distinctly known.

This unconsciousness of piety is natural with a child. In early life it is unavoidable; only now and then some rare and precious boy or girl opens from out its husk of unconsciousness his childish bud of faith, and blossoms right early with the consciousness of God, a "strong and flame-like flower." This instinctiveness of piety is the beauty of childhood, the morning-red widely and gorgeously diffused before the rising of the sun. But as a man becomes mature, adds reflection to instinct, transmutes sentiments into ideas, he should also become conscious of his religious action, of his love of God in this fourfold form; when he loves truth, justice, love, he should know that it is God he loves underneath these special forms, and should unite them all into one great act of total piety. As the state of self-consciousness is a more advanced state than unconsciousness; as the reflective reason of the man is above the unreflective instinct of the child;

so the man's conscious piety belongs to a higher stage of development, and is above the mere instinctive and unconscious piety of the girl. Accordingly, the philosopher who loved truth for its own sake, and with his mind denied in words the God of truth, was less a philosopher for not knowing that he loved God. He had less intellectual power because he was in an abnormal state of intellectual religious growth. The man who loved justice for its own sake, and would not for an empire do a conscious wrong, whom the popular hell could not scare, nor the popular heaven allure from right, — he had less power of justice for not knowing that in loving right he loved the God of right. That philanthropist who has such love of love, that he would lay down his life for men, is less a philanthropist, and has less affectional power, because he knows not that in his brave benevolence he loves the God of love. The man full of profound love of the universe, of reverence for its order, its beauty, its justice, and the love which fills the lily's cup with fragrant loveliness, who wonders at the mighty cosmic force he sees in these fractions of power, — he is less a man because he does not know it is God's world that he admires, reverences, and worships; aye, far less a man because he does not know he loves and worships God. When he becomes conscious of his own spiritual action, conscious of God, of loving God with mind and conscience, heart and soul, his special love will increase, he will see the defects there are in his piety; if it be disproportionate, through redundance here or failure there, he can correct the deformity and make his entire inner life harmonious, a well-proportioned whole. Then he feels that he goes in and out, continually, in the midst of the vast forces of the universe, which are only the forces of God; that in his studies, when he attains a truth, he confronts the thought of God; when he learns the right, he learns the will of God laid down as a rule of conduct for the universe; and when he feels disinterested love, he knows that he partakes the feeling of the infinite God. Then, when he reverences the mighty cosmic force, it is not a blind Fate in an atheistic or a pantheistic world, it is the Infinite God that he confronts, and feels, and knows. He is then mindful of the mind of God, conscious of God's conscience, sensible of God's sentiment, and his own existence is in the Infinite Being of God. Thus he joins into a whole integral state of piety the various parts developed by the several faculties; there is a new growth of each, a new development of all.

If these things be so, then it is plain what relation piety sustains to manly life; — it is the basis of all the higher excellence of man, and when the man is mature, what was instinctive at first becomes a state of conscious love of God.

Now, when this universal fourfold force is once developed and brought to consciousness, and the man has achieved something in this way, his piety may be left to take its natural form of expression, or it may be constrained to take a form not natural. Mankind has made many experiments upon piety; books of history are full of them. Most of these, as of all the experiments of man in progress, are failures. We aim many times before we hit the mark. The history of religion is not exceptional or peculiar in this respect. See how widely men experiment in agriculture, navigation, government, before they learn the one right way. The history of science is the history of mistakes. The history of religion and the history of astronomy are equally marked by error. It is not surprising that mistakes have been made in respect to the forms of piety after it is procured.

For there are various helps which are needful, and perhaps indispensable, in childhood, to the development of the love of God, but which are not needed after the religious character is somewhat mature. Then the man needs not those former outward helps; he has other aids suited to his greater strength. This is true of the individual, repeating no more the hymns of his nursery, — true also of mankind, that outgrows the sacrifices and the mythologies of the childhood of the world. Yet it is easy for human indolence to linger near these helps, and refuse to pass further on. So the unadventurous nomad in the Tartarian wild keeps his flock in the same close-cropped circle where they first learned to browse, while the progressive man roves ever forth "to fresh fields and pastures new." See how parents help develop the body of the child. The little boy is put into a standing-stool, or baby-jumper, till he learns to walk. By and by he has his hoop, his top, his ball; each in turn is laid aside. He has helps to develop his mind not less, — little puzzles, tempting him to contrive, — prints set off with staring colors; he has his alphabet of wooden letters, in due time his primer, his nursery rhymes, and books full of most wonderful impossibilities. He has his early reader, his first lessons in arithmetic, and so goes on with new helps proportionate to his strength. It is a long slope from counting the fingers up to calculating the orbit of a planet not yet seen. But the fingers and the solar system are alike helps to mathematic thought. When the boy is grown up to man's estate, his body vigorous and mature, he tries his strength in the natural work of society, is a merchant, a sailor, a mechanic, a farmer; he hews stones, or lifts up an axe upon the thick timber. For a long time his body grows stronger by his work, and he gets more skill. His body pays for itself, and refunds to mankind the cost of its training up. When his mind is mature, he applies that also to the various works of society, to transact private business, or manage the affairs of the public; for a long time his mind grows stronger, gaining new knowledge and increase of power. Thus his mind pays for its past culture, and earns its tuition as it goes along.

In this case the physical or mental power of the man assumes its natural form, and does its natural work. He has outgrown the things which pleased his childhood and informed his youth. Nobody thinks it necessary or beautiful for the accomplished scholar to go back to his alphabet, and repeat it over, to return to his early arithmetic and paradigms of grammar, when he knows them all; for this is not needful to keep an active mind in a normal condition, and perform the mental work of a mature man. Nobody sends a lumberer from the woods back to his nursery, or tells him he cannot keep his strength without daily or weekly sleeping in his little cradle, or exercising with the hoop, or top, or ball, which helped his babyhood. Because these little trifles sufficed once, they cannot help him now. Man, reaching forward, forgets the things that are behind.

Now the mischief is, that, in matters of religion, men demand that he who has a mature and well-proportioned piety should always go back to the rude helps of his boyhood, to the A B C of religion and the nursery books of piety. He is not bid to take his power of piety and apply that to the common works of life. The Newton of piety is sent back to the dame-school of religion, and told to keep counting his fingers, otherwise there is no health in him, and all piety is wiped out of his consciousness, and he hates God and God hates him. He must study the anicular lines on the school-dame's slate, not the diagrams of God writ on the heavens in points of fire. We are told that what once thus helped mould a religious character must be continually resorted to, and become the permanent form thereof.

This notion is exceedingly pernicious. It wastes the practical power of piety by directing it from its natural work; it keeps the steam-engine always fanning and blowing itself, perpetually firing itself up, while it turns no wheels but its own, and does no work but feed and fire itself. This constant firing up of one's self is looked on as the natural work and only form of piety. Ask any popular minister, in one of the predominant sects, for the man most marked for piety, and he will not show you the men with the power of business who do the work of life, — the upright mechanic, merchant, or farmer; not the men with the power of thought, of justice, or of love; not him whose whole life is one great act of fourfold piety. No, he will show you some men who are always a dawdling over their souls, going back to the baby-jumpers and nursery rhymes of their early days, and everlastingly coming to the church to fire themselves up, calling themselves "miserable offenders," and saying, "save us, good Lord." If a man thinks himself a miserable offender, let him away with the offence, and be done with the complaint at once and for ever. It is dangerous to reiterate so sad a cry.

You see this mistake, on a large scale, in the zeal with which nations or sects cling to their religious institutions long after they are obsolete. Thus the Hebrew cleaves to his ancient ritual and ancient creed, refusing to share the religious science which mankind has brought to light since Moses and Samuel went home to their God. The two great sects of Christendom exhibit the same thing in their adherence to ceremonies and opinions which once were the greatest helps and the highest expression of piety to mankind, but which have long since lost all virtue except as relics. The same error is repeated on a small scale all about us, men trying to believe what science proves ridiculous, and only succeeding by the destruction of reason. It was easy to make the mistake, but when made it need not be made perpetual.

Then this causes another evil: not only do men waste the practical power of piety, but they cease to get more. To feed on baby's food, to be dandled in mother's arms, — to play with boys' playthings, to learn boys' lessons, and be amused with boys' stories, — this helps the boy, but it hinders the man. Long ago we got from these helps all that was in them. To stay longer is waste of time. Look at the men who have been doing this for ten years; they are where they were ten years ago. They have done well if they have not fallen back. If we keep the baby's shoes for ever on the child, what will become of the feet? What if you kept the boy over his nursery rhymes for ever, or tried to make the man grown believe that they contained the finest poetry in the world, that the giant stories and the fairy tales therein were all true; what effect would it have on his mind? Suppose you told him that the proof of his manhood consisted in his fondness for little boys' playthings, and the little story-books and the little games of little children, and kept him securely fastened to the apron-strings of the school-dame; suppose you could make him believe so! You must make him a fool first. What would work so bad in intellectual affairs works quite as ill in the matter of piety. The story of the flood has strangled a world of souls. The miracles of the New Testament no longer heal, but hurt mankind.

Then this method of procedure disgusts well-educated and powerful men with piety itself, and with all that bears the name of religion. "Go your ways," say they, "and cant your canting as much as you like, only come not near us with your grimace." Many a man sees this misdirection of piety, and the bigotry which environs it, and turns off from religion itself, and will have nothing to do with it. Philosophers always have had a bad name in religious matters; many of them have turned away in disgust from the folly which is taught in its name. Of all the great philosophers of this day, I think no one takes any interest in the popular forms of religion. Do we ever hear religion referred to in politics? It is mentioned officially in proclamations and messages; but in the parliamentary debates of Europe and America, in the State papers of the nations, you find hardly a trace of the name or the fact. Honest men and manly men are ashamed to refer to this, because it has been so connected with unmanly dawdling and niggardly turning back, — they dislike to mention the word. So religion has ceased to be one of the recognized forces of the State. I do not remember a good law passed in my time from an alleged religious motive. Capital punishment, and the laws forbidding work or play on Sunday, are the only things left on the statute-book for which a strictly "religious motive" is assigned! The annual thanksgivings and fast-days are mementos of the political power of the popular religious opinions in other times. Men of great influence in America are commonly men of little apparent respect for religion; it seems to have no influence on their public conduct, and, in many cases, none on their private character; the class most eminent for intellectual culture, throughout all Christendom, is heedless of religion. The class of rich men has small esteem for it; yet in all the great towns of America the most reputable churches have fallen under their control, with such results as we see. The life of the nation in its great flood passes by, and does not touch the churches, — "the institutions of religion." Such fatal errors come from this mistake.

But there is a natural form of piety. The natural use of the strength of a strong man, or the wisdom of a wise one, is to the work of a strong man or a wise one. What is the natural work of piety? Obviously it is practical life; the use of all the faculties in their proper spheres, and for their natural function. Love of God, as truth, justice, love, must appear in a life marked by these qualities; that is the only effectual "ordinance of religion." A profession of the man's convictions, joining a society, assisting at a ceremony, — all these are of the same value in science as in religion; as good forms of chemistry as of piety. The natural form of piety is goodness, morality, living a true, just, affectionate, self-faithful life, from the motive of a pious man. Real piety, love of God, if left to itself, assumes the form of real morality, loyal obedience to God's law. Thus the power of religion does the work of religion, and is not merely to feed itself.

There are various degrees of piety, the quality ever the same, the quantity variable, and of course various degrees of goodness as the result thereof. Where there is but little piety, the work of goodness is done as a duty, under coercion as it were, with only the voluntary, not the spontaneous will; it is not done from a love of the duty, only in obedience to a law of God felt within the conscience or the soul, a law which bids the deed. The man's desires and duty are in opposition, not conjunction; but duty rules. That is the goodness of a boy in religion, the common goodness of the world.

At length the rising man shoots above this rudimentary state, has an increase of love of God, and therefore of love of man; his goodness is spontaneous, not merely enforced by volition. He does the good thing which comes in his way, and because it comes in his way; is true to his mind, his conscience, heart, and soul, and feels small temptation to do to others what he would not receive from them; he will deny himself for the sake of his brother near at hand. His desire attracts in the line of his duty, both in conjunction now. Not in vain does the poor, the oppressed, the hunted fugitive look up to him. This is the goodness of men well grown in piety. You find such men in all Christian sects, Protestant and Catholic; in all the great religious parties of the civilized world, among Buddhists, Mahometans, and Jews. They are kind fathers, generous citizens, unimpeachable in their business, beautiful in their daily lives. You see the man's piety in his work, and in his play. It appears in all the forms of his activity, individual, domestic, social, ecclesiastic, or political.

But the man goes on in his growth of piety, loving truth, justice, love, loving God the more. What is piety within must be morality without. The quality and quantity of the outward must increase as the quality and quantity of the inward. So his eminent piety must become eminent morality, which is philanthropy. He loves not only his kindred and his country, but all mankind; not only the good, but also the evil. He has more goodness than the channels of his daily life will hold. So it runs over the banks, to water and to feed a thousand thirsty plants. Not content with the duty that lies along his track, he goes out to seek it; not only willing, he has a salient longing to do good, to spread his truth, his justice, his love, his piety, over all the world. His daily life is a profession of his conscious piety to God, published in perpetual good-will to men.

This is the natural form of piety; one which it assumes if left to itself. Not more naturally does the beaver build, or the blackbird sing her own wild gushing melody, than the man of real piety lives it in this beautiful outward life. So from the perennial spring wells forth the stream to quicken the meadow with new access of green, and perfect beauty bursting into bloom.

Thus piety does the work it was meant to do: the man does not sigh and weep, and make grimaces, for ever in a fuss about his soul; he lives right on. Is his life marked with errors, sins, — he ploughs over the barren spot with his remorse, sows with new seed, and the old desert blossoms like a rose. He is free in his spiritual life, not confined to set forms of thought, of action, or of feeling. He accepts what his mind regards as true, what his conscience decides is right, what his heart deems lovely, and what is holy to his soul; all else he puts far from him. Though the ancient and the honorable of the earth bid him bow down to them, his stubborn knees bend only at the bidding of his manly soul. His piety is his freedom before God, not his bondage unto men. The toys and child's stories of religion are to him toys and child's stories, but no more. No baby-shoes deform his manly feet.

This piety, thus left to obey its natural law, keeps in sound health, and grows continually more and more. Doing his task, the man makes no more ado about his soul than about his sense. Yet it grows like the oak-tree. He gets continually more love of truth and right and justice, more love of God, and so more love of man. Every faculty becomes continually more. His mind acts after the universal law of the intellect, his conscience according to the universal moral law, his affections and his soul after the universal law thereof, and so he is strong with the strength of God, in this fourfold way communicating with him. With this strengthening of the moral faculties there comes a tranquillity, a calmness and repose, which nothing else can give, and also a beauty of character which you vainly seek elsewhere. When a man has the intellectual, the moral, the affectional part of piety, when he unites them all with conscious love of God, and puts that manifold piety into morality, his eminent piety into philanthropy, he attains the highest form of loveliness which belongs to mortal man. His is the palmy loftiness of man,—such strength, such calmness, and such transcendent loveliness of soul.

I know some men mock at the name of piety; I do not wonder at their scoff; for it has been made to stand as the symbol of littleness, meanness, envy, bigotry, and hypocritical superstition; for qualities I hate to name. Of what is popularly called piety there is no lack; it is abundant everywhere, common as weeds in the ditch, and clogs the wheels of mankind in every quarter of the world. Yet real piety, in manly quantity and in a manly form, is an uncommon thing. It is marvellous what other wants the want of this brings in: look over the long list of brilliant names that glitter in English history for the past three hundred years, study their aims, their outward and their inner life; explore the causes of their manifold defeat, and you will see the primal curse of all these men was lack of piety. They did not love truth, justice, or love; they did not love God with all their mind and conscience, heart and soul. Hence came the failure of many a mighty-minded man. Look at the brilliant array of distinguished talent in France for the last five generations; what intellectual gifts, what understanding, what imagination, what reason, but with it all what corruption, what waste of faculty, what lack of strong and calm and holy life, in these great, famous men! Their literature seems marvellously like the thin, cold dazzle of Northern Lights upon the wintry ice. In our own country it is still the same; the high intellectual gift or culture is ashamed of religion, and flouts at God; and hence the faults we see.

But real piety is what we need; we need much of it, — need it in the natural form thereof. Ours is an age of great activity. The peaceful hand was never so busy as to-day; the productive head never created so fast before. See how the forces of nature yield themselves up to man: the river stops for him, content to be his servant, and weave and spin; the ocean is his vassal, his toilsome bondsman; the lightning stoops out of heaven, and bears thoughtful burdens on its electric track from town to town. All this comes from the rapid activity of the lower intellect of man. Is there a conscious piety to correspond with this, — a conscious love of truth and right and love, — a love of God?

Ask the State, ask the church, ask society, and ask our homes.

The age requires a piety most eminent. What was religion enough for the time of the Patriarchs, or the Prophets, or the Apostles, or the Reformers, or the Puritans, is not enough for the heightened consciousness of mankind to-day. When the world thinks in lightning, it is not proportionate to pray in lead. The old theologies, the philosophies of religion of ancient times, will not suffice us now. We want a religion of the intellect, of the conscience, of the affections, of the soul,—the natural religion of all the faculties of man. The form also must be natural and new.

We want this natural piety in the form of normal human life,—morality, philanthropy. Piety is not to forsake, but possess the world; not to become incarnate in a nun and a monk, but in women and in men. Here are the duties of life to be done. You are to do them, do them religiously, consciously obedient to the law of God, not atheistically, loving only your selfish gain. Here are the sins of trade to be corrected. You are to show that a good merchant, mechanic, farmer, doctor, lawyer, is a real saint, a saint at work. Here are the errors of philosophy, theology, politics, to be made way with. It is the function of piety to abolish these and supply their place with new truths all radiant with God.

Here are the great evils of church and State, of social and domestic life, wrongs to be righted, evils to be outgrown: it is the business of piety to mend all this. Ours is no age when Religion can forsake the broad way of life. In the public street must she journey on, open her shop in the crowded square, and teach men by deeds, her life more eloquent than any lips. Hers is not now the voice that is to cry in the wilderness, but in the public haunts of men must she call them to make straight their ways.

We must possess all parts of this piety, — the intellectual, moral, affectional, — yea, total piety. This is not an age when men in religion's name can safely sneer at philosophy, call reason "carnal," make mouths at immutable justice, and blast with their damnation the faces of mankind. Priests have had their day, and in dull corners still aim to protract their favorite and most ancient night; but the sun has risen with healing in his wings. Piety without goodness, without justice, without truth or love, is seen to be the pretence of the hypocrite. Can philosophy satisfy us without religion? Even the head feels a coldness from the want of piety. The greatest intellect is ruled by the same integral laws with the least, and needs this fourfold love of God; and the great intellects that scorn religion are largest sufferers from their scorn.

Any man may attain this piety; it lies level to all.

Yet it is not to be won without difficulty, manly effort, self-denial of the low for the sake of the highest in us. Of you, young man, young maid, it will demand both prayer and toil. Not without great efforts are great heights won. In your period of passion you must subordinate instinctive desire to your reason, your conscience, your heart and soul; the lust of the body to the spirit's love. In the period of ambition you must coördinate all that is personal or selfish with what is absolutely true, just, holy, and good. Surely this will demand self-denial, now of instinctive desire, now of selfish ambition. Much you must sacrifice. But you will gain the possession, the use, the development, and the joy of your own mind and conscience, heart and soul. You will never sacrifice truth, justice, holiness, or love. All these you will gain; gain for to-day, gain for ever. What inward blessedness will you acquire! what strength, what tranquillity, what loveliness, what joy in God! You will have your delight in Him; He his in you. Is it not worth while to live so that you know you are in unison with God; in unison, too, with men; in quantity growing more, in quality superior? Make the trial for manly excellence, and the result is yours, for time and for eternity.

II.

OF TRUTH AND THE INTELLECT.

BUY THE TRUTH, AND SELL IT NOT; ALSO WISDOM, AND INSTRUCTION, AND UNDERSTANDING.—Prov. xxiii. 23.

TEMPERANCE is corporeal piety; it is the preservation of divine order in the body. It is the harmony of all the members thereof; the true symmetry and right proportion of part with part, of each with all, and so the worship of God with every limb of the body. Wisdom is to the mind what temperance, in this sense, is to the body; it is intellectual piety; the presence of divine order in the mind; the harmony of all the faculties thereof; the true symmetry and right proportion of faculty with faculty, of each with all. It is a general power of intellect, which may turn in any one or in all directions; the poet is a wise man in what relates to poetry; the philosopher, the statesman, the man of business, each in what relates to his particular function. So it is a general power of mind. We say "knowledge is power," but mean wisdom, which is general intellectual ability, the power of knowing and of using truth.

This wisdom implies two things: the love of truth as truth, which I spoke of the other day as the intellectual side of piety; and, secondly, the power to possess and use this truth, either in the specific form which is sought by the philosopher, poet, statesman, and man of business, or else in some more general form including all these; the power of getting truth either by the mode of reflection, as truth demonstrated, or by the mode of intuition, as truth seen and known at sight. For the acquisitive part of wisdom is the generic power which includes both the specific powers, — of intuition and of reflection.

Truth is the object which corresponds to the mind. As the eye has the power of sight, and as the special things we see are the object of the eye, so is truth, in its various forms, the object of the mind. If a man keep the law of his body, in the large sense of the word Temperance, he acquires three good things, health, strength, and beauty. As a general rule these three will come; there are, indeed, particular and personal exceptions, but such is the rule. Let any race of men, say the New Englanders, for a hundred years fulfil all the conditions of the body, and observe the laws thereof, they will become distinguished for these three things.

In like manner, if a man keep the law of his mind, and fulfil its natural conditions, he acquires wisdom, — acquires intellectual health, strength, and beauty. Here also there may be particular and personal exceptions, but such is the rule. Let any race of men, say the New Englanders, for a hundred years fulfil the natural condition of mind and keep the law thereof, we should have these three qualities to a greater degree than the ancient inhabitants of Athens, long regarded as the most intellectual race in the world; we should have the quality of wisdom which they had, but with more intellectual health, strength, and loveliness, more truth and more power to use it, inasmuch as the human race has acquired a greater intellectual development in the two thousand years that have passed since the days of Aristotle and Alexander. The laws which regulate the development of mind, in the individual or the race, are as certain as the laws of matter. Observance thereof is sure to bring certain consequences to the individual, the nation, and mankind. The intellectual peculiarity of a nation is transmitted from age to age, and only disappears when the nation perishes or mingles with some other tribe inferior to itself; then it does not cease, but is spread more thinly over a wider field, and does not appear in its ancient form for years to come. Intellectual talent dies out of a particular family. There are seldom two men of genius of the same name. Stuarts and Tudors, Guelphs and Bourbons, there are in abundance, but only one Luther, Shakspeare, Milton, Cromwell, Burns; only a single Franklin or Washington. But the intellectual power which once rose up in such men does not perish from the race, only from the special family. It comes up in other names, for the fee of all the genius that is born, as well as the achievements won, vests perpetually in mankind; not in the special family which holds only its life-estate of talent under the race and of it. The wisdom which this generation shall develop, foster, and mature, will not perish with this age; it will be added to the spiritual property of mankind, and go down, bequeathed as a rich legacy, to such as come after us, all the more valuable because it is given in perpetual entail, a property which does not waste, but greatens in the use. Yet probably no great man of this age will leave a child as great as himself. At death the father's greatness beoomes public property to the next generation. The piety of Jesus of Nazareth did not die out of mankind when he gave up the ghost; the second century had more of Christ than the first; there has been a perpetual increase of Socratic excellence ever since the death of the Athenian sage.

This is a remarkable law of Providence, but a law it is; and cheering is it to know that all the good qualities you give example of, not only have a personal immortality in you beyond the grave, but a national, even a human, immortality on earth, and, while they bless you in heaven, are likewise safely invested in your brother man, and shall go down to the last posterity, blessing your nation and all mankind. So the great men of antiquity continue to help us, — Moses, Confucius, Buddha, Zoroaster, Pythagoras, Socrates, Plato, — not to dwell upon the name dearest of all. These men and their fellows, known to all or long since forgotten of mankind, — the aristocracy of heaven, whose patent of nobility dates direct from God, — they added to the spiritual power of mankind. The wisdom they inherited or acquired was a personal fief, which at their death reverted to the human race. Not a poor boy in Christendom, not a man of genius, rejoicing in the plenitude of power, but is greater and nobler for these great men; not barely through his knowledge of their example, but because, so to say, they raised the temperature of the human world. For, as there is a physical temperature of the interstellar spaces, betwixt sun and sun, which may be called the temperature of the universe, so is there a spiritual temperature of the interpersonal spaces, a certain common temperature of spirit, not barely personal, not national alone, but human and of the race, which may be called the temperature of mankind. On that in general we all depend, as on our family in special, or in particular upon our personal genius and our will. Those great men added wisdom to mankind, brought special truths to consciousness, which now have spread throughout the enlightened nations of the world, and penetrate progressively the human mass, giving mankind continual new power. So shall you see an iron bar become magnetic; first it was a single atom of the metal which caught the electric influence, spark by spark; that atom could not hold the subtile fire, whose nature was to spread, and so one atom gave the spark to the next, and soon it spread through the whole, till the cold iron, which before seemed dead as stone, is all magnetic, acquires new powers, and itself can hold its own, yet magnetize a thousand bars if rightly placed.

According to his nature man loves truth with a pure and disinterested love, the strongest intellectual affection. The healthy eye does not more naturally turn to the light, than the honest mind turns toward the truth. See how we seek after it in nature. All the National Academies, Institutes, and Royal Societies are but so many companies organized for the pursuit of truth, — of truth chiefly in some outward form, materialized in the visible world. These societies propose no corporeal benefit to themselves, none to the human race. They love each truth of nature for its own fair sake. What is the pecuniary value of the satellites of Neptune to us? See how laborious naturalists ransack the globe to learn the truths writ in its elements. One goes to Florida to look after the bones of a mastodon, hid in a bog some thousands of years ago; another curiously collects chips of stone from all the ledges of the world, lives and moves and has his being in the infra-carboniferous sandstones and shales, a companion of fossil plants and fossil shells. This crosses land and ocean to study the herbage of the earth; that, careless of ease and homefelt joys, devotes his life to mosses and lichens, which grow unheeded on the rocks; he loves them as if they were his own children, yet they return no corresponding smile, nor can he eat and drink of them. How the astronomer loves to learn the truth of the stars, which will not light his fire nor fill his children's hungry mouths! No Inquisition can stop Galileo in his starry quest. I have known a miser who loved money above all things; for this, would sacrifice reason, conscience, and religion, and break affection's bond; but it was the use of money that was loved, with a mean and most ignoble selfish lust, vulgarizing and depraving the man. The true disciple of science loves truth far more, with a disinterested love; will endure toil, privation, and self-denial, and encounter suffering, for that. This love of truth will bless the lover all his days; yet when he brings her home, his fair-faced bride, she comes empty-handed to his door, herself her only dower.

How carefully men look after the facts of human history! how they study the tragic tale of Greece and Rome, and explore the remains of nations that long since have perished from the earth! Of what material consequence is it to us who composed the Iliad, twenty-five hundred years ago, or whether Homer wrote, or only sung, his never-dying song? Yet what a mass of literature has come into being within the last sixty years to settle these two questions! How the famous scholars light their lamps and dim their eyes over this work, and how the world rejoices in their books, which will not bake bread, nor make two blades of grass grow where only one rose up before; which will not build a railroad, nor elect a president, nor give a man an office in any custom-house of the wide world! There is a deep love of truth in men, even in these poor details. A natural king looks royal at the plough.

How men study yet higher modes of truth, writ in the facts of human consciousness! How the ablest men have worked at the severest forms of intellectual toil, yet proposing no gain to themselves, only the glorious godliness of truth! A corporeal gain to men does come from every such truth. There is such a solidarity betwixt the mind and body, that each spiritual truth works welfare in the material world, and the most abstract of ideas becomes concrete in the widest universe of welfare. But philosophers love the truth before they learn its material use. Aristotle, making an exhaustive analysis of the mind of man, did not design to build a commonwealth in New England, and set up public schools.

This love of truth, instinctive and reflective both, is so powerful in human nature, that mankind will not rest till we have an idea corresponding to every fact of Nature and of human consciousness, and the contents of the universe are repeated in the cosmic mind of man, which grasps the whole of things. The philosophic work of observation, analysis, and synthesis, will not be over, till the whole world of material nature is comprehended by the world of human nature. Such is our love, not only of special truths, but of total truth.

Consider what an apparatus man has devised

to aid the search for truth: not only visible tools to magnify the little and bring near us the remote, but the invisible weapons of the mind, — mathematics and the various sciences, the mining-tools with which we dig for truth, — logic, the Lydian stone to test the true, — rhetoric, the art to communicate, — language, speech itself, the most amazing weapon of the human mind, an instrument half made on purpose, and half given without our thought.

This love of truth is the natural and instinctive piety of the mind. In studying the facts of nature, material or human, I study the thought of God; for in the world of real things a fact is the direct speech of the Father. Words make up the language of men; facts and ideas are the words of God, his universal language to the Englishman and the Chinese, in which He speaks from all eternity to all time. Man made "in the image of God" loves his Father's thought, and is not contented till he hears that speech; then he is satisfied. All intellectual error is but the babble of the baby-man. Every truth which I know is one point common to my consciousness and the consciousness of God; in this we approach, and, so far as that goes, God's thought is my thought, and we are at one. Mankind will not be content till we also are conscious of the universe, and have mastered this Bible of God writ in the material world, a perpetual lesson for the day.

I cannot think we value wisdom high enough; not in proportion to other things for more vulgar use. We prize the material results of wisdom more than the cause which produces them. Let us not undervalue the use. What is it which gives Christendom its rank in the world? What gives Old England or New England her material delight, — our comfortable homes, our mills and ships and shops, these iron roads which so cover the land? It is not the soil, hard and ungrateful; not the sky, cold and stormy half the year; it is the educated mind, the practical wisdom of the people. The Italian has his sunnier sky, his labored land, which teems with the cultured luxuriance of three thousand years. Our outfit was the wilderness and our head. God gave us these, and said, "Subdue the earth;" and we have toiled at the problem, not quite in vain. The mind is a universal tool, the abstract of all instruments; it concretizes itself in the past present and future weapons of mankind.

We value wisdom chiefly for its practical use, as the convenience of a weapon, not the function of a limb; and truth as a servant, not a bride. The reason of this seeming falseness to the intellectual instinct is found partly in the low development of man, — the external precedes the spiritual in order of unfolding, — and partly in this, that the human race is still too poor to indulge in merely intellectual delights, while material wants are not yet satisfied. Mankind rejoices in rough aprons of camel's hair, and feeds on locusts and wild honey, before there is purple and fine linen for all, with sumptuous faring every day. Even now a fourth part of the human family is as good as naked. It is too soon to ask men to rejoice exclusively in the beauty of wisdom, when they need its convenience so much. Let us not be too severe in our demands of men. God "suffereth long, and is kind."

Then, sour theologies confront us, calling wisdom "foolish," reason "carnal," scoffing at science with a priestly sneer, as if knowledge of God, of God's world, and of its laws, could disturb the natural service of God. We are warned against the "arrogance of the philosopher," but by the arrogance of the priest. We are told to shun "the pride of wisdom;" alas! it is sometimes the pride of folly which gives the caution.

It seems to me, that the value of the intellect is a little underrated by some writers in the New Testament, and wisdom sometimes turned off rather rudely. Perhaps the reason was, that then, as now, men often cultivated the mind alone, and not the highest faculties of that; and, though ever learning, never hit the truth. Doubtless men of accomplished mind and manners sneered at the rudeness of the Galilean, and with their demonstrations sought to parry the keen intuitions of great-souled men. It is not to be wondered at, that James attacked the rich, and Paul the learned, of their time. Fox and Bunyan did the same. Many a Christian Father has mocked at all generous culture of the mind. Even now, with us, amongst men desiring to be religious, there is an inherited fear of reason and of common sense. Science is thought a bad companion for religion. Men are cautioned against "free thinking" in religion, and, as all thinking must be free, against all thinking in that quarter. Even common sense is thought dangerous. Men in pews are a little afraid, when a strong man goes into the pulpit, lest he should shake the ill-bottomed fabric to the ground; men in pulpits are still more fearful. It is a strange fear, that the mind should drive the soul out of us, and our knowledge of God annihilate our love of God. Yet some earnest men quake with this panic terror, and think it is not quite safe to follow the records writ in the great Bible of Nature, its world-wide leaves laid open before us, with their "millions of surprises."

Let me say a word in behalf of the largest culture of the intellect, of all faculties thereof, — understanding, imagination, reason. I admit there have been men of able mind and large intellectual development who have turned off from religion, their science driving them away from the doctrines taught in this name. But such men have been few. Did they oppose the truths of religion? Oftener the follies taught in its name. All the attacks made on religion itself by men of science, from Celsus to Feuerbach, have not done so much to bring religion into contempt as a single persecution for witchcraft, or a Bartholomew massacre, made in the name of God. At this day, in America, the greatest argument against the popular form of religion is offered by the churches of the land, a twofold argument: first, the follies taught as religious doctrine, the character assigned to God, the mode of government ascribed to him, both here and hereafter, the absurdities and impossibilities taught as the history of God's dealing with mankind; next, the actual character of these churches, as a body never rebuking a popular and profitable sin, but striking hands by turns with every popular form of wrong. Men of science, as a class, do not war on the truths, the goodness, and the piety that are taught as religion, only on the errors, the evil, the impiety, which bear its name.

Science is the natural ally of religion. Shall we try and separate what God has joined? We injure both by the attempt. The philosophers of this age have a profound love of truth, and show great industry and boldness in search thereof. In the name of truth they pluck down the strong-holds of error, venerable and old. But what a cry has been raised against them! It was pretended that they would root out religion from the hearts of mankind! It seems to me it would be better for men who love religion to understand philosophy before they declaim against "the impiety of modern science." The study of Nature, of human history, or of human nature might be a little more profitable than the habit of "hawking at geology and schism." A true philosophy is the only cure for a false philosophy. The sensational scheme of philosophy has done a world of harm, it seems to me, in its long history from Epicurus to Comte; but no-philosophy would be far worse. The abnegation of mind must be the abnegation of God. The systems built by priests, who deemed reason not fit to trust, are more dangerous than "infidel science." Those have been found sad periods of time, when the ablest men were forced to spend their strength in pulling down the monstrous pagodas built in the name of religion, full of idols and instruments of torture. Epicurus, Lucretius,

Voltaire, even Hobbes and Hume, performed a work indispensable to the religious development of mankind. Yet destruction is a sad work; — set your old house afire, you do not know how much of it will burn down. It was the ignorance, the folly, the arrogance, and the tyranny of a priesthood which made necessary the scoff of Lucian and the haughty scorn of D'Holbach. The science of philosophers cannot be met by the ignorance of the priests; the pride of wisdom is more than a match for the pride of folly; the philosophy of an unwelcome demonstration is ill answered by the preaching of foolishness. How can a needle's eye embrace a continent? In the name of religion, I would call for the spirit of wisdom without measure; have free thinking on the Bible, on the Church, on God and man, — the largest liberty of the intellect. I would sooner have an unreasonable form of agriculture than of religion. The state of religion is always dependent, in a good measure, on the mental culture of mankind. A foolish man cannot give you a wise form of piety. All men by nature love truth. Cultivate their mind, they will see it, know it, value it. Just now we need a large development of mind in the clergy, who fall behind the men of leading intellect in England, America, and France. Thinking men care little for the "opinions of the clergy," except on the mere formalities of a ritual and church-show. Depend upon it, the effect will be even more baneful for the future than at present.

I love to look on the wise mind as one means of holding communion with the Infinite God; for I believe that He inspires men, not only through the conscience, the affections, and the soul, but also through the intellect — through the reason, imagination, and understanding. But he does this, not arbitrarily, miraculously, against the nature of the mind, but by a mode of operation as constant as the gravitation of planets or the chemical attraction of atoms of metal. Yet I do not find that He inspires thoughtless men with truth, more than malicious men with love. Tell me God inspired the Hebrew saints with wisdom, filled the vast urns of Moses and of Jesus; I believe it, but not Hebrew saints alone. The Grecian saints, the saints of Rome, of Germany, of France, of either England, Old or New; all the sons of men hang on the breasts of Heaven, and draw inspiration from Him "in whom we live and move and have our being." Intellectual inspiration comes in the form of truth, but the income from God is proportionate to the wisdom which seeks and so receives. A mind small as a thimble may be filled full thereof, but will it receive as much as a mind whose ocean-bosom is thirsty for a whole heaven of truth?

Bring larger intellect, and you have the more. A drop would overflow a hollow cherry-stone, while whole Mediterranean Seas fill but a fraction of the Atlantic's mighty deep. There still is truth in the sweet heaven, near and waiting for mankind. A man of little mind can only take in the contents of his primer; he should not censure his neighbor whose encyclopedic head dines on the science of mankind, and still wanders crying for lack of meat.

How mankind loves the truth! We will not let it go;

> "One accent of the Holy Ghost
> The heedless world hath never lost;"

so native is it to the mind of man. Look on the power of a special truth, a great idea; view it merely as a force in the world of men. At first, nothing seems so impotent. It has no hands nor feet; how can it go alone? It seems as if the censor of the press could blot it out for ever. It flatters no man, offers to serve no personal and private interest and then forbear its work, will be no man's slave. It seems ready to perish; surely it will give up the ghost the next moment. There now, a priest has it in the dust and stamps it out! O idle fear! stamp on the lightning of the sky! Of all things truth is the most lasting; invulnerable as God; "of the Eternal coeternal beam," shall we call it an accident of his being, or rather substance of the substance of God, inseparable from Him? The pyramids may fall, in ages of time the granite be crumbled into dust and blown off by the sirocco of the wilderness; the very mountains, whence they first were hewn, may all vanish, evaporate to the sky and spread over the world; but truth shall still remain, immortal, unchanging, and not growing old. Heaven and earth may pass away, but a truth never. A true word cannot fail from amongst men; it is indorsed by the Almighty, and shall pass current with mankind for ever. Could the armies of the world alter the smallest truth of mathematics; make one and one greater or less than two? As easily as they can alter any truth, or any falsehood, in morals, in politics, or in religion. A lie is still a lie, a truth a truth.

See the power of some special truth upon a single man. Take an example from a high mode of truth, a truth of religion. Saul of Tarsus sees that God loves the Gentile as well as the Jew. It seems a small thing to see that. Why did men ever think otherwise? Why should not God love the Gentile as well as the Jew? It was impossible that He should do otherwise. Yet this seemed a great truth at that time, the Christian Church dividing upon that matter. It burnt in the bosom of Paul of Tarsus, then a young man. What heroism it wakens in him! what self-denial he can endure! Want, hardships, persecution, the contempt and loathing of his companions and former friends, shipwreck, scourging, prison, death, — all these are nothing to him. A truth has inspired him; he is eloquent with its new force, his letters powerful. Go where he will he finds foes, the world bristling with peril; but go where he may he makes friends, makes them by this truth and the heroism it awoke in him. Men saw the new doctrine, and looked back on the old error, — that Jove loved Rome, Pallas Athens, Juno Samos and Carthage most of all, Jehovah Mount Zion, and Baal his Tyrian towns; that each several deity looked grim at all the rest of men, and so must have his own forms and ceremonies, unwelcome to the rest. Men see this is an error now; they see the evil which came thereof, — the wars and ages full of strife, national jealousies, wrangling betwixt Babylonian or Theban priests, and the antagonism of the Gentile and the Jew. Now all are "one in Christ." They bless the lips which taught the doctrine and brought them freedom by the truth. Meantime the truth uplifts the Apostle; his mind expands, his conscience works more freely than before, no longer burdened with a law of sin and death. His affections have a wider range, knowing no man after his national flesh. His soul has a better prospect of God, now the partition-wall between the Jew and Gentile is thrown down.

We often estimate the value of a nation by the truths it brings to light. To take the physical census, and know how many shall vote, we count the heads, and tell men off by millions, — so many square miles of Russians, Tartars, or Chinese. But to take the spiritual census, and see what will be voted, you count the thoughts, tell off the great men, enumerate the truths. The nations may perish, the barbarian sweep over Thebes, the lovely places of Jerusalem become a standing pool, and the favorite spot of Socrates and Aristotle be grown up to brambles, — yet Egypt, Judea, Athens, do not die; their truths live on, refusing death, and still these names are of a classic land. I do not think that God loves the men or the nations He visits with this lofty destiny better than He loves other ruder tribes or ruder men: but it is by this standard that we estimate the nations; a few truths make them immortal.

A great truth does not disdain to ride on so humble a beast as interest. Thus ideas go abroad in the ships of the desert, or the ships of the sea. Some nations, like the English and others, seem to like this equipage the best, and love to handle and taste a truth in the most concrete form; so great truths are seen and welcomed as political economy before they are thought of as part of political morality, human affection, and cosmic piety. All the great truths of political science seem to have been brought to the consciousness of men stimulated by fear, or by love of the results of the truth, not of itself. Nations have sometimes adopted their ideal children only for the practical value of the dress they wore; but the great Providence of the Father sent the truth as they were able to bear it. So earthly mothers sometimes teach the alphabet to their children in letters of sugar, eaten as soon as learned.

But even with us it is not always so. In our own day we have seen a man possessed with this great idea, — that every man has a right to his own body and soul, and consequently that it is wrong to hold an innocent man in bondage; that no custom, no law, no constitution, no private or national interest, can justify the deed; nothing on earth, nothing beneath it or above. He applies this to American slavery. Here is a conflict between an acknowledged truth and what is thought a national interest. What an influence did the idea have on the man! It enlarged him, and made him powerful, opened the eye of his conscience to the hundred-headed injustice in the Lernæan Marsh of modern society; widened his affections, till his heart prayed, ay, and his hands, for the poor negro in the Southern swamps,—for all the oppressed. It touched and wakened up his soul, till he felt a manly piety in place of what might else have been a puny sentimentalism, mewling and whining in the Church's arms. The idea goes abroad, sure to conquer.

See how a great idea, a truth of morals or religion, has an influence on masses of men. Some single man sees it first, dimly for a long time, without sight enough to make it clear, the quality of vision better than his quantity of sight. Then he sees it clearly and in distinct outline. The truth burns mightily within him, and he cannot be still; he tells it, now to one, then to another; at each time of telling he gets his lesson better learned. Other men see the idea, dimly at first as he. It wakens a love for itself; first, perhaps, in the recipient heart of some woman, waiting for the consolation. Then a few minds prepared for the idea half welcome it; thence it timidly flashes into other minds, as light reflected from the water. Soon the like-minded meet together to sun themselves in one another's prayers. They form a family of the faith, and grow strong in their companionship. The circle grows wider. Men oppose the new idea, with little skill or much, sometimes with violence, or only with intellect. Then comes a little pause, — the ablest representatives of the truth must get fully conscious of their truth, and of their relation to the world; a process like that in the growing corn of summer, which in hot days spindles, as the farmers say, but in cool nights gets thick, and has a green and stocky growth. The interruptions to a great idea are of corresponding value to its development in a man, or a nation, or the world. Our men baptized with a new idea pause and reflect to be more sure, — perfecting the logic of their thought; pause and devise their mode to set it forth, — perfecting their rhetoric, and seek to organize it in an outward form, for every thought must be a thing. Then they tell their idea more perfectly; in the controversy that follows, errors connected with it get exposed; all that is merely accidental, national, or personal gets shaken off, and the pure truth goes forth to conquer. In this way all the great ideas of religion, of philanthropy, have gone their round. Yet every new truth of morals or religion which blesses the world conflicts with old notions, binds a new burden on the men who first accept it; demands of them to lay aside old comforts, accept a hard name, endure the coldness of their friends, and feel the iron of the world. What a rough wind winnowed the early Christians and the Quakers! They bear all that, and still the truth goes on.

Soon it has philosophers to explain it, apologists to defend it, orators to set it forth, institutions to embody its sacred life. It is a new force in the world, and nothing can dislodge or withstand it. It was in this way that the ideas of Christianity got a footing in the world. Between the enthusiasm of Peter and James at the Pentecost, and the cool demonstrations of Clarke and Schleiermacher, what a world of experience there lay!

Some four hundred years ago this truth began to be distinctly seen: Man has natural empire over all institutions; they are for him, accidents of his development, not he for them. That is a very simple statement, each of you assents to it. But once it was a great new truth. See what it has led to. Martin Luther dimly saw its application to the Catholic Church, the institution that long had ruled over the souls of men. The Church gave way and recoiled before the tide of truth. That helpless truth,—see what it has done, what millions it has inspired, what institutions it has built, what men called into life! By and by men saw its application to the despotic state which long had ruled over the bodies and souls of men. Revolutions followed thick and fast in Holland, England, America, and France, and one day all Europe and the world will be ablaze with that idea. Men opposed; one of the Stuarts said, "It shall not cross the four seas of England;" but it crossed the Stuart's neck, and drove his children from the faithful soil. It came to America, that idea so destructive at first, destined to be so creative and conservative. It brought our fathers here, grim and bearded men, full of the fear of God; they little knew what fruit would come of their planting. See the institutions which have sprung up on the soil then cumbered by a wilderness, and hideous with wild beasts and wilder men. See what new ideas blossomed out of the old truth: All men have natural, equal, and unalienable rights to life, liberty, and the pursuit of happiness;—that was a new flower from the old stem. See the one-and-thirty States which have sprung up under the shadow of this great idea.

That truth long since recognized as true, now proved expedient by experiment, goes back over the sea, following the track the Mayflower broke, and earnest nations welcome it to their bosom, that sovereign truth: Man is supreme over institutions, not they over him. How it has thundered and lightened over Europe in the last few years! It will beat to the dust many a godless throne, and the palm of peace shall occupy the ground once reserved for soldiers' feet; here and there a city ditch of defence has already become a garden for the town.

Here in America, men full of this truth rise up against ungodly customers, now become a law, and under this demand the freedom of the slave. See how it spreads! It cannot be written down, nor voted down, nor sneered and frowned down; it cannot be put down by all the armies of the world. This truth belongs to the nature of man, and can only perish when the race gives up the ghost. Yet it is nothing but an idea; it has no hands, no feet. The man who first set it agoing on the earth, — see what he has done! Yet I doubt not the villagers around him thought the ale-house keeper was the more useful man; and when beer fell a penny in the pot, or the priest put on a new cassock, many a man thought it was a more important event than the first announcement of this truth to men. But is not the wise man stronger than all the foolish? Truth is a part of the celestial machinery of God; whoso puts that in gear for mankind has the Almighty to turn his wheel. When God turns the mill, who shall stop it? There is a spark from the good God in us all.

> "O, joy that in our embers
> Is something that doth live,
> That nature yet remembers
> What was so fugitive."

Methinks I see some thoughtful man, studious of truth, his intellectual piety writ on his tall pale brow, coming from the street, the field, or shop, pause and turn inward all his strength; now he smiles as he gets glimpses of this bashful truth, which flies, yet wishes to be seen,—a daughter of the all-blessed God. It is at her beauty that he smiles, the thought of kindred loveliness, she is to people earth withal. And then the smile departs, and a pale sadness settles down upon his radiant face, as he remembers that men water their gardens for each new plant with blood, and how much must be shed to set a truth like this! He shows his thought to other men; they keep it nestled in the family awhile. In due time the truth has come of age, and must take possession of the estate. Now she wrestles with the Roman Church; the contest is not over yet, but the deadly wound will never heal. Now she wrestles with the Northern kings; see how they fall, their sceptres broken, their thrones overturned; and the fair-faced daughter of the Eternal King leads forward happy tribes of men, and with pious vow inaugurates the chiefs of peace, of justice, and of love, and on the one great gospel of the human heart swears them to keep the constitution of the universe, written by God's own hand.

But this last is only prophecy; men say, "It cannot be; the slaves of America must be bondmen for ever; the nations of Europe can never be free."

I laugh at such a word. Let me know a thing is true, I know it has the omnipotence of God on its side, and fear no more for it than I fear for God. Politics is the science of exigencies. The eternal truth of things is the exigency which controls the science of men as the science of matter. Depend upon it, the Infinite God is one of the exigencies not likely to be disregarded in the ultimate events of human development. Truth shall fail out of geometry and politics at the same time; only we learn first the simpler forms of truth. Now folly, passion, and fancied interest pervert the eye, which cannot always fail to see.

Truth is the object of the intellect; by human wisdom we learn the thought of God, and are inspired by his mind, — not all of us with the same mode, or form, or quantity of truth; but each shall have his own, proportionate to his native powers and to the use he makes thereof. Love of truth is the intellectual part of piety. Wisdom is needful to complete and manly religion; a thing to be valued for itself, not barely for its use. Love of the use will one day give place to love of truth itself.

To keep the body's law brings health and strength, and in long ages brings beauty too; to keep the laws of mind brings in the higher intellectual health and strength and loveliness, as much nobler than all corporeal qualities as the mind is nobler than the muscles it controls. Truth will follow from the lawful labor of the mind, and serve the great interest of men. Many a thousand years hence, when we are forgotten, when both the Englands have perished out of time, and the Anglo-Saxon race is only known as the Cherethites and Pelethites, — nothing national left but the name, — the truths we have slowly learned will be added to the people that come after us; the great political truth of America will go round the world, and clothe the earth with greenness and with beauty. All the power of mind that we mature and give examples of shall also survive; in you and me it will be personally immortal, — a portion of our ever-widening consciousness, though all the earthly wisdom of Leibnitz or Aristotle must soon become a single drop in the heavenly ocean of the sages whom death has taught; but it will be not less enduring on the earth, humanly immortal; for the truths you bring to light are dropped into the world's wide treasury, — where Socrates and Kant have cast in but two mites, which made only a farthing in the wealth of man, — and form a part of the heritage which each generation receives, enlarges, holds in trust, and of necessity bequeathes to mankind, the personal estate of man entailed of nature to the end of time. As the men who discovered corn, tamed the ox, the horse, invented language and letters, who conquered fire and water, and yoked these two brute furious elements with an iron bond, as gentle now as any lamb, — as they who tamed the lightning, sending it of their errands, and as they who sculptured loveliness in stone two thousand years ago, a thing of beauty and a joy for ever, — as these and all such transmit their wealthy works to man, so he who sets forth a truth and develops wisdom, any human excellence of gift or growth, greatens the spiritual glory of his race. And a single man, who could not make one hair white or black, has added a cubit to the stature of mankind.

All the material riches inherited or actively acquired by this generation, our cultivated land, our houses, roads of earth, of wood, of iron, our factories and ships, — mechanical inventions which make New England more powerful than Russia to create, though she have forty-fold our men, — all these contrivances, the crown-jewels of the human race, the symbols of our kingly power over the earth, we leave to the next age; your children's burden will be lighter, their existence larger, and their joy more delightful, for our additions to this heritage. But the spiritual truths we learn, the intellectual piety which we acquire, all the manly excellence that we slowly meditate and slowly sculpture into life, goes down in blessing to mankind, the cup of gold hid in the sack of those who only asked for corn, richer than all the grain they bought. Into our spiritual labors other men shall enter, climb by our ladder, then build anew, and so go higher up towards heaven than you or I had time and power to go. There is a spiritual solidarity of the human race, and the thought of the first man will help the wisdom of the last. A thousand generations live in you and me.

It is an old world, mankind is no new creation, no upstart of to-day, but has lived through hard times and long. Yet what is the history of man to the nature that is in us all! The instinctive hunger for perfect knowledge will not be contented with repetitions of the remembered feast. There are new truths to come,— truths in science, morals, politics, religion; some have arrived not long ago upon this planet,— many a new thing underneath the sun. At first men give them doubtful welcome. But if you know that they are truths, fear not; be sure that they will stay, adding new treasures to the consciousness of men, new outward welfare to the blessedness of earth. No king nor conqueror does men so great a good as he who adds to human kind a great and universal truth; he that aids its march, and makes the thought a thing, works in the same line with Moses, has intellectual sympathy with God, and is a fellow-laborer with Him. The best gift we can bestow upon man is manhood. Undervalue not material things; but remember that the generation which, finding Rome brick, left it marble and full of statues and temples too, as its best achievement bequeathed to us a few words from a young Carpenter of Galilee, and the remembrance of his manly life.

III.

OF JUSTICE AND THE CONSCIENCE.

TURN AND DO JUSTICE. — Tobit xiii. 6.

EVERYWHERE in the world there is a natural law, that is a constant mode of action, which seems to belong to the nature of things, to the constitution of the universe: this fact is universal. In different departments we call this mode of action by different names, as the law of Matter, the law of Mind, the law of Morals, and the like. We mean thereby a certain mode of action which belongs to the material, mental, or moral forces, the mode in which commonly they are seen to act, and in which it is their ideal to act always. The ideal laws of matter we only know from the fact that they are always obeyed; to us the actual obedience is the only witness of the ideal rule, for in respect to the conduct of the material world the ideal and the actual are the same.

The laws of matter we can learn only by observation and experience. We cannot divine them and anticipate, or know them at all, unless experience supply the facts of observation. Before experience of the fact, no man could foretell that a falling body would descend sixteen feet the first second, twice that the next, four times the third, and sixteen times the fourth. The law of falling bodies is purely objective to us; no mode of action in our consciousness anticipates this rule of action in the outer world. The same is true of all the laws of matter. The ideal law is known because it is a fact. The law is imperative; it must be obeyed, without hesitation. In the solar system, or the composition of a diamond, no margin is left for any oscillation of disobedience; margins of oscillation there always are, but only for vibration as a function, not as the refusal of a function. Only the primal will of God works in the material world, no secondary finite will.

In Nature, the world spread out before the senses,—to group many specific modes of action about a single generic force,—we see there is the great general law of Attraction, which binds atom to atom in a grain of sand, orb to orb, system to system, gives unity to the world of things, and rounds these worlds of systems to a universe. At first there seem to be exceptions to this law,—as in growth and decomposition, in the repulsions of electricity; but at length all these are found to be instantial cases of this great law of attraction acting in various modes. We name the attraction by its several modes,—cohesion in small masses, and gravitation in large. When the relation seems a little more intimate, we call it affinity, as in the atomic union of molecules of matter. Other modes we name electricity, and magnetism; when the relation is yet more close and intimate, we call it vegetation in plants, vitality in animals. But for the present purpose all these may be classed under the general term Attraction, considered as acting in various modes of cohesion, gravitation, affinity, vegetation, and vitality.

This power gives unity to the material world, keeps it whole; yet, acting under such various forms, gives variety at the same time. The variety of effect surprises the senses at first; but in the end the unity of cause astonishes the cultivated mind. Looked at in reference to this globe, an earthquake is no more than a chink that opens in a garden-walk, of a dry day in summer. A sponge is porous, having small spaces between the solid parts; the solar system is only more porous, having larger room between the several orbs; the universe yet more so, with vast spaces between the systems; a similar attraction keeps together the sponge, the system, and the universe. Every particle of matter in the world is related to each and all the other particles thereof; attraction is the common bond.

In the spiritual world, the world of human consciousness, there is also a law, an ideal mode of action for the spiritual forces of man. To take only the moral part of this sphere of consciousness, we find the phenomenon called Justice, the law of right. Viewed as a force, it bears the same relation in the world of conscience, that attraction bears in the world of sense. I mean justice is the normal relation of men, and has the same to do amongst moral atoms, — individual men, — moral masses, — that is, nations, — and the moral whole, — I mean all mankind, — which attraction has to do with material atoms, masses, and the material whole. It appears in a variety of forms not less striking.

However, unlike attraction, it does not work free from all hinderance; it develops itself through conscious agents, that continually change, and pass by experiment from low to high degrees of life and development, to higher forms of justice. There is a certain private force, personal and peculiar to each one of us, controlled by individual will; this may act in the same line with the great normal force of justice, or it may conflict for a time with the general law of the universe, having private nutations, oscillations, and aberrations, personal or national. But these minor forces, after a while, are sure to be overcome by the great general moral force, pass into the current, and be borne along in the moral stream of the universe.

What a variety of men and women in the world! Two hundred million persons, and no two alike in form and lineament! in character and being how unlike! how very different as phenomena and facts! What an immense variety of wish, of will, in these thousand million men! of plans, which now rise up in the little personal bubble that we call a reputation or a great fortune, then in the great national bubble which we call a State! for bubbles they are, judging by the space and time they occupy in this great and age-outlasting sea of human kind. But underneath all these bubbles, great and little, resides the same eternal force which they shape into this or the other special form; and over all the same paternal Providence presides, and keeps eternal watch above the little and the great, producing variety of effect from unity of force. This Providence allows the little bubbles of his child's caprice, humors him in forming them, gives him time and space for that, understands his little caprices and his whims, and lets him carry them out awhile;

but Himself, with no whim and no caprice, rules there as universal justice, omniscient and all-powerful. Out of His sea these bubbles rise; by His force they rise; by His law they have their consistence, and the private personal will, which gives them size or littleness and normal or abnormal shape, has its limitation of error marked out for it which cannot be passed by. In this human world there is a wide margin for oscillation; refusal to perform the ideal function has been provided for, redundance made to balance deficiency; checks are provided for every form of abnormal action of the will.

Viewed as an object not in man, justice is the constitution or fundamental law of the moral universe, the law of right, a rule of conduct for man in all his moral relations. Accordingly all human affairs must be subject to that as the law paramount; what is right agrees therewith and stands, what is wrong conflicts and falls. Private cohesions of self-love, of friendship, or of patriotism, must all be subordinate to this universal gravitation towards the eternal right.

We learn the laws of matter, that of attraction, for example, by observation and reflection; what we know thereof is the result of long experience, — the experienced sight and the experienced thought of many a thousand years. We might learn something of the moral law of justice, the law of right, in the same way, as a merely external thing. Then we should know it as a phenomenon, as we know attraction; as a fact so general, that we called it universal and a law of nature. Still it would be deemed only an arbitrary law, over us, indeed, but not in us,— or in our elements, not our consciousness,— which we must be subordinate to, but could not become coördinate with; a law like that of falling bodies, which had no natural relation with us, which we could not anticipate or divine by our nature, but only learn by our history. We should not know why God had made the world after the pattern of justice, and not injustice, any more than we now know why a body does not fall as rapidly the first as the last second of its descent.

But God has given us a moral faculty, the conscience, which is able to perceive this law directly and immediately, by intuitive perception thereof, without experience of the external consequences of keeping or violating it, and more perfectly than such experience can ever disclose it. For the facts of man's history do not fully represent the faculties of his nature as the history of matter represents the qualities of matter. Man, though finite, is indefinitely progressive, continually unfolding the qualities of his nature; his history, therefore, is not the whole book of man, but only the portion thereof which has been opened and publicly read. So the history of man never completely represents his nature; and a law derived merely from the facts of observation by no means describes the normal rule of action which belongs to his nature. The laws of matter are known to us because they are kept; there the ideal and actual are the same; but man has in his nature a rule of conduct higher than what he has come up to, — an ideal of nature which shames his actual of history. Observation and reflection only give us the actual of morals; conscience, by gradual and successive intuition, presents us the ideal of morals. On condition that I use this faculty in its normal activity, and in proportion as I develop it and all its kindred powers, I learn justice, the law of right, the divine rule of conduct for human life; I see it, not as an external fact which might as well not be at all as be, or might have been supplanted by its opposite, but I see it as a mode of action which belongs to the infinitely perfect nature of God; belongs also to my own nature, and so is not barely over me, but in me, of me, and for me. I can become co-ordinate with that, and not merely subordinate thereto; I find a deep, permanent, and instinctive delight in justice, not only in the outward effects, but in the inward cause, and by my nature I love this law of right, this rule of conduct, this justice, with a deep and abiding love. I find that justice is the object of my conscience, fitting that as light the eye and truth the mind. There is a perfect agreement between the moral object and the moral subject. Finding it fit me thus, I know that justice will work my welfare and that of all mankind.

Attraction is the most general law in the material world, and prevents a schism in the universe; temperance is the law of the body, and prevents a schism in the members; justice is the law of conscience, and prevents a schism in the moral world, amongst individuals in a family, communities in a State, or nations in the world of men. Temperance is corporeal justice, the doing right to each limb of the body, and is the mean proportional between appetite and appetite, or one and all; sacrificing no majority to one desire, however great, — no minority, however little, to a majority, — but giving each its due, and to all the harmonious and well-proportioned symmetry that is meet for all. It keeps the proportions betwixt this and that, and holds an even balance within the body, so that there shall be no excess. Justice is moral temperance in the world of men. It keeps just relations between men; one man, however little, must not be sacrificed to another, however great, to a majority, or to all men. It holds the balance betwixt nation and nation, for a nation is but a larger man; betwixt a man and his family, tribe, nation, race; between mankind and God. It is the universal regulator which coördinates man with man, each with all, — me with the ten hundred millions of men, so that my absolute rights and theirs do not interfere, nor our ultimate interests ever clash, nor my eternal welfare prove antagonistic to the blessedness of all or any one. I am to do justice, and demand that of all, — a universal human debt, a universal human claim.

But it extends further; it is the regulator between men and God. It is the moral spontaneousness of the Infinite God, as it is to be the moral volition of finite men. The right to the justice of God is unalienable in men, the universal human claim, the never-ending gift for them. Can God ever depart from his own justice, deprive any creature of a right, or balk it of a natural claim? Philosophically speaking, it is impossible, — a contradiction to our idea of God; religiously speaking, it is impious, — a contradiction to our feeling of God. Both the philosophic and the religious consciousness declare it impossible that God should be unjust. The nature of finite men claims justice of God; His infinite nature adjusts the claim. Every man in the world is morally related to each and all the rest. Justice is the common human bond. It joins us also to the infinite God. Justice is his constant mode of action in the moral world.

So much for justice, viewed as objective; as a law of the universe, the mode of action of the universal moral force.

Man naturally loves justice, for its own sake, as the natural object of his conscience. As the mind loves truth and beauty, so conscience loves the right; it is true and beautiful to the moral faculties. Conscience rests in justice as an end, as the mind in truth. As truth is the side of God turned towards the intellect, so is justice the side of Him which conscience looks upon. Love of justice is the moral part of piety.

When I am a baby, in my undeveloped moral state, I do not love justice, nor conform to it; when I am sick, and have not complete control over this republic of nerves and muscles, I fail of justice, and heed it not; when I am stung with beastly rage, blinded by passion, or over attracted from my proper sphere of affection, another man briefly possessing me, I may not love the absolute and eternal right, private capillary attraction conflicting with the universal gravitation. But in my maturity, in my cool and personal hours, when I am most myself, and the accidents of my bodily temperament and local surroundings are controlled by the substance of my manhood, then I love justice with a firm, unwavering love. That is the natural fealty of my conscience to its liege-lord. Then I love justice, not for its consequences for bodily gain, but for itself, for the moral truth and loveliness thereof. Then if justice crown me I am glad, not merely with my personal feeling, because it is I who wear the crown, but because it is the crown of justice. If justice discrown and bind me down to infamy, I still am glad with all my moral sense, and joy in the universal justice, though I suffer with the private smart. Though all that is merely selfish and personal of me revolts, still what is noblest, what I hold in common with mankind and in common with God, bids me be glad if justice is done upon me; to me or upon me, I know it is justice still, and though my private injustice be my foe, the justice of the universe is still my friend. God, acting in this universal mode of moral force, acts for me, and the prospect of future suffering has no terror.

Men reverence and love justice. Conscience is loyal; moral piety begins early, the ethical instinct prompting mankind, and in savage ages bringing out the lovely flower in some woman's character, where moral beauty has its earliest spring. Commonly, men love justice a little more than truth;

they are more moral than intellectual; have ideas of the conscience more than of the mind. This is not true of the more cultivated classes in any civilization, but of the mass of men in all; their morals are better than their philosophy. They see more absolute truth with the moral than with the intellectual faculty. The instinct for the abstract just of will is always a little before the instinct for the abstract true of thought. This is the normal order of development. But in the artificial forms of culture, what is selfish and for one takes rank before what is human and for all. So cultivated men commonly seek large intellectual power, as an instrument for their selfish purposes, and neglect and even hate to get a large moral power, the instrument of universal benevolence. They love the exclusive use of certain forms of truth, and neglect justice, which would make the convenience of every truth serve the common good of all. Men with large moral power must needs work for all; with merely large intellectual power they may work only for themselves. Hence crafty aristocracies and monopolists seek for intellectual culture as a mode of power, and shun moral culture, which can never serve a selfish end. This rule holds good of all the great forms of civilization, from the Egyptian to the British; of all the higher seminaries of education, from the Propaganda of the

Jesuits to a New England college. In all the civilized nations at this day, the controlling class is intellectual more than moral; has more power of thought than power of righteousness. The same fact appears in the literature of the world. The foremost class in culture, wealth, and social rank have less than the average proportion of morality. Hence comes the character of laws, political, social, and ecclesiastical institutions, — not designed for all, but for a few, at best a part, because the makers did not start with adequate moral power, nor propose justice as an end.

Yet the mass of men are always looking for the just; all this vast machinery which makes up a State, a world of States, is, on the part of the people, an attempt to organize justice; the minute and wide-extending civil machinery which makes up the law and the courts, with all their officers and implements, on the part of mankind, is chiefly an effort to reduce to practice the theory of right. Alas! with the leaders of civil and political affairs it is quite different, often an organization of selfishness. Mankind reaches out after the absolute right, makes its constitutions to establish justice, and provide for the common defence. We report the decisions of wise men, and of courts; we keep the record of cases decided, to help us judge more wisely in time to come. The nation would enact laws: it aims to get the justest men in the State, that they may incorporate their aggregate sense of right into a statute. We set twelve honest men to try an alleged offender; they are to apply their joint justice to the special case. The people wish law to be embodied justice, administered without passion. I know the government seldom desires this; the people as seldom fail of the wish. Yet the mass of men commonly attribute their own moral aims to every great leader. Did they know the actual selfishness and injustice of their rulers, not a government would stand a year. The world would ferment with universal revolution.

In savage times, duelling and private revenge grew out of this love of justice. They were rude efforts after the right. In its name a man slew his father's murderer, or, failing thereof, left the reversion of his vengeance as a trust in the hands of his own son, to be paid to the offender or his heir. With the Norsemen it was deemed a crime against society to forgive a grievous wrong, and "nidding" is a word of contempt to this day. It was not merely personal malice which led to private revenge; which bade the Scottish mother train up one son after another filled with a theological hatred against their father's murderer; not a private and selfish lust of vengeance alone which sustained her after the eldest and then the next of age perished in the attempt, and filled her with a horrid joy when the third succeeded. It was "wild justice" in a wild age, but always mixed with passion, and administered in hate; private vengeance edged the axe with which wild justice struck the blow. Even now, in the ruder portions of America, South and West, where the common law is silent, and of statutes there are none, or none enforced, when a wrong is done, the offended people come forth and hold their court, with summary process, brief and savage, to decree something like justice in a brutal way; rage furnishing the occasion, conscience is still the cause.

All these things indicate a profound love of justice inherent in mankind. It takes a rude form with rude men, is mixed with passion, private hate; in a civilized community it takes a better form, and attempts are made to remove all personal malice from the representatives of right. A few years ago men were surprised to see the people of a neighboring city for the first time choose their judges: common elections had been carried there by uncommon party tricks; but when this grave matter came before the people, they laid off their party badges, and as men chose the best officers for that distinguished trust.

The people are not satisfied with any form of government, or statute law, until it comes up to their sense of justice; so every progressive State revises its statutes from time to time, and at each revision comes nearer to the absolute right which human nature demands. Mankind, always progressive, revolutionizes constitutions, changes and changes, seeking to come close to the ideal justice, the divine and immutable law of the world, to which we all owe fealty, swear how we will.

In literature men always look for poetical justice, desiring that virtue should have its own reward, and vice appropriate punishment, not always outward, but always real, and made known to the reader. All students of English history rejoice at the downfall of Judge Jeffries. In romances we love to read of some man or maid oppressed by outward circumstances, but victorious over them; hawked at by villains whose foot is taken in their own snare. This is the principal charm in the ballads and people's poetry of England and Germany, and in the legends of Catholic countries. All men sympathize in the fate of Blue Beard, and "the guardian uncle fierce." The world has ready sympathy with the Homeric tale of Ulysses returning to his Penelope, long faithful, but not grown old with baffling the suitors for twenty years. It is his justice and humanity which give such a wide audience to the most popular novelist of our day. But when a writer tries to paint vice beautiful, make sin triumphant, men shrink away from the poison atmosphere he breathes. Authors like Filmer, Machiavel, and Hobbes arouse the indignation of mankind. The fact of personal error it is easy to excuse, but mankind does not forgive such as teach the theory of sin. We always honor men who forget their immediate personal interests, and use an author's sacred function to bear witness to the right.

The majority of men who think have an ideal justice better than the things about them, juster than the law. Some paint it behind them, on the crumbling walls of history, and tell us of "the good old times;" others paint it before them, on the morning mist of youthful life, and in their prayers and their daily toil strive after this,—their New Jerusalem. We all of us have some ideal; our dream is fairer than our day; we will not let it go. If the wicked prosper, it is but for a moment, say we; the counsel of the froward shall be carried headlong. What an ideal democracy now floats before the eyes of earnest and religious men,—fairer than the "Republic" of Plato, or More's "Utopia," or the "golden age" of fabled memory! It is justice that we want to organize,—justice for all, for rich and poor There the slave shall be free from his master. There shall be no want, no oppression, no fear of man, no fear of God, but only love. "There is a good time coming,"—so we all believe when we are young and full of life and healthy hope.

God has made man with the instinctive love of justice in him, which gradually gets developed in the world. But in Himself justice is infinite. This justice of God must appear in the world, and in the history of men; and, after all "the wrongs that patient merit of the unworthy takes," still you see that the ploughshare of justice is drawn through and through the field of the world, uprooting the savage plants. The proverbs of the nations tell us this: "The mills of the gods grind slow, but they grind to powder;" "Ill got ill spent;" "The triumphing of the wicked is but for a moment;" "What the Devil gives, he also takes;" "Honesty is the best policy;" "No butter will stick to a bad man's bread." Sometimes these sayings come from the instinct of justice in man, and have a little ethical exaggeration about them, but yet more often they represent the world's experience of facts more than its consciousness of ideas.

Look at the facts of the world. You see a continual and progressive triumph of the right. I do not pretend to understand the moral universe; the arc is a long one, my eye reaches but little ways; I cannot calculate the curve and complete the figure by the experience of sight; I can divine it by conscience. And from what I see I am sure it bends towards justice. Things refuse to be mismanaged long. Jefferson trembled when he thought of slavery and remembered that God is just. Erelong all America will tremble. The Stuarts in England were tyrannical and strong: respectable and peaceful men kept still a while, and bore the tyranny; but men who loved God and his justice more than house and land fled to the wilderness, and built up a troublesome commonwealth of Puritans. Such as stayed at home endeavored for a while to submit to the wrong; some of them made theories to justify it. But it could not be; the tyranny became unbearable even to barons and bishops; one tyrant loses his head, another his crown; no Stuart must tread again the English soil; legitimacy becomes a pretender.

England would rule America, not for our good, but hers alone. We forgot the love which bound the two people into one family; the obstinate injustice of the mother weakened the ties of language, literature, religion, — the Old England and the New read the same Bible, — kindred blood and institutions inherited from the same fathers; we thought only of the injustice; and there was an ocean between us and the mother country. The fairest jewel fell from the British crown.

In France, kings, nobles, clergy, trod the people down. Men bore it with the slow, sad patience of humanity, bore it out of regard for the "divinity that doth hedge a king," for the nobility of the noble, and the reverence of the priest. But in a few years outraged humanity forgot its slow, sad patience, and tore away this triple torment,—as Paul, escaped from wreck, shook off the viper from his hand,—and trod the venomous beast to dust. Napoleon came, king of the people. Justice was his word, his action for a while. The nation gathered about him, gave him their treasure and their trust. He was strong through the people's faith; his foes fell before him; ancient thrones tottered and reeled, and came heavy to the ground. The name of justice, of the rights of man, shook down their thrones, and organized victory at every step. But he grows giddy with his height; selfishness takes the place of justice in his counsels; a bastard giant sits on the throne whence the people had hurled off "legitimate" oppression; he fights no more the battles of mankind; justice is exiled from his upstart court. The people fall away; victory perches no more on his banner. The snows of Russia cut off his army, but it was his own injustice that brought Napoleon to the ground. Self-shorn of this great strength, the ablest monarch since Charlemagne sits down on a little island in the tropic sea, and dies upon that lonely rock, his life a warning, to bid mankind be just and not despise the Lord. No mightiness of genius could save him, cut off from the moral force of the human race. Can any tyrant prosper where such a master fell?

Look at the condition of Christendom at this day; what tyrant sits secure? Revolution is the Lynch-law of nations; it creates an anarchy, and then organizes its provisional government of momentary despotism. It is a bloody process, but justice does not disdain a rugged road; the Desire of all nations comes not always on an ass's colt. All Europe is, just now, in a great ferment; terrible questions are getting ready for a swift tribunal. Injustice cannot stand. No armies, no "Holy Alliance," can hold it up. Human nature is against it; and so is the nature of God! "Justice has feet of wool," no man hears her step, "but her hands are of iron," and where she lays them down, only God can uplift and unclasp. It is vain to trust in wrong: As much of evil, so much of loss, is the formula of human history.

I know men complain that sentence against an evil work is not presently executed. They see but half; it is executed, and with speed; every departure from justice is attended with loss to the unjust man, but the loss is not reported to the public.

Sometimes a man is honored as a brave, good man, but trial rings him and he gives an empty, hollow sound. All the ancient and honorable may bid the people trust that man, — they turn off their affections from him.

So have I seen an able man, witty and cunning, graceful, plausible, elegant, and rich; men honored him for a time, tickled by his beauty to eye and ear. But gradually the mean soul of the man appeared in his conduct, selfish, grasping, inhuman, and fraudulently unjust. The public heart forgot him, and when he came to die, the town which once had honored him so much gave him only earth to rest his coffin on. He had the official praises which he paid for, that was all. Silence is a figure of speech, unanswerable, short, cold, but terribly severe.

How differently do men honor such as stood up for truth and right, and never shrank! What monuments the world builds to its patriots! Four great statesmen, organizers of the right, embalmed in stone, look down upon the lawgivers of France as they pass to their hall of legislation, silent orators to tell how nations love the just. What a monument Washington has built in the heart of America and all the world! not by great genius, — he had none of that, — but by his effort to be just. The martyrs of Christendom, of Judaism, and of every form of heathen faith, — how men worship those firm souls who shook off their body sooner than be false to conscience.

Yet eminent justice is often misunderstood. Littleness has its compensation. A small man is seldom pinched for want of room. Greatness is its own torment. There was once a man on this earth whom the world could not understand. He was too high for them, too wide, was every way too great. He came, the greatest moral genius of our history, to bless mankind. Men mocked him, gave him a gallows between two thieves. "Saviour, save thyself," said they, as they shot out the lip at him. "Father, forgive them, for they know not what they do!" was the manly answer to the brutal taunt. Now see how the world avenges its conscience on itself for this injustice: for sixteen hundred years men worship him as God throughout the Western World. His name goes like the morning sun around the earth, like that to waken beauty into life. This conscience of ours is loyal; only let us see the man and know that he is King of Righteousness, and we will do him homage all our days.

But we do not see that justice is always done on earth; many a knave is rich, sleek, and honored, while the just man is poor, hated, and in torment. The Silesian merchant fattens on the weavers' tears, and eats their children's bones. Three million slaves earn the enjoyment of Americans, who curse them in the name of Christ; in the North, capital is a tyrant over labor. How sad is the condition of the peasantry of Christendom! The cry of a world of suffering, from mythic Abel to the actual slaves of America, comes up to our ear, and the instinct of justice paints a world beyond the grave, where exact justice shall be done to all and each, to Abel and to Cain. The moral instinct, not satisfied on earth, reaches out to the future world, and in an ideal heaven would realize ideal justice. But even there the tyranny of able-minded men has interfered, painting immortality in such guise that it would be a curse to mankind. Yet the instinct of justice prevails above it all, and few men fear to meet the eternal Mother of us all in heaven.

We need a great and conscious development of the moral element in man, and a corresponding expansion of justice in human affairs; an intentional application thereof to individual, domestic, social, ecclesiastical, and political life. In the old military civilization that was not possible; in the present industrial civilization it is not thought desirable by the mercantile chiefs of church and State. Hitherto, the actual function of government, so far as it has been controlled by the will of the rulers, has commonly been this: To foster the strong at the expense of the weak, to protect the capitalist and tax the laborer. The powerful have sought a monopoly of development and enjoyment, loving to eat their morsel alone. Accordingly, little respect is paid to absolute justice by the controlling statesmen of the Christian world. Not conscience and the right is appealed to, but prudence and the expedient for to-day. Justice is forgotten in looking at interest, and political morality neglected for political economy; instead of national organization of the ideal right, we have only national housekeeping. Hence come the great evils of civilization at this day, and the questions of humanity, so long adjourned and put off, that it seems they can only be settled with bloodshed. Nothing rests secure save in the law of God. The thrones of Christian Europe tremble; a little touch and they fall. Capitalists are alarmed, lest gold ill got should find an equilibrium. Behind the question of royalty, nobility, slavery, — relics of the old feudalism, — there are other questions yet more radical, soon to be asked and answered.

There has been a foolish neglect of moral culture throughout all Christendom. The leading classes have not valued it; with them the mind was thought better than the moral sense, and conscience a dowdy. It is so in the higher education of New England, as of Europe. These men seek the uses of truth, not truth itself; they scorn duty and its higher law; to be ignorant and weak-minded is thought worse than to be voluntarily unjust and wicked; idiocy of conscience is often thought an excellence, is never out of fashion. Morality is thought no part of piety in the Church, it "saves" no man; "belief" does that with the Protestants, "sacraments" with the Catholics; it is no part of politics in the State,—not needed to save the nation or the soul.

Of late years there has been a great expansion of intellectual development in Europe and America. Has the moral development kept pace with it? Is the desire to apply justice to its universal function as common and intense with the more intellectual classes, as the desire to apply special truths to their function? By no means. We have organized our schemes of intellectual culture: it is the function of schools, colleges, learned societies, and all the special institutions for agriculture, manufactures, and commerce, to develop the understanding and apply it to various concrete interests. No analogous pains have been taken with the culture of conscience. France has the only academy for moral science in the Christian world! We have statistical societies for interest, no moral societies for justice. We rely only on the moral instinct; its development is accidental, not a considerable part of our plan; or else is involuntary, no part of the will of the most intellectual class. There is no college for the conscience.

Do the churches accomplish this educational purpose for the moral sense? The popular clergy think miracles better than morality; and have even less justice than truth. They justify the popular sins in the name of God; are the allies of despotism in all its forms, military or industrial. Oppression by the sword and oppression by capital successively find favor with them. In America there are two common ecclesiastical defences of African slavery: The negroes are the descendants of Ham, who laughed at his father Noah, — overtaken with drink, — and so it is right that Ham's children, four thousand years later, should be slaves to the rest of the world; Slavery teaches the black men "our blessed religion." Such is ecclesiastical justice; and hence judge the value of the churches to educate the conscience of mankind! It is strange how little the clergy of Christendom, for fifteen hundred years, have done for the morality of the world; much for decorum, little for justice; a deal for ecclesiastical ceremony, but what for ecclesiastical righteousness? They put worship with the knee before the natural piety of the conscience. "Trusting in good works" is an offence to the Christian Church, as well Protestant as Catholic.

In Europe the consequences of this defect of moral culture have become alarming, even to such as fear only for money. That intellectual culture, which was once the cherished monopoly of the rich, has got diffused amongst wide ranks of men, who once sat in the shadow of intellectual darkness. There is no development of conscience to correspond therewith. The Protestant clergy have not enlightened the people on the science of religion. The Catholics had little light to spare, and that was spent in exhibiting "the holy coat of Treves," or images of "the Virgin," and in illuminating cardinals and popes set in the magic-lantern of the great ecclesiastical show-box. No pains, or little, have been taken with the moral culture of the people; none scientifically and for the sake of justice and human kind. So the selfishness of the rich has spread with their intellectual culture. The few have long demanded a monopoly for themselves, and with their thunder blasted the mortal life of the prophets of justice sent by God to establish peace on earth and good-will amongst men. Now the many begin to demand a monopoly for themselves. Education, wealth, political power, was once a privilege, and they who enjoyed it made this their practical motto: "Down with the poor!" The feudal system fell before Dr. Faustus and his printing-press. Military civilization slowly gives way to industrial. Common schools teach men to read. The steam-press cheapens literature; the complicated tools of modern industry make the shop a college for the understanding; the laborer is goaded by his hate of wrong, which is the passion of morality, as love of right is the affection thereof;—he sees small respect for justice in church or State. What shall save him from the selfishness about him, long dignified as philosophy, sanctified as religion, and reverenced as the law of God! Do you wonder at "atheism" in Germany; at communism in France? Such "atheism" is the theory of the Church made popular; the worst communism is only the principle of monopoly translated out of aristocracy into democracy; the song of the noble in the people's mouth. The hideous cry, "Down with the rich!"—is that an astonishment to the leaders of Europe, who have trod down the poor these thousand years? When ignorance, moral and intellectual stupidity, brought only servile obedience from the vassal, the noble took delight in the oppression which trod his brother down. Now numbers are power; that is the privilege of the people, and if the people, the privileged class of the future, have the selfishness of the aristocracy, what shall save the darling dollars of the rich? "They that laughed at the grovelling worm, and trod on him, may cry and howl when they see the stoop of the flying and fiery-mouthed dragon!"

The leaders of modern civilization have scorned justice. The chiefs of war, of industry, and the Church are joined in a solidarity of contempt; in America, not harlots, so much as politicians debauch the land. Conscience has been left out of the list of faculties to be intentionally developed in the places of honor. Is it marvellous if men find their own selfishness fall on their own heads? No army of special constables will supply the place of morality in the people. If they do not reverence justice, what shall save the riches of the rich? Ah me! even the dollar flees to the Infinite God for protection, and bows before the Higher Law its worshippers despise.

What moral guidance do the leading classes of men offer the people in either England, — the European or American? Let the laboring men of Great Britain answer; let Ireland, about to perish, groan out her reply; let the three million African slaves bear the report to Heaven. "Ignorance is the mother of devotion," once said some learned fool; monopolists act on the maxim. Ignorance of truth, ignorance of right, — will these be good directors, think you, of the class which has the privilege of numbers and their multitudinous agglomerated power? "Reverence the eternal right," says Conscience, "that is moral piety!" "Reap as you sow," quoth human History. Alas for a church without righteousness, and a State without right! All history shows their fate! What is false to justice cannot stand; what is true to that cannot perish. Nothing can save wrong.

A sentence is written against all that is unjust, written by God in the nature of man and the nature of the universe, because it is in the nature of the Infinite God. Fidelity to your faculties, trust in their convictions, that is justice to yourself; a life in obedience thereto, that is justice towards men. Tell me not of successful wrong. The gain of injustice is a loss, its pleasure suffering. Iniquity seems to prosper, but its success is its defeat and shame. The knave deceives himself. The miser, starving his brother's body, starves also his own soul, and at death shall creep out of his great estate of injustice, poor and naked and miserable. Whoso escapes a duty avoids a gain. Outward judgment often fails, inward justice never. Let a man try to love the wrong, and do the wrong, it is eating stones, and not bread; the swift feet of justice are upon him, following with woollen tread, and her iron hands are round his neck. No man can escape from this, no more than from himself.

At first sight of the consequences of justice, redressing the evils of the world, its aspect seems stern and awful. Men picture the palace of this king as hell: there is torment and anguish; the waters are in trouble. The chariot of justice seems a car of Juggernaut crushing the necks of men; they cry for mercy. But look again: the sternness all is gone; nothing is awful there; the palace of justice is all heaven, as before a hell; the water is troubled only by an angel, and to heal the sick; the fancied car of Juggernaut is the triumphal chariot of mankind riding forth to welfare. With swift and noiseless feet justice follows the transgressor and clutches the iron hand about his neck; it was to save him that she came with swift and noiseless tread. This is the angel of God that flies from east to west, and where she stoops her broad wings it is to bring the counsel of God, and feed mankind with angels' bread. As an eagle stirreth up her nest, from her own beak to feed its young, broods over their callow frame, and bears them on her wings, teaching them first to fly, so comes justice unto men.

Sometimes men fear that justice will fail, wickedness appears so strong. On its side are the armies, the thrones of power, the riches, and the glory of the world. Poor men crouch down in despair. Shall justice fail and perish out from the world of men? shall any thing that is wrong continually endure? When attraction fails out of the world of matter, when God fails and there is no God, then shall justice fail, then shall wrong be able continually to endure; not till then.

The unity of the material world is beautiful, kept by attraction's universal force; temperance in the body has fair effects, and wisdom in the mind. The face of Nature, how fair it is; the face of strong and healthy, beauteous manhood is a dear thing to look upon. To intellectual eyes, the countenance of truth has a majestic charm. Wise men, with cultivated mind, understanding, imagination, reason well developed, discovering and disclosing truth and beauty to mankind, are a fair spectacle. But I love the moral side of Deity yet more; love God as justice. His justice, our morality working with that, shall one day create a unity amongst all men more fair than the face of Nature, and add a wondrous beauty, wondrous happiness, to this great family of men. Will you fear lest a wrong should prove immortal? So far as any thing is false, or wrong, it is weak; so far as true and right, is omnipotently strong. Never fear that a just thought shall fail to be a thing; the power of God, the wisdom of God, and the justice of God are on its side, and it cannot fail, — no more than God himself can perish. Wrong is the accident of human development. Right is of the substance of humanity, justice the goal we are to reach.

But in human affairs the justice of God must work by human means. Men are the measures of God's principles; our morality the instrument of his justice, which stilleth alike the waves of the sea, the tumult of the people, and the oppressor's brutal laugh. Justice is the idea of God, the ideal of man, the rule of conduct writ in the nature of mankind. The ideal must become actual, God's thought a human thing, made real in a reign of righteousness, and a kingdom — no, a Commonwealth — of justice on the earth. You and I can help forward that work. God will not disdain to use our prayers, our self-denial, and the little atoms of justice that personally belong to us, to establish his mighty work, — the development of mankind.

You and I may work with Him, and, as on the floor of the Pacific Sea little insects lay the foundation of firm islands, slowly uprising from the tropic wave, — the ocean working with their humble toil, — so you and I in our daily life, in house, or field, or shop, obscurely faithful, may prepare the way for the republic of righteousness, the democracy of justice that is to come. Our own morality shall bless us here; not in our outward life alone, but in the inward and majestic life of conscience. All the justice we mature shall bless us here, yea, and hereafter; but at our death we leave it added to the common store of humankind. Even the crumbs that fall from our table may save a brother's life. You and I may help deepen the channel of human morality in which God's justice runs, and the wrecks of evil, which now check the stream, be borne off the sooner by the strong, all-conquering tide of right, the river of God that is full of blessing.

IV.

OF LOVE AND THE AFFECTIONS.

LOVE IS OF GOD.—1 John iv. 7.

CONSCIENCE deals with universal principles of morals. It has for its object justice, the divine law of the world, to be made ideal in the consciousness of mankind, and then actual in the facts of our condition and history. The affections deal with persons; with nothing but persons, for animate, and even inanimate, things get invested with a certain imaginary personality as soon as they become objects of affection. Ideas are the persons of the intellect, and persons the ideas of the heart. Persons are the central point of the affectional world. The love of persons is the function of the affections, as it is that of the mind and conscience to discover and accept truth and right.

This love is a simple fact of consciousness; a simple feeling, not capable of analysis, not easily described, yet not likely to be confounded with any other fact of consciousness, or simple feeling. It is not directly dependent on the will, so is free from all immediate arbitrariness and caprice of volition. It is spontaneous, instinctive, disinterested, not seeking the delight of the loving subject, but of the object loved. So it is not a desire of enjoying, but of delighting. As we love truth for itself, justice for its own sake, so we love persons not for their use, but for themselves; we love them independently of their convenience to us. Love is its own satisfaction; it is the love of loving, not merely of enjoying, another.

Such is love itself, described by its central character; but it appears in many forms, and is specifically modified by the character and condition of the person loved, the object of affection; by the person who loves, the loving subject, and by the various passions and emotions mingling therewith. So it appears as fraternal, filial, connubial, and parental love; as friendship, love of a few who reciprocate the feeling; as charity, love of the needy; as patriotism, love of your nation; and a philanthropy, the love of all mankind without respect to kin or country. In all these cases love is the same thing in kind, but modified specifically by other emotions which connect themselves with it. Love is the piety of the affections.

Of course there are not only forms of love, where the quality is modified, but degrees which measure the different quantity thereof. The degree depends on the subject, and also on the object, of love.

There is a state of consciousness in which we wish no ill to a man, but yet wish him no good. That is the point of affectional indifference. The first remove above that may be regarded as the lowest degree of love, hardly worthy of the name, a sort of zoöphytic affection. You scarcely know whether to call it love or not.

The highest degree of love is that state of feeling in which you are willing to abandon all, your comfort, convenience, and life, for the sake of another, to sacrifice your delight in him to his delight in you, and to do this not merely by volition, as an act of conscience, and in obedience to a sense of duty,— not merely by impulse, in obedience to blind feeling, as an act of instinct,—but to do all this consciously, yet delightedly, with a knowledge of the consequences, by a movement which is not barely instinctive, and not merely of the will, but spontaneous; to do all this not merely out of gratitude for favors received, for a reward paid in advance, nor for the sake of happiness in heaven, a recompense afterwards; with no feeling of grateful obligation, no wish for a recompense, but from pure, entire, and disinterested affection.

This highest ideal degree of love is sometimes attained, but, like all the great achievements of human nature, it is rare. There are few masterpieces in sculpture, painting, architecture, in poetry or music. The ideal and actual are seldom the same in any performance of mankind. It is rarely that human nature rises to its highest ideal mark; some great hearts notch the mountains and leave their line high up above the heads of ordinary men,—a history and a prophecy. Yet the capacity for this degree of love belongs to the nature of man as man. The human excellence which is actual in Jesus, is possible in Iscariot; give him time and opportunity, the man will appear in him also. I doubt not that the worst man ever hanged or even honored for his crime, will one day attain a degree of love which the loftiest men now cannot comprehend. This power of loving to this degree, it seems to me, is generic, of the nature of man; the absence of it is a mark of immaturity, of greenness, and clownishness of the heart. But at this day the power of affection is distributed as diversely as power of mind or conscience, and so the faculty of loving is by no means the same in actual men. All are not at once capable of the same quantity of love.

There are also different degrees of love occasioned by the character of the object of affection. All cannot receive the same quantity. Thus you cannot love a dog so well as a man, nor a base, mean man so much as a great, noble man, with the excellences of mind and conscience, heart and soul. Can you and I love an Arnold as well as a Washington? a kidnapper as well as a philanthropist? God may do so, not you and I. So with finite beings the degree of love is affected by the character of both the subject and the object of affection.

It is unfortunate that we have but one word in English to express affectional action in respect to myself and to other men; we speak of a man loving himself, and loving another. But it is plain that I cannot love myself at all in the sense that I love another; for self-love is intransitive,—subject and object are identical. It is one thing to desire my own delight, and something quite opposite to desire the delight of another. So, for the sake of clearness, I will use the words Self-love for the normal feeling of a man towards himself; Selfishness for the abnormal and excessive degree of this; and Love for the normal feeling towards others.

Self-love is the lesser cohesive attraction which keeps the man whole and a unit, which is necessary for his consistency and existence as an individual. It is a part of morality, and is to the man what impenetrability is to the atoms of matter, and what the centripetal force is to the orbs of heaven; without it, the man's personality would soon be lost in the press of other men.

Selfishness is the excess of this self-love; no longer merely conservative of myself, I become invasive, destructive of others, and appropriate what is theirs to my own purposes.

Love is the greater gravitation which unites me to others; the expansive and centrifugal power that extends my personality, and makes me find my delight in others, and desire them to have theirs in me. In virtue of this I feel for the sorrows of another man; they become, in some measure, my sorrows, just in proportion to the degree of my love; his joys also are my joys just in the same degree; I am gladdened with his delights, honored in his honors; and so my consciousness is multiplied by all the persons that I love, for my affectional personality is extended to them all, and with a degree of power exactly proportionate to my degree of love. So affection makes one man into many men, as it were.

The highest action of any power is in combination with all the rest. Yet there is much imperfect action of the faculties, working severally, not jointly. The affections may act independent of the conscience, as it of them. It is related that an eminent citizen of Athens had a son who committed an offence for which the law demanded the two eyes of the offender; the father offered one of his to save one of his son's. Here his heart, not his conscience, prompted the deed. When the affections thus control the conscience, we have the emotion called Mercy, which is the preponderance of love for a person, not love for right, of love for the concrete man over the abstract idea of justice. In a normal condition, it seems to me that love of persons is a little in advance of love of the abstract right, and that spontaneous love triumphs over voluntary morality; the heart carries the day before the conscience. This is so in most women, who are commonly fairer examples of the natural power of both the moral and affectional faculties, and represent the natural tendency of human nature better than men. I think they seldom sacrifice a person to an abstract rule of conduct; or at least, if there is a collision between conscience and the heart, with them the heart carries the day. Non-resistants, having a rule of conduct which forbids them to hurt another, will yet do this for a wife or child, though not for themselves, their love being greater than their selfishness. This is so common that it seems a rule of nature,—that the affectional is a little stronger than the moral instinct, and where both have received due culture, and there is still a collision between the two, that mercy is the law. But here no private love should prevail against right, and only universal love come in to its aid to supply the defect of conscience. Brutus, so the story goes, finds his son committing a capital offence, and orders his head struck off, sacrificing his private and paternal love to his universal and human love of justice, his love of a special man to his love of what is right for all men. This is as it should be.

Conscience may be cultivated in an exclusive manner to the neglect of the affections. Then conscience is despotic; the man always becomes hard and severe, a stern father, a cold neighbor, a harsh judge, a cruel magistrate. He will err often, but always on the side of vengeance. Love improves the quality of finite morality, for it is the same as divine justice. Absolute justice and absolute love are never antagonistic, but identical.

The affections may be cultivated at the expense of conscience. This often happens with such as limit the range of their love to a few friends, to their own family, class, or nation. The world is full of examples of this. Here is one who loves her own family with intense love, — her husband, children, grandchildren, and collateral relations, — the love always measured by their propinquity to her. Like the crow in the fable, she thinks her own young the fairest of the fair, heedless of their vulgarity, and worldly and ignoble materialism. She is generous to them, no she-crow more bounteous to her young, but no hawk was ever more niggardly to all beyond. Here neglect of justice and scorn of conscience have corrupted her affections; and her love is only self-love, — for she loves these but as limbs of herself, — and has degenerated into selfishness in a wider form, not simple, but many-headed selfishness.

I once knew of a man who was a slave-trader on the Atlantic, and a proverb for cruelty among the felons of that class; he was rich, and remarkably affectionate in his own family; he studied the comfort of his daughters and wife, was self-denying for their sake. Yet he did not hesitate to break up a thousand homes in Africa, that he might adorn his own in New England. The lion, the tiger, the hyena, each is kind to his whelps, — for instinctive love affects the beast also. No man has universal love; conscience gives the rule thereof, and so in applying justice applies God's universal love to that special case. Seek to exercise love without justice, and you injure some one.

The same form of affection appears on a larger scale in the members of a class in society, or a sect in religion; it leads to kindliness within the circle of its range, but intense cruelty is often practised beyond that limit. All the aristocracies of the world, the little sects of Christendom, and the great sects of the human race, furnish examples of this.

What is called patriotism is another form of the same limited love, — a culture of the affections without regard to justice. Hence it has been held patriotic to build up your country by the ruin of another land, to love Jacob and hate Esau. This feeling is of continual occurrence. "Lands intersected by a narrow frith abhor each other," cities that are rivals in trade seek to ruin each other; nations do the same.

In all these cases, where ove is limited to the family, class, sect, or nation, the aim is this: Mutuality of love within the narrow circle; without its range, mutuality of selfishness. Thus love is deemed only a privilege of convention and for a few, arbitrarily limited by caprice; not a right, of nature and for all, the extension thereof to be limited only by the power, not the will, of the man who loves.

All the above are common forms of limited affection. The domestic, social, ecclesiastical, and political institutions of the world, the educational and commercial machinery of the world, tend to produce this result. All the religions of the world have practically fostered this mistake, by starting with the idea, that God loved best the men who worshipped Him in a certain conventional form.

But this expansive and centrifugal power may be cultivated to the neglect of natural and well-proportioned self-love. This also is a defect, for the conservative or self-preserving power is quite as necessary as the beneficent and expansive power. Impenetrability is the necessary concomitant of attraction. The individual is first an integer, then a fraction of society; he must keep his personal integrity and discreteness of person, and not be lost in the press and crowd of other persons. What is true of bodies is not less so of spirits. Here is a man with so little self-love, that his personality seems lost; he is no person, but now this man, now that, — a free port of trade, where all individualities are unloaded and protected; but he has none. His circumference is everywhere; his centre nowhere. He keeps other men's vineyards, not his own. This is a fault; doubtless a rare one, still a fault which destroys the individual character of the man.

There is, doubtless, a large difference amongst men in respect to the original power of the affections, — a difference of nature; a great difference in respect to the acquired power of love, — a difference of culture; a difference, also, in respect to the mode of culture of the heart, which may be developed jointly with mind and conscience, or independent of them, — a difference in proportion. Thus, practically, the affectional power of men varies as much as the intellectual or the moral power.

Look at the place which the affections occupy in the nature of man. In point of time they precede the intellectual and moral powers in their order of development, they have a wider range in the world than those other faculties. You find affection in animals. In some, love is very powerful. True, it appears there as rudimentary, and for a short time, as in birds, grouping them into brief cohesions. In some animals it is continual, yet not binding one individual to another in a perpetual combination, but grouping many individuals into a flock. The flock remains; all the individuals sustain a constant relation to the flock, but most unconstant relations to one another, — the male and female parting fellowship when the annual season of passion is over, the parents neglecting their child as soon as it outgrows the mother's care. Throughout the animal world love does not appear to exist for its own sake, but only as a means to a material end; now to create, then to protect, the individual and the race. Besides, it is purely instinctive, not also self-conscious and voluntary action. The animal seems not an agent, but only a tool of affection, his love necessitated, not spontaneous. Accordingly, in its more permanent forms, love is merely gregarious, and does not come to individual sociality; it seems but a more subtle mode of gravitation. A herd of buffaloes is only an aggregation of members, not a society of free individuals, who group from choice. Friendship, I think, never appears amongst animals, excepting such as are under the eye of man, and have, in some manner not easily understood, acquired his habits. The animal does not appear to have private affinities, and to attach himself to this or that fellow-being with the discrimination of love; development of the affections is never sought for as a thing good in itself, but only as a means to some other good.

With man there is this greater gravitation of men into masses; which, without doubt, is at first as instinctive as the grouping of bees or beavers; but man is capable of modifying the action of this gregarious instinct so, on the one side, as to form minute cohesions of friendship, wherein each follows his private personal predilections, his own elective affinities; and, also, on the other, to form vast associations of men gravitating into a nation, ruled by a common will; and one day we shall, no doubt, group all these nations into one great family of races, with a distinct self-consciousness of universal brotherhood.

It is instructive to look on the rudimentary love in animals, and see the beginnings of human nature, as it were, so low down, and watch the successive risings in successive creations. It helps us to see the unity of the world, and also to foretell the development of human nature; for what is there accomplished by successive creation of new races, with us takes place by the continual development of the same individual.

It is according to the order of nature, that the power to love should be developed before the power to think. All things with us begin with a feeling; next enlarge to an idea; then take the form of action, the mind mediating between the inward sentiment and the outward deed. We delight in love long before we have any conscious joy in truth or justice. In childhood we are acquainted with persons before we know things; indeed, things are invested with a dim personality in the mind of children and of savages. We know father and mother long before we have any notion of justice or of truth. The spontaneous development of the heart in children is one of the most beautiful phenomena in nature. The child has self-love, but no selfishness; his nebulous being not yet solidified to the impenetrability which is to come. His first joys are animal, the next affectional, the delight of loving and of being loved!

Indeed, with most men the affections take the lead of all the spiritual powers; only they act in a confined sphere of the family, class, sect, or nation. Men trust the heart more than the head. The mass of men have more confidence in a man of great affection than in one of great thought; pardon is commonly popular, mercy better loved than severity. Men rejoice when the murderer is arrested; but shout at his acquittal of the crime. The happiness of the greater part of men comes from affectional more than intellectual or moral sources. Hence the abundant interest felt in talk about persons, the popular fondness for personal anecdotes, biographies, ballads, love-stories, and the like. The mass of men love the person of their great man, not his opinions, and care more to see his face and hear his voice than to know his ideas of truth and of justice. It is so with religious teachers. Men sympathize with the person before they take his doctrine. Hence the popular fondness for portraits of great men, for their autographs, and even for relics. The person of Jesus of Nazareth has left a much greater impression on the hearts of men, than his doctrines have made on the mind and conscience of Christendom. For this reason, religious pictures preserve scenes which have nothing to do with the truth or the right that the man represented, but are merely personal details, often destitute of outward beauty, of no value to the mind, of much to the affections. This explains the popular fondness for stories and pictures of the sufferings of martyrs. A crucifix is nothing to the mind and conscience; — how much to the heart of Christendom! Hence, too, men love to conceive of God in the person of a man.

Now and then you find a man of mere intellectual or moral power, who takes almost his whole delight in the exercise of his mind or conscience. Such men are rare and wonderful, but by no means admirable.

Without the culture of the affections life is poor and unsatisfactory; truth seems cold, and justice stern. Let a man have the piety of the body, of the mind and conscience, it is not satisfactory without the piety of the heart. Let him have this also, and what a world of delight it opens to him!

Take the whole population of Christendom, there are but one or two in a thousand who have much delight in intellectual pursuits, who find a deep and reconciling joy in science, or literature, or any art; even music, the most popular of all, has a narrow range. But almost every one has a delight in the affections which quite transcends his intellectual joy. When a new book comes into being, if it be brave and good, it will quicken the progress of mankind; men rejoice, and the human race slowly folds to its bosom the works of Homer, Dante, Shakspeare, Milton, and will not willingly let them die. When a new child is born into some noble and half-starved family, it diminishes their "comforts," it multiplies their toil, it divides their loaf, it crowds their bed, and shares the unreplenished fire; but with what joy is it welcomed there! Men of great genius, who can judge the world by thought, feel less delight at the arrival of some great poet at his mind's estate, than many a poor mother feels at the birth of a new soul into the world; far less than she feels in the rude affection of her home, naked, comfortless, and cold. I know there is a degradation caused by poverty, when the heart dies out of the man, and "the mother hath sodden her own child." But such depravity is against nature, and only takes place when physical suffering has worn off the human qualities, one by one, till only impenetrability is left.

You find men that are ignorant, rich men too; and they are not wholly ashamed of it. They say, "Early circumstances hindered my growth of mind, for I was poor. You may pity, but you should not blame me." If you should accuse a man of lacking heart, of having no culture of affection, every one would feel it was a great reproach, and, if true, a fault without excuse. No man ever confesses this, —a sin against human nature.

All men need something to poetize and idealize their life a little, something which they value for more than its use, and which is a symbol of their emancipation from the mere materialism and drudgery of daily life. Rich men attempt to do this with beautiful houses, with costly furniture, with sumptuous food, and "wine too good for the tables of pontiffs," thereby often only thickening and gilding the chain which binds the soul to earth. Some men idealize their life a little with books, music, flowers; with science, poetry, and art; with thought. But such men are comparatively rare, even in Scotland and New England, — two or three in the hundred, not more. In America the cheap newspaper is the most common instrument used for this purpose, — a thing not without great value. But the majority of men do this idealizing by the affections, which furnish the chief poetry of their life, — the wife and husband delighting in one another, both in their children. Burns did not exaggerate in his Cotter's Saturday Night, when he painted the laborer's joy:

> "His wee bit ingle, blinkin' bonnily,
> His clean hearth-stane, his thriftie wifie's smile,
> The lisping infant prattling on his knee,
> Does a' his weary kiaugh and care beguile,
> An' makes him quite forget his labor an' his toil."

I have heard a boorish pedant wonder how a woman could spend so many years of her life with little children, and be content! In her satisfaction he found a proof of her "inferiority," and thought her but the "servant of a wooden cradle," herself almost as wooden. But in that gentle companionship she nursed herself and fed a higher faculty than our poor pedant, with his sophomoric wit, had yet brought to consciousness, and out of her wooden cradle got more than he had learned to know. A physician once, with unprofessional impiety, complained that we are not born men, but babies. He did not see the value of infancy as a delight to the mature, and for the education of the heart. At one period of life we need objects of instinctive passion, at another, of instinctive benevolence without passion.

I am not going to undervalue the charm of wisdom, nor the majestic joy which comes from loving principles of right; but if I could have only one of them, give me the joy of the affections,—my delight in others, theirs in me,—the joy of delighting, rather than the delight of enjoying. Here is a woman with large intellect, and attainments which match her native powers, but with a genius for love, developed in its domestic, social, patriotic, human form, with a wealth of affection which surpasses even her affluence of intellect. Her chief delight is to bless the men who need her blessing. Naturalists carry mind into matter, and seek the eternal truth of God in the perishing forms of the fossil plant, or the evanescent tides of the sea; she carries love into the lanes and kennels of society, to give bread to the needy, eyes to the blind, mind to the ignorant, and a soul to men floating and weltering in this sad pit of society. I do not undervalue intellect in any of its nobler forms, but if God gave me my choice to have either the vast intellect of a Newton, an Aristotle, a Shakspeare, a Homer, the ethical insight of the great legislators, the moral sense of Moses, or Menu, the conscience of men who discover justice and organize unalienable right into human institutions, — or else to take the heroic heart which so loves mankind, and I were to choose what brought its possessor the greatest joy, — I would surely take, not the great head, but the great heart, the power of love before the power of thought.

I know we often envy the sons of genius, men with tall heads and brain preternaturally delicate and nice, thinking God partial. They are not to be envied: the top of Mount Washington is very lofty; it far transcends the neighboring hills, and overlooks the mountain tops from the Mississippi to the Atlantic main, and has no fellow from the

Northern Sea down to the Mexique Bay. Men look up and wonder at its tall height; but it must take the rude blasts of every winter upon its naked, granite head; its sides are furrowed with the storm. It is of unequalled loftiness, but freezing cold; while in the low valleys and on the mountain's southern slopes the snow melts quick away, early the grass comes green, the flowers lift up their modest, lovely face, and shed their fragrance on the sudden spring. Who shall tell me that intellectual or moral grandeur is higher in the scale of powers than the heart! It is not so. Mind and conscience are great and noble; truth and justice are exceeding dear, but love is dearer and more precious than both.

See the array of natural means provided for the development and education of the heart. Spiritual love, joining with the instinctive passion which peoples the world, attracts mankind into little binary groups, families of two. Therein we are all born of love. Love watches over our birth. Our earliest knowledge of mankind is of one animated by the instinctive power of affection, developed into conscious love. The first human feeling extended towards us is a mother's love. Even the rude woman in savage Patagonia turns her sunniest aspect to her child; the father does the same. In our earliest years we are almost wholly in the hands of women, in whom the heart emphatically prevails over the head. They attract and win, while man only invades and conquers. The first human force we meet is woman's love. All this tends to waken and unfold the affections, to give them their culture, and hasten their growth. The other children of kindred blood, asking or giving kind offices; affectionate relations and friends, who turn out the fairest side of nature and themselves to the new-born stranger, — all of these are helps in the education of the heart. All men unconsciously put on amiable faces in the presence of children, thinking it is not good to cause these little ones to offend. As the roughest of men will gather flowers for little children, so in their presence he turns out "the silver lining" of his cloudy character to the young immortals, and would not have them know the darker part. The sourest man is not wholly hopeless when he will not blaspheme before his son.

The child's affection gets developed on the smallest scale at first. The mother's love tempts forth the son's; he loves the bosom that feeds him, the lips which caress, the person who loves. Soon the circle widens, and includes brothers and sisters, and familiar friends; then gradually enlarges more and more, the affections strengthening as their empire spreads. So love travels from person to person, from the mother or nurse to the family at home; then to the relatives and frequent guests; next to the children at school, to the neighborhood, the town, the State, the nation; and at last manly love takes in the whole family of mankind, counting nothing alien that is human.

You often find men lamenting the lack of early education of the intellect; it is a grievous deficiency; and it takes the hardest toil in after years to supply the void, if indeed it can ever be done. It is a misfortune to fail of finding an opportunity for the culture of conscience in childhood, and to acquire bad habits in youth, which at great cost you must revolutionize at a later day. But it is a yet greater loss to miss the opportunity of affectional growth; a sad thing to be born, and yet not into a happy home, — to lack the caresses, the fondness, the self-denying love, which the child's nature needs so much to take, and the mother's needs so much to give. The cheeks which affection does not pinch, which no mother kisses, have always a sad look, that nothing can conceal, and in childhood get a scar which they will carry all their days. What sad faces one always sees in the asylums for orphans! It is more fatal to neglect the heart than the head.

In a world like this, not much advanced as yet in any high qualities of spirit, but still advancing, it is beautiful to see the examples of love which we sometimes meet, the exceptional cases that to me are prophecies of that good time which is so long in coming. I will not speak of the love of husband and wife, or of parent and child, for each of these is mainly controlled by a strong generic instinct, which deprives the feeling of its personal and voluntary character. I will speak of spontaneous love not connected with the connubial or parental instincts. You see it in the form of friendship, charity, patriotism, and philanthropy, where there is no tie of kindred blood, no impulsion of instincts to excite, but only a kindred heart and an attractive soul. Men tell us that the friendship of the ancients has passed away. But it is not so; Damon and Pythias are perpetually reproduced in every walk of life, save that where luxury unnerves the man, or avarice coins him into a copper cent, or ambition degrades him to lust of fame and power. Every village has its tale of this character. The rude life of the borderers on the frontiers of civilization, the experience of men in navigation, in all the difficult emergencies of life, bring out this heroic affection of the heart.

What examples do we all know of friendship and of charity! Here is a woman of large intellect, well disciplined, well stored, gifted with mind and graced with its specific piety, whose chief delight it is to do kind deeds to those beloved. Her life is poured out, like the fair light of heaven, around the bedside of the sick. She comes like a last sacrament to the dying man, bringing back a reminiscence of the best things of mortal life, and giving a foretasted prophecy of the joys of heaven, her very presence an alabaster box of ointment, exceeding precious, filling the house with the balm of its thousand flowers. Her love adorns the paths wherein she teaches youthful feet to tread, and blooms in amaranthine loveliness above the head laid low in earth. She would feel insulted by gratitude; God can give no greater joy to mortal men than the consciousness whence such a life wells out. Not content with blessing the few whom friendship joins to her, her love enlarges and runs over the side of the private cup, and fills the bowl of many a needy and forsaken one. Self-denial is spontaneous, — self-indulgence of the noble heart to her. In the presence of such affection as this, the intellect of a Plato would be abashed, and the moral sense of a saint would shrink and say to itself: "Stand back, my soul, for here is somewhat far holier than thou!" In sight of such excellence I am ashamed of intellect; I would not look upon the greatest mind that ever spoke to ages yet unborn.

There is far more of this charity than most men

imagine. You find it amid the intense worldliness of this city, where upstart Mammon scoffs at God; in the hovels of the poor, in the common dwellings of ordinary men, and in the houses of the rich; drive out nature with a dollar, still she comes back. This love is the feminine saviour of mankind, and bestows a peace which nothing else can give, which nought can take away. From its nature this plant grows in by-places, where it is not seen by ordinary eyes, till wounded you flee thither; then it heals your smart, or when beheld fills you with wonder at its human loveliness.

The calling of a clergyman in a great, wicked town brings him acquainted with ghastly forms of human wickedness, — with felons of conscience, and men idiotic in their affections, who seem born with an arithmetic instead of a conscience, and a vulture for a heart: but we also find those angels of affection in whom the dearest attribute of God becomes incarnate, and his love made flesh; else an earnest minister might wear a face grim, stony, battered all over by the sad sight of private suffering, and the sadder sight of conscious and triumphant wickedness trampling the needy down to dust, and treating the Almighty with sneer and scoff.

Books tell us of but few examples of patriotism: they are common. Let us see examples in its vulgarest, and so most honored form, — love of country, to the exclusion and hate of other lands. Men tell of Regulus, how he laid down his life for his country, the brave old heathen that he was. But in the wickedest of modern wars, when America plundered Mexico of soil and men, many a deluded volunteer laid down his life, I doubt not, with a heroism as pure, and a patriotism as strong, as that of Regulus or Washington. Detesting the unholy war, let us honor the virtue which it brought to light.

This virtue of patriotism is common with the mass of men in this republic. In aristocratic governments the rich men and nobles have it in a large degree; it is, however, somewhat selfish, — a love of their private privileges more than of the general rights of their countrymen. With us in America, especially in the seat of riches and of trade, there seems little patriotism in the wealthy, or more educated class of men; small fondness for the commonwealth in that quarter. Exclusive love of gain drives that out of their heart. To the dollar, all lands, all governments, are the same.

But apart from patriotism, charity, friendship, I have seen most noble examples of the same affection on a yet wider scale, — I mean philanthropy, the love of all mankind. You all know men, whose affection, at first beginning at home, and loving only the mother who gave her baby nature's bread, has now transcended family and kin, gone beyond all private friendships with like-minded men, overleaped the far barriers of our native land, and now, loving family, friend, and country, loves likewise all humankind. This is the largest expanse of affection; the man's heart, once filled with love for one, for a few, for men in need beneath his eye, for his countrymen, has now grown bountiful to all. To love the lovely, to sympathize with the like-minded,—everybody can do that;—all save an ill-born few, whom we may pity, but must not blame, for their congenital deformity and dwarfishness;—but to love the unlovely, to sympathize with the contrary-minded, to give to the uncharitable, to forgive such as never pity, to be just to men who make iniquity a law, to pay their sleepless hate with never-ceasing love,—that is the triumph of the affections, the heroic degree of love; you must be but little lower than the angels to do that. It is one of the noblest attainments of man, and in this he becomes most like God. The intellect acquaints you with truth, the thought of God; conscience informs you with his justice, the moral will of God; and the heart fitly exercised gives you a fellowship with his eternal love, the most intimate feeling of the Infinite Father; having that, you can love men spite of the imperfections of their conduct and character, — can love the idiot, the criminal, hated or popular, — be towardly to the froward, kind to the unmerciful, and on them bestow the rain and the sunshine of your benevolence, your bounty limited only by your power, not your will, to bless, asking no gratitude, expecting no return.

I do not look for this large philanthropy in all men here, only in a few. All have a talent for loving, though this is as variously distributed as any intellectual gift; few have a genius for benevolence. The sublime of patriotism, the holy charity, and the delicate friendship, are more common. The narrower love between husband and wife, child and parent, has instinct to aid it, and is so common, that, like daily bread and nightly sleep, we forget to be thankful for it, not heeding how much depends thereon.

The joys of affection are the commonest of joys; sometimes the sole poetic ornament in the hutch of the poor, they are also the best things in the rich man's palace. They are the Shekinah, the presence of God in the dwellings of men. It is through the affections that most men learn religion. I know they often say, "Fear first taught us God." No! Fear first taught us a devil, — often worshipped as the God, — and with that fear all devils fade away, they and their misanthropic hell. Ghosts cannot stand the light, nor devils love. My affections bind me to God, and as the heart grows strong my ever-deepening consciousness of God grows more and more, till God's love occupies the heart, and the sentiment of God is mine.

Notwithstanding the high place which the affections hold in the natural economy of man, and the abundant opportunities for their culture and development furnished by the very constitution of the family, but little value is placed thereon in what is called the "superior education" of mankind. The class of men that lead the Christian world have but a small development of affection. Patriotism is the only form of voluntary love which it is popular with such men to praise, — that only for its pecuniary value; charity seems thought a weakness, to be praised only on Sundays; avarice is the better weekday virtue; friendship is deemed too romantic for a trading town. Philanthropy is mocked at by statesmen and leading capitalists; it is the standing butt of the editor, whereat he shoots his shaft, making up in its barb and venom for his arrows' lack of length and point. Metropolitan clergymen rejoice in calumniating philanthropy; "Even the golden rule hath its exceptions," says one of them just now. It is deemed important to show that Jesus of Nazareth was "no philanthropist," and cared nothing for the sin of the powerful, which trod men into a mire of blood! In what is called the "highest education," only the understanding and the taste get a considerable culture. The piety of the heart is thought "inelegant" in society, unscholarly with the learned, and a dreadful heresy in the churches. In literature it is not love that wins the palm; it is power to rule by force,—force of muscles or force of mind: "None but the brave deserve the fair." In popular speech it is the great fighters that men glorify, not the great lovers of mankind. Interest eats out the heart from commerce and politics; controlling men have no faith in disinterested benevolence; to them the nation is a monstrous shop, a trading city but a bar-room in a commercial tavern, the church a desk for the accountant, the world a market; men are buyers and sellers, employers and employed. Governments are mainly without love, often without justice. This seems their function: To protect capital and tax toil.

Hitherto justice has not been done to the affections in Religion. We have been taught to fear God, not to love Him, to see Him in the earthquake and the storm, in the deluge, or the "ten plagues of Egypt," in the "black death," or the cholera; not to see God in the morning sun, or in the evening full of radiant gentleness. Love has little to do with the popular religion of our time. God is painted as a dreadful Eye, which bores through the darkness to spy out the faults of men who must sneak and skulk about the world; or as a naked, bony Arm, uplifted to crush his children down with horrid squelch to endless hell. The long line of scoffers from Lucian, their great hierophant, down to Voltaire and his living coadjutors, have not shamed the priesthood from such revolting images of deity. Sterner men, who saw the loveliness of the dear God and set it forth in holy speech and holy life, — to meet a fate on earth far harder than the scoffer's doom, — they cannot yet teach men that love of God casts every fear away. In the Catholic mythology the Virgin Mary, its most original creation, represents pure love, — she, and she alone. Hence is she, (and deservedly,) the popular object of worship in all Catholic countries. But the sterner Protestant sects have the Roman Godhead after Mary is taken away.

When this is so in religion, do you wonder at the lack of love in law and custom, in politics and trade? Shall I write satires on mankind? Rather let me make its apology. Man is a baby yet; the time for the development of conscious love has not arrived. Let us not say, "No man eat fruit of thee hereafter;"

let us wait; dig about the human tree and encourage it; in time it shall put forth figs.

Still affection holds this high place in the nature of man. Out of our innermost hearts there comes the prophecy of a time when it shall have a kindred place in history and the affairs of men. In the progress of mankind, love takes continually a higher place; what was adequate and well-proportioned affection a century ago, is not so now. Long since, prophets rose up to declare the time was coming when all hate should cease, there should be war no more, and the sword should be beaten into the ploughshare. Were they dreamers of idle dreams? It was human nature which spoke through them its lofty prophecy; and mankind fulfils the highest prediction of every noble man. The fighter is only the hod-carrier of the philanthropist. Soldiers build the scaffolding; with the voice of the trumpet, with the thunder of the captain, and manifold shouting, are the stones drawn to the spot, the cement of human architecture has been mixed with human blood, but it is a temple of peace which gets builded at the last.

In every man who lives a true life the affections grow continually. He began with his mother and his nurse, and journeyed ever on, pitching his tent each night a day's march nearer God. His own children helped him love others yet more; his children's children carried the old man's heart quite out beyond the bounds of kin and country, and taught him to love mankind. He grows old in learning to love, and now, when age sets the silver diadem upon his brow, not only is his love of truth and justice greater than before, — not only does he love his wife better than in his hour of prime, when manly instinct added passion to his heart, — not only does he love his children more than in their infancy, when the fatherly instinct first began its work, — not only has he more spontaneous love for his grandchildren than he felt for his first new-born babe, — but his mature affection travels beyond his wife, and child, and children's child, to the whole family of men, mourns in their grief, and joys in their delight. All his powers have been greatened in his long, industrious, and normal life, and so his power of love has continually enlarged. The human objects do not wholly satisfy his heart's desire. The ideal of love is nowhere actual in the world of men, no finite person fills up the hungry heart, so he turns to the Infinite Object of affection, to the great Mother of mankind; and in the sentiment of love he and his God are one. God's thought in his mind, God's justice in his conscience, God's love in his heart, — why should not he be blessed?

In mankind, as in a faithful man, there has been the same enhancement of the power to love. Already Affection begins to legislate, even to administer the laws of love. Long ago you see intimation of this in the institutes of Moses and Menu. "The qualitative precedes the quantitative," as twilight precedes day. Slowly vengeance fades out of human institutions, slowly love steals in: — the wounded soldier must be healed, and paid, his widow fed, and children comforted; the slaves must be set free; the yoke of kings and nobles must be made lighter, be broken, and thrown away; all men must have their rights made sure; the poor must be fed, must have his human right to a vote, to justice, truth, and love; the ignorant must be educated, the State looking to it that no one straggles in the rear and so is lost; the criminals — I mean the little criminals committing petty crimes — must be instructed, healed, and manlified; the lunatic must be restored to his intellect; the blind, the deaf and dumb, the idiots, must be taught, and all mankind be blessed. The attempt to banish war out of the world, odium from theology, capital punishment out of the State, the Devil and his hell from the Christian mythology, — the effort to expunge hate from the popular notion of God, and fear from our religious consciousness, — all this shows the growth of love in the spirit of men. A few men see that while ir-religion is fear of a devil, religion is love: one half is piety, — the love of God as truth, justice, love, as Infinite Deity; the rest is morality, — self-love, and the love of man, a service of God by the normal use, development, and enjoyment of every limb of the body, every faculty of the spirit, every particle of power we possess over matter or over man. A few men see that God is love, and makes the world of love as substance, from love as motive, and for love as end.

Human nature demands the triumph of pure, disinterested love at last; the nature of God is warrant that what is promised in man's nature shall be fulfilled in his development. Human nature is human destiny; God's nature, universal Providence. The mind tells us of truth which will prevail; conscience, of justice sure to conquer; the heart gives us the prophecy of infinite love certain to triumph. One day there shall be no fear before men, no fear before God, no tyrant in society, no Devil in theology, no hell in the mythology of men; love and the God of love shall take their place. Hitherto Jesus is an exceptional man, the man of love; Cæsars and Alexanders are instantial men, men of force and fight. One day this will be inverted, these conquerors swept off and banished, the philanthropists become common, the kingdom of hate forgot in the commonwealth of love. Here is work for you and me to do;

for our affectional piety, assuming its domestic, social, national, universal form, will bless us with its delight, and then go forth to bless mankind; and long after you and I shall have gone home to the God we trust, our affectional piety shall be a sentiment living in the hearts of men; — yes, a power in the world to bless mankind for ever and ever.

"Serene will be our days and bright,
And happy will our nature be,
When love is an unerring light,
And joy its own security.
And they a blissful course may hold
Even now, who, not unwisely bold,
Live in the spirit of this creed,
Yet find that other strength, according to their need."

V.

OF CONSCIOUS RELIGION AND THE SOUL.

WORSHIP THE LORD IN THE BEAUTY OF HOLINESS. — Ps. xxix. 2.

THE mind converses with things indirectly, by means of the senses; with ideas directly, independent of the senses, by spiritual intuition, whereto the senses furnish only the occasion, not the power, of knowledge; so the mind arrives at truth, in various forms or modes, rests contented therein, and has joy in the love thereof. Conscience is busied with rules of right, by direct intuition learns the moral law of the universe as it is writ in human nature, — outward experience furnishing only the occasion, not the power, of knowing right, — arrives at justice, rests contented therein, and has its joy in the love thereof. The affections deal with persons, whom it is their function to love, travel ever on to wider and wider spheres, joying in the men they love, but always seeking the perfect object with which they may be contented and have the absolute joy of the heart. To think truth, to will justice, to feel love, is the highest act respectively of the intellectual, moral, and affectional powers of man, which seek the absolutely true, just, and lovely, as the object of their natural desire.

The soul has its own functions. God is the object thereof. As the mind and conscience by their normal activity bring truth and justice to human consciousness, so the soul makes us conscious of God.

We see what intellectual, moral, and affectional creations have come from the action of the mind, the conscience, and the heart of man; we see the human use thereof and joy therein. But the religious faculty has been as creative and yet more powerful, overmastering all the other powers of man. The profoundest study of man's affairs, or the hastiest glance thereat, shows the power of the soul for good and ill. The phenomena of man's religious history are as varied and important as they are striking. The surface of the world is dotted all over with the temples which man has built in his acts of reverence; religious sentiments and ideas are deeply ploughed into the history of every tribe that has occupied time or peopled space. Consider mankind as one man, immortal and not growing old, universal history as his biography; study the formation of his religious consciousness, the gradual growth of piety in all its forms, normal or monstrous; note his stumblings in the right way, his wanderings in the wrong, his penitence, his alarm and anxiety, his remorse for sin, his successive attainments of new truth, new justice, and new love, the forms in which he expresses his inward experience, — and what a strange, attractive spectacle this panorama of man's religious history presents to the thoughtful man.

The religious action of a child begins early; but like all early activity it is unconscious. We cannot remember that; we can only recollect what we have known in the form of consciousness, or, at best, can only dimly remember what lay dimly and half conscious in us, though the effects thereof may be as lasting as our mortal life. You see the tendency to the superhuman in quite little children asking, "But who made God?" the child's causality heedlessly leaping at the Infinite, he having a dim sentiment of the Maker of all itself unmade. You have seen little babies, early deprived of their mother, involuntarily and by instinct feeling with their ill-shapen mouths after what nature provided for their nourishment. So in our childhood as involuntarily and instinctively do we feel with our soul after the Infinite God, often, alas! to be beguiled by our nurses with some sop of a deity which fills our mouth for the time and keeps us from perishing. Perhaps a few of you remember a time when you had a sentiment — it was more a feeling than a thought — of a vague, dim, mysterious somewhat, which lay at the bottom of all things, was above all, about all, and in all, which you could not comprehend nor yet escape from. You seemed a part of it, or it of you; you wondered that you could not see with your eyes, nor hear with your ears, nor touch with your hands, what you yet felt and longed after with such perplexity of indistinctness. Sometimes you loved it; sometimes you feared. You dared not name it, or if you did, no one word was name enough for so changeable a thing. Now you felt it in the sunshine, then in the storm; now it gave life, then it took life away. You connected it with all that was strange and uncommon; now it was a great loveliness, then an ugliness of indefinite deformity. In a new place you missed it at first; but it soon came back, travelling with the child, a constant companion at length.

All men do not remember this, I think; only a few, in whom religious consciousness began early. But we have all of us been through this nebulous period of religious history, when the soul had emotions for which the mind could not frame adequate ideas.

You see the same phenomena drawn on a large scale in the history of ancient nations, whose monuments still attest these facts of consciousness; you find nations at this day still in this nebulous period of religion, the Divine not yet resolved to Deity. Sphinxes and pyramids are fossil remains of old facts of consciousness which you and I and every man have reproduced. Savages are baby nations, feeling after God, and trying to express with their reflective intellect the immediate emotions of the soul. When language is a clumsy instrument, men try to carve in stone what they fail to express in speech. Is the soul directly conscious of a superhuman power? they seek to legitimate the feeling in the mind, and so translate it to a thought; at least they legitimate it to the senses, and make it a thing. This vague, mysterious, superhuman something, before it is solidified into deity, let me call The Divine. Man does not know what it is. "It is not myself," says he. "What is it, then? Some outward thing?" He takes the outward thing which seems most wondrous to himself, — a reptile, beast, bird, insect; an element, the wind, the lightning, the sun, the moon, a planet, or a star. Outward things embody his inward feeling; but while there are so many elements of confusion within him, no one embodiment is enough; he must have many, each one a step beyond the other. His feeling becomes profounder, his thought more clear. At length he finds that man is more mighty than the elements, and seeks to consolidate the Divine in man, and has personifications thereof, instead of his primitive embodiments in Nature. Then his feeling of the Divine becomes an idea of Deity; he has his personal gods, with all the accidents of human personality, — the passions, feelings, thoughts, mistakes, and all the frailties of mortal men.

Age after age this work goes on; the human idea of God has its metempsychosis, and transmigrates through many a form, rising higher at every step until this day. In studying mathematics man has used for counters the material things of earth, has calculated by the help of pebbles from the beach, learned the decimal system from his ten fingers, and wonders of abstract science from the complicated diagrams of the sky. So he has used reptiles, beasts, and all the elements and orbs of nature, in studying his sentiment of God, transferring each excellence of Nature to the Divine, and then each excellence of man. Nature is the rosary of man's prayer. The successive embodiments and personifications of God in matter, animals, or men were in religion what the hypotheses of

Thales and Ptolemy, Galileo and Kepler, were in science, — helps to attain a more general form of truth. Every idol-fetish, every embodiment of a conception of God in matter, every personification thereof in man, has been a step forward in religious progress. The grossest fetichism is only the early shoot from the instinctive seed, one day to blossom into the idea of the Infinite God. The confusion of past and present mythologies is not only a witness to the confusion in the religious consciousness of men, but the outward expression helps men to understand the inward fact, and so to bring truth out of error.

The religious history of mankind could not have been much different from what it has been; the margin for human caprice is not a very wide one. All mankind had the same process to pass through. The instinct of development in the human race is immensely strong, even irrepressible; checked here, in another place it puts out a limb. The life of mankind is continual growth. There is a special progress of the intellectual, moral, affectional, and religious faculties; so a general progress of man; with that, a progress in the ideas which men form of God. Each step seems to us unavoidable and not to be dispensed with. Once unconscious reverence of the Divine was all man had attained to; next he reached the worship of the Deity in the form of material or animal nature then personified in man. Let us not libel the human race: we are babies before we are men. "Live and learn" applies to mankind, as to Joseph and Jane.

You and I are born as far from pure religion as the first men, and have passed over the same ground which the human race has painfully trod, only mankind has been before us, and made a road to travel on; so we journey more swiftly; and in twenty or thirty years an ordinary man accomplishes what it took the human race five or six hundred generations to achieve. But hitherto the majority of Christians have not attained unity, or even concord, in their conception of the Deity. There is a God, a Christ, a Holy Ghost, and a Devil, with angels and saints, demons and damned; it takes all these to represent the popular ecclesiastical conception of the Deity; and a most heterogeneous mixture of contradictions and impossibilities do they make. The Devil is part of the popular Godhead. Here and there is a man conscious of God as Infinite; but such are only exceptional men, and accordingly disowned as heretics, condemned, but no longer burnt, as of old time.

It is plain that the religious faculty is the strongest spiritual power in the constitution of man. Accordingly, what is called religion is always one of the mightiest forces in the world of men. It overrides the body, mutilates every instinct, and hews off every limb; it masters the intellect, the conscience, and the affections. Lightning shows us the power of electricity, shattering that it may reach its end, and shattering what it reaches; the power of the religious faculty hitherto has been chiefly shown in this violent exhibition. A crusade is only a long thunderstorm of the religious forces.

In the greater part of the world, men who speak in the name of God are looked on with more reverence than any other. So every tyrant seeks to get the priesthood on his side. Hard Napoleon got the Pope to assist at the imperial coronation; even the cannons must yield to the Cross. All modern wickedness must be banked up with Christianity. If the State of the Philistines wishes to sow some eminently wicked seed, it ploughs with the heifer of the Church.

A nation always prepares itself for its great works with consecration and prayer; both the English and American revolutions are examples of this. The religious sentiment lies exceeding deep in the heart of mankind. Even to-day the nations look on men who die for their country as a sacrifice offered to God. No government is so lasting as that based on religious sentiments and ideas; with the mass of men the State is part of the Church, and politics a national sacrament. Nothing so holds a nation together as unity of religious conviction. Men love to think their rulers have a religious sanction. "Kings rule by divine right," says the monarchist; "Civil government is of God," quoth the Puritan. The mass of men love to spread acts of religion along their daily life, having the morning sacrament for birth, the evening sacrament for death, and the noonday sacrament of marriage for the mature beauty of maid and man. Thus in all the sects, the morning, the evening, and the noon of life are connected with sentiments and ideas of religion. In New England we open a town-meeting, a banquet, or a court with prayer to God.

You see the strength of the religious instinct in the power of the sacred class, which has existed in all nations, while passing from the savage state to the highest civilization, — a power which only passes away when the class which bears the name ceases to represent the religious feeling and thought of the nation, and merely keeps the traditions and ceremonies of old time. So long as the priests represent God to the people, they are the strongest class. What are the armies of Saul, if Samuel pleases to anoint a shepherd-lad for king? You see examples of this power of the sacred class in Egypt, in India, in Judea, in Greece and Rome, before the philosopher outgrew the priest. You see it in Europe during the Middle Ages; what monuments thereof are left, marking all the land from Byzantium to Upsala with convents, basilicas, minster, cathedral, dome, and spire! At this day the Mormons, on the borders of American civilization, gather together the rudest white men of the land, and revive the ancient priestly power of darker times, a hierarchic despotism under a republic. In such communities the ablest men and the most ambitious form a sacred class; the Church offers the fairest field for activity. There religion is obviously the most powerful form of power. Men who live in a city where the tavern is taller, costlier, more beautiful and permanent, than the temple, and the tavern-keeper thought a more important man than the minister of religion, who is only a temple-keeper now, can hardly understand the period when such works as the Cathedral at Milan or the Duomo at Venice got built: but a Mormon city reveals the same state of things; Nauvoo and Deseret explain Jerusalem and Carnak.

The religious faculty has overmastered all others; the mind is reckoned "profane" in comparison. Does the priest tell men in its name to accept what contradicts the evidence of the senses, and all human experience, millions bow down before the Grand Lama or the Pope. It is the faith of the Christian world, that a Galilean woman bore the Almighty God in her bosom, and nursed Him at her breast. Augustine and Aquinas stooped their proud intellects and accepted the absurdity. The priests have told the people that three persons are one God, or three Gods one person, — that the world was created in six days; the people give up their intellect and try to believe the assertion, Grotius and Leibnitz assenting to the tale. Every thing written in the Bible, the Koran, the Book of Mormon, is thus made to pass current with their respective worshippers. In the name of religion men sacrifice reason. St. James says, "Is any sick among you? let him call for the elders of the Church; and let them pray over him, anointing him with oil in the name of the Lord, and the prayer of faith shall save the sick, and the Lord shall raise him up." Thousands of men, in the name of religion, believe that this medical advice of a Hebrew fisherman was given by the infallible inspiration of God; and it is clerically thought wicked and blasphemous to speak of it as I do this day. I only mention these facts to show the natural strength of the religious instinct, working in a perverted and unnatural form, and against the natural action of the mind.

In like manner religion is made to silence the moral faculties. The Hebrews will kill the Canaanites by thousands; Catholic Spaniards will build the Inquisition for their countrymen; English Protestants, under the bloody Elizabeth, will dip their hands in their Catholic brothers' blood; Puritan Boston has had her AUTOS DA FE, hanging Quakers for "non-resistance" and the "inner light," or witches for a "compact with the Devil." Do we not still hang murderers throughout all Christendom as an act of worship? This is not done as political economy, but as "Divine service;" not for the conversion of man, but in the name of God,— one of the few relics of human sacrifice. "Reason is carnal," says one priest,—men accept a palpable absurdity as a "revealed truth;" "Conscience must not be trusted," says another,—and human sacrifice is readily assented to. Nothing is so unjust, but men, meaning to be pious, will accept and perform it, if commanded in the name of religion. In such cases even interest is a feeble ally to conscience, and money is sometimes sacrificed in New England.

The religious instinct is thus made to trample on the affections. At the priest's command, men renounce the dearest joys of the heart, degrading woman to a mere medium of posterity, or scoffing at nature, and vowing shameful oaths of celibacy. Puritan mothers feared lest they should "love their children too much." How many a man has made his son "pass through the fire unto Moloch?" The Protestant thinks it was an act of religion in Abraham to sacrifice his only son unto Jehovah; the

Catholic still justifies the St. Bartholomew massacre. Mankind did not shrink at human sacrifice which was demanded in the name of religion terribly perverted. These facts are enough to show that the religious faculty is the strongest in human nature, and easily snaps all ties which bind us to the finite world, making the lover forswear his bride, and even the mother forget her child.

See what an array of means is provided for the nurture and development of the religious instinct,—provided by God in the constitution of men and of the universe. All these things about us, things magnificently great, things elegantly little, continually impress mankind. Even to the barbarian Nature reveals a mighty power and a wondrous wisdom, and continually points to God. I do not wonder that men worshipped the several things of the world, at first reverencing the Divine in the emmet or the crocodile. The world of matter is a revelation of fear to the savage in northern climes: he trembles at his deity throned in ice and snow. The lightning, the storm, the earthquake, startle the rude man, and he sees the Divine in the extraordinary.

The grand objects of Nature perpetually constrain men to think of their Author. The Alps are the great altar of Europe; the nocturnal sky has been to mankind the dome of a temple, starred all over with admonitions to reverence, trust, and love. The Scriptures for the human race are writ in earth and heaven. Even now we say, "An undevout astronomer is mad." What a religious mosaic is the surface of the earth, — green with vegetable beauty, animated with such swarms of life. No organ or Pope's Miserere touches my heart like the sonorous swell of the sea, and the ocean wave's immeasurable laugh. To me, the works of men who report the aspects of Nature, like Humboldt, and of such as Newton and Laplace, who melt away the facts, and leave only the laws, the forces of Nature, the ideas and ghosts of things, are like tales of a pilgrimage to the Holy Land, or poetical biographies of a saint; they stir religious feelings, and I commune with the Infinite.

This effect is not produced on scholarly men so much as on honest and laborious mankind, all the world over. Nature is man's religious book, with lessons for every day. In cities men tread on an artificial ground of brick or stone, breathe an unnatural air, see the heavens only a handful at a time, think the gas-lights better than the stars, and know little how the stars themselves keep the police of the sky. Ladies and gentlemen in towns see Nature only at second hand. It is hard to deduce

God from a brick pavement. Yet ever and anon the mould comes out green and natural on the walls, and through the chinks of the sidewalks bursts up the life of the world in many a little plant, which to the microscopic eye of science speaks of the presence of the same Power that slowly elaborates a solar system and a universe. In the country men and women are always in the presence of Nature, and feel its impulse to reverence and trust. Every year the old world puts on new bridal beauty, and celebrates its Whitsunday, — each bush putting its glory on. Spring is our Dominica in Albis. Is not autumn a long All-Saints' day? The harvest is Hallowmass to mankind. How men have marked each annual crisis of the year, — the solstice and the equinox, — and celebrate religious festivals thereon! The material world is the element of communion between man and God. To heedful men God preaches on every mount, utters beatitudes in each little flower of spring.

Our own nature also reminds us of God. Thoughtful men are conscious of their dependence, their imperfection, their finiteness, and naturally turn to the Independent, the Perfect, the Infinite. The events of life, its joys and its sorrows, have a natural tendency to direct the thoughts to the good Father of us all. Religious emotions spring up spontaneously at each great event in the lives of earnest men.

When I am sick I become conscious of the Infinite Mother in whose lap I lay my weary head. The lover's eyes see God beyond the maid he loves; Heaven speaks out of the helpless face which the young mother presses to her bosom; each new child connects its parents with the eternal duration of human kind. Who can wait on the ebb and flow of mortal life in a friend, and not return to Him who holds that ocean also in the hollow of his hand! The old man looking for the last time upon the sun turns his children's face towards the Sun which never sets. Even in cities men do not pause at a funeral or look on a grave without a thought of the eternal life beyond the tomb, and the dependence of rich and poor on the God who is father of body and soul. The hearse obstructs the omnibus of commerce, and draws the eyes of even the silly and the vain and empty creatures who buzz out their ephemeral phenomena in wealthy towns, the butterflies of this garden of bricks, and forces them to confront one reality of life, and reverence, though only with a shudder, the Author of all. The undertaker is a priest to preach terror, if no more, to the poor flies of metropolitan frivolity, reminding them at least of the worm.

The outward material world forms a temple where all invites us to reverence the Soul which inspires it with life; the spiritual powers within are all instinctively astir with feelings infinite. Thus material nature joins with human nature in natural fellowship; outward occasions and inward means of piety are bountifully given, and man is led to develop his religious powers. The soul of man cannot well be still; religion has always had a powerful activity in the world, and a great influence upon the destiny of mankind. The soul has been as active as the sense, and left its monuments.

An element thus powerful, thus well appointed with outward and with inward helps, must have a purpose for the individual and the race commensurate with its natural power. The affections tell me it is not good for man to be alone in the body without a friend; the soul as imperatively informs us that we cannot well be alone in the spirit without a consciousness of God. If the religious faculty has overpowered all others, and often trod them underfoot, its very power shows for what great good to mankind it was invested with this formidable force. It will act jointly or alone; if it have not its proper place in the mass of men, working harmoniously with the intellect, the conscience, and the affections, then it will tyrannize as a brute instinct, lusting after God, and, like a river that bursts its bounds, sweep off the holy joys of men before its desolating flood.

The mind may work without a corresponding action of the conscience or the heart. You can comprehend the worth of a man all head, with no sense of right, no love of men, with nothing but a demon-brain. Conscience may act with no corresponding life of the affections and the mind. You can understand the value of a man all conscience and will,— nothing but an incarnate moral law, the "categorical Imperative" exhibited in the flesh, with no wisdom and no love. A life domineered over by conscience is unsatisfying, melancholy, and grim. The affections may also have a development without the moral and the mental powers. But what is a man domineered over by his heart; with no justice, no wisdom, nothing but a lump of good-nature, partial and silly? It is only the rareness of such phenomena that makes them bearable. Truth, justice, love,—it is not good for them to be alone; each loses two thirds of the human power when it expels the sister virtues from it. What God has joined must not be put asunder.

The religious faculty may be perverted, severed from the rest and made to act alone, with no corresponding action of the mind, the conscience, and the heart. Attempts are often made to produce this independent development of the soul. It is no new thing to seek to develop piety while you omit its several elements, the intellectual love of truth, the moral love of justice, and the affectional love of men. But in such a case what is the value of the "piety" thus produced? The soul acting without the mind goes to superstition and bigotry. It has its conception of God, but of a God that is foolish and silly. Reason will be thought carnal, science dangerous, and a doubt an impiety; the greatest absurdities will be taught in the name of religion; the philosophy of some half-civilized, but God-fearing people, will be put upon the minds of men as the word of God; the priest will hate the philosopher, and the philosopher the priest; men of able intellect will flee off and loathe ecclesiastical piety. If the churches will have a religion without philosophy, scholars will have a philosophy without religion. The Roman Church forbid science, burnt Jordano Bruno, and reduced Galileo to silence and his knees. So much the worse for the Church. The French philosophy of the last century, its Encyclopædia of scoffs at religion, were the unavoidable counterpart. Voltaire and Diderot took vengeance for the injustice done to their philosophic forerunners. The fagots of the Middle Ages got repaid by the fiery press of the last generation.

You may try and develop the soul to the neglect of conscience: — your Antinomian will recognize no moral law: " All things are permissible to the elect; let them do what they will, they cannot sin, for they are born of God; the moral law is needless under the Gospel," says he. Religion will be made the pander of wrong, and priests will pimp for respectable iniquity. God is thus represented as unjust, partial, cruel, and full of vengeance. The most unjust things will be demanded in his name; the laws and practices of a barbarous nation will be ascribed to God, and men told to observe and keep them. Religion will aim to conserve the ritual barbarities of ruder times. Moral works will be thought hostile to piety, — goodness regarded as of no value, rather as proof that a man is not under the "covenant of grace," but only of works. Conscience will be declared an uncertain guide. No "higher law" will be allowed in religion, — only the interest of the politician and the calculation of the merchant must bear rule in the State. The whim of some priest, a new or an old traditionary whim, must be the rule in the Church. It will then be taught that religion is for the Sunday and "holy communion;" business for the week, and daily life. The "most respectable churches" will be such as do nothing to make the world a better place, and men and women fitter to live in it. The catechism will have nothing to do with the conduct, nor prayers with practice. But if the churches will have religion without morals, many a good and conscientious man will go to the opposite extreme, and have morals without religion, — will jeer and mock at all complete and conscious piety; eminently moral men will flee off from the churches, which will be left with their idle mummeries and vain conceits.

Men sometimes seek to develop the religious element while they depress the affectional. Then they promote fanaticism — hate before God, which so often has got organized in the world. Then God is represented as jealous, partial, loving only a few, and of course Himself unlovely. He sits as a tyrant on the throne of the world, and with his rod of iron rules the nations whom he has created for his glory, to damn for his caprice. He is represented as having a little, narrow heaven, where he will gather a few of his children, whining and dawdling out a life of eternal indolence; and a great, wide hell, full of men, demons, and torments lasting for ever and ever. Then, in the name of God, men are bid to have no fellowship with unbelievers, no sympathy with sinners. Nay, you are bidden to hate your brethren of a different mode of religious belief. This fanaticism organizes itself, now into brief and temporary activity, to persecute a saint, or to stone a philanthopist; now into permanent institutions for the defence of heathenism, Judaism, Mohammedanism, or Christianity. The fires in which Catholics and Protestants have burnt their brother Christians, the dreadful tortures which savage heathens have inflicted on the followers of Jesus, have all been prepared by the same cause, hatred in the name of God. It is this which has made many a temporary hell on earth, and fancied and taught an eternal hell beneath it. Brief St. Bartholomew massacres, long and lasting crusades against Albigenses or Saracens, permanent Inquisitions, laws against unbelievers, atheists, quakers, deists, and Christians, all spring from this same wantonness of the religious sentiment rioting with ungodly passions of the flesh. The malignant priest looks out of the storm of his hate, and smites men in the name of religion and of God. But then the affectionate man turns off from the God who is "a consuming fire," from the "religion" that scorches and burns up the noblest emotions of mankind, and, if others will have a worship without love in the worshippers or the worshipped, he will have love without religion, and philanthropy without God. So, in the desert, the Arab sees the whirlwind coming with its tornado of fiery sand, and hastens from its track, or lies down, he and his camels, till the horrid storm has spent its rage and passed away; then he rises and resumes his peaceful pilgrimage with thanks to God.

How strong is the family instinct! how beautiful is it when, passion and affection blending together, it joins man and maid into one complete and perfect solidarity of human life, each finding wholeness and enjoyment while seeking only to delight! What beautiful homes are built on marriages like that! what families of love are born and bred therein! but take away the affection, the self-denial, the mutual surrender, aggravate the instinctive love to the unnatural selfishness of lust seeking its own enjoyment, heedless of its victim, and how hateful is the beastly conjunction of David, Solomon, Messallina, Mohammed, of Gallic Cassanova, or Moscovian Catharine. Religion bereft of love to men becomes more hateful yet, — a lusting after God. It has reddened with blood many a page of human history, and made the ideal torments of hell a flaming fact in every Christian land. The Catharines of such a religion, the Cassanovas of the soul, are to me more hideous than Bacchanalians of the flesh. Let us turn off our eyes from a sight so foul.

Piety of mind, the love of truth, is only a fragment of piety; piety of conscience, the love of right, is also fragmentary; so is love of men, piety of the heart. Each is a beautiful fragment, all three not a whole piety. We want to unite them all with the consciousness of God, into a complete, perfect, and total religion, the piety of mind and conscience, heart and soul, — to love God with all the faculties, — to love Him as truth, as justice, as love, as God, who unites in Himself infinite truth, infinite justice, infinite love, and is the Father of all. We need to do this consciously, to be so wonted to thus loving Him, that it is done spontaneously, without effort, and yet not merely by instinct; done personally, not against our own consent. Then we want to express this fourfold total piety by our outward morality, in its natural forms and various degrees.

I mentioned, that in human history the religious faculty had often tyrannized over the other powers of men; I think it should precede them in its development, should be the controlling power in every man, the universal force which sways the several parts. In the history of man the soul has done so, but in most perverse forms of action. In the mass of men the religious element is always a little in advance of all the rest. Last Sunday I said that the affections often performed an idealizing and poetizing function in men who found it not in the intellect or the moral sense. In the vast majority of men it is religion that thus idealizes and adorns their life, and gives the rude worshipper an intimate gladness and delight beyond the reach of art. The doctrine of Fate and Foreordination idealizes the life of the Mohammedan; he feels elevated to the rank of an instrument of God; he has an inflexible courage, and a patience which bears all that courage cannot overcome. The camel-driver of the Arabian prophet rejoiced in this intimate connection with

God, a spoke in the wheel of the Unalterable. The thought that Jehovah watched over Israel with special love, consoled the Hebrews who hung their harps on the willows of Babylon, and sat down and wept; it brought out of their hearts stories like that of Jonah, Esther, and Daniel, and the sweet Psalms of comfort which the world will not forget to sing. How it has sustained the nation, wandering, exiled and hated, in all the corners of the world! The God of Jacob is their refuge and the Holy One of Israel the joy of their hearts. Faith in God sustained and comforted our fathers here in New England. Their affections went wandering over the waters to many a pleasant home in the dear old island of the sea, and a tear fell on the snow, at the thought that, far over the waters, the first violet was fragrant on a mother's grave; but the consciousness of God lit a smile in the Puritan's heart which chased the tear from his manly cheek.

The thought that God sees us, knows us, loves us, idealizes the life of all religious men. How it blunts the edge of pain, takes away the sting of disappointment, abates the bitterness of many a sorrowful cup which we are called to drink! If you are sure of God, is there any thing which you cannot bear? The belief in immortality is so intimately connected with the development of religion, that no nation ever doubted of eternal life. How that idealizes and embellishes all our daily doing and suffering! What a power is there that hangs over me, within a day's march perhaps, nay, within an easy walk of an hour, or a minute it may be, certainly not far off, its gates wide open night and day! The weary soul flees thither right often. Poor, weary, worn-out millions, it is your heaven! No king can shut you out. The tyrants, shooting their victim's body, shoot his soul into the commonwealth of heaven. The martyr knows it, and laughs at the bullets which make an involuntary subject of despotism an immortal republican, giving him citizenship in the democracy of everlasting life. There the slave is free from his master; the weary is at rest; the needy has no want of bread; all tears are wiped from every eye; justice is done; souls dear to ours are in our arms once more; the distractions of life are all over; no injustice, no sorrow, no fear. That is the great comfort with the mass of mankind,—the most powerful talisman which enchants them of their weary woe. Men sing Anacreontic odes, amid wine and women, and all the voluptuousness of art, buying a transient jollity of the flesh; but the Methodist finds poetry in his mystic hymn to take away the grief of a wound and leave no poison in its place. The rudest Christian, with a real faith in immortal life, has a means of adorning the world which puts to shame the poor finery of Nicholas and Nebuchadnezzar.

What are the prizes of wealth, of fame, of genius, nay, of affection, compared with what we all anticipate erelong? The worst man that ever lived may find delight overmastering terror here. "I am wicked," he may say; "God knows how I became so; his infinite love will one day save me out of my bitterness and my woe!" I once knew a man tormented with a partner, cruel and hard-hearted, ingenious only to afflict. In the midst of her torment he delighted to think of the goodness of God, and of the delights of heaven, and in the pauses of her tongue dropped to a heaven of lovely dreams unsullied by any memory of evil words.

Religion does not produce its fairest results in persons of small intellectual culture; yet there it often spreads a charm and a gladness which nothing else can give. I have known men, and still oftener women, nearly all of whose culture had come through their religious activity. Religion had helped their intellect, their conscience, even their affections; by warming the whole ground of their being, had quickened the growth of each specific plant thereof. Young observers are often amazed at this, not knowing then the greener growth and living power of a religious soul. In such persons, spite of lack of early intellectual culture, and continual exclusion from the common means of refinement, you find piety without narrowness, zeal without bigotry, and trust in God with no cant. Their world of observation was not a wide world, not much varied, not rich; but their religious experience was deep, their consciousness of divine things extended high. They were full of love and trust in God. Religion was the joy of their heart, and their portion for ever. They felt that God was about them, immanent in matter, within not less, dwelling in their spirit, a present help in their hour of need, which was their every hour. Piety was their only poetry; out of ignorance, out of want, out of pain, which lay heavy about them, — a triple darkness that covered the people, — they looked up to heaven, and saw the star of everlasting life, which sent its mild beams into their responsive soul. Dark without, it was all-glorious within. Men with proud intellect go haughtily by these humble souls; but Mohammeds, Luthers, are born of such a stock, and it is from these little streams that the great ocean of religion is filled full.

Yet it is not in cases like these that you see the fairest effects of religion. The four prismatic rays of piety must be united into one natural and fourfold beam of light, to shine with all their beauty, all their power; then each is enhanced. I love truth the more for loving justice; both the more for loving love; all three the more, when I see them as forms of God; and in a totality of religion I worship the

Father, who is truth, justice, and love, who is the Infinite God.

The affections want a person to cling to; — my soul reveals to me God, without the limitations of human personality; Him I can love, and not be narrowed by my affections. If I love a limited object, I grow up to the bigness thereof, then stop; it helps my growth no more. The finiteness of my friend admits no absolute affection. Partial love must not disturb the universal sweep of impersonal truth and justice. The object of the heart must not come between me and the object of mind or conscience, and enfeeble the man. But if you love the Infinite God, it is with all your faculties, which find their complete and perfect object, and you progressively grow up towards him, to be like him. The idea of God becomes continually more, your achievement of the divine becomes more. You love with no divided love; there is no collision of faculties, the head forbidding what the soul commands, the heart working one way and the conscience another. The same Object corresponds to all these faculties, which love Him as truth, as justice, as love, as God who is all in all; one central sun balances and feeds with fire this system of harmonious orbs.

Consider the power of religion in a man whose mind and conscience, heart and soul, are all well developed. He has these four forms of piety; they all unite, each to all, and all to each. His mind gives him knowledge of truth, the necessary condition for the highest action of his conscience; that furnishes him with the idea of justice, which is the necessary condition for the highest action of the affections; they in their development extend to all in their wide love of men; this affords the necessary condition for the highest action of the soul, which can then love God with absolute love, and, joining with all the other activity of the man, helps the use, development, and enjoyment of every faculty. Then truth has lost its coldness; justice is not hard and severe; love is not partial, as when limited to family, tribe, or nation; but, coextensive with justice, applies to all mankind; faith is not mystical or merely introversive and quietistic. This fourfold action joins in one unity of worship, in love of God, —love with the highest and conjoint action of all the faculties of man. Then love of the Infinite God is no mystical abstraction, no dreamy sentimentalism, but the normal action of the entire man, every faculty seeking its finite contentment, and finding also its infinite satisfaction by feeling the life of God in the soul of man.

In our time, as often before, attempts are making to cultivate the soul, in the narrowest way, without

15

developing the other parts of man's spiritual nature. The intellect is called "carnal," conscience "dangerous," and the heart "deceitful." We are told to trust none of these in matters of religion. Accordingly, ecclesiastical men complain that "science is not religious," because it breaks down the "venerable doctrines" of the Church, — because geologists have swept away the flood, grammarians annihilated the tower of Babel, and physiologists brushed off the miracles of the Jews, the Greeks, the Hindoos, and the Christians, to the same dust-hole of the ages and repository of rubbish. It is complained that "morality is not religious," because it refuses to be comforted with the forms of religious ceremony, and thinks "divine service" is not merely sitting in a church, or listening to even the wisest words. The churches complain also that "philanthropy is not religious," but love of men dissuades us from love of God. The philanthropist looks out on the evils of society, — on the slavery whose symbol is the lash, and the slavery whose symbol is the dollar; on the avarice, the intemperance, the licentiousness of men; and calls on mankind in the name of God to put away all this wickedness. The churches say: "Rather receive our sacraments. Religion has nothing to do with such matters."

This being the case, men of powerful character no longer betake themselves to the Church as their fortress whence to assail the evils of the age, or as their hermitage wherein to find rest to their souls. In all England there are few men, I think, of first-rate ability who speak from a pulpit. Let me do no injustice to minds like three great men honoring her pulpits now, but has England a clerical scholar to rival the intellectual affluence of Hooker, and Barrow, and Taylor, and Cudworth, and South? The great names of English literature at this day, Carlyle, Hallam, Macaulay, Mill, Grote, and the rest, seem far enough from the Church, or its modes of salvation. The counting-house sends out men to teach political economy, looking always to the kitchen of the nation, and thinking of the stomach of the people. Does the Church send out men of corresponding power to think of the soul of the nation, and teach the people political morality? Was Bishop Butler the last of the great men who essayed to teach Britain from her established pulpit? Even Priestley has few successors in the ranks of religious dissent. The same may be said of Church poets: they are often well-bred; what one of them is there that was well-born for his high vocation?

In the American Church there is the same famine of men. Edwards and Mayhew belonged to a race now extinct, — great men in pulpits. In our literature there are names enough once clerical. The very fairest names on our little hill of the Muses are of men once clergymen. Channing is the only one in this country who continued thus to the end of life. A crowd of able men, with a mob of others, press into all departments of trade, into the profession of the law, and the headlong race of American politics, — where a reputation is gained without a virtue or lost without a crime, — but no men of first-rate powers and attainments continue in the pulpit. Hence we have strong-minded men in business, in politics, and law, who teach men the measures which seem to suit the evanescent interests of the day, but few in pulpits, to teach men the eternal principles of justice, which really suit the present and also the everlasting interests of mankind. Hence no popular and deadly sin of the nation gets well rebuked by the Church of the Times. The dwarfs of the pulpit hide their diminished heads before the Anakim of politics and trade. The almighty dollar hunts wisdom, justice, and philanthropy out of the American Church. It is only among the fanatical Mormons that the ablest men teach in the name of God.

The same is mainly true of all Christendom. The Church which in her productive period had an Origen, a Chrysostom, an Augustine, a Jerome, an Aquinas, its Gregories and its Basils, had real saints and willing martyrs, in the nineteenth century cannot show a single mind which is a guide of the age.

The great philosophers of Europe are far enough from Christian.

It is, doubtless, a present misfortune that the positions most favorable to religious influence are filled with feeble men, or such as care little for the welfare of mankind, — who have all of religion except its truth, its justice, its philanthropy, and its faith. Still, such is the fact just now; a fact which shows plainly enough the position of what is popularly called "Christianity" in the world of men. The form of religion first proclaimed by the greatest religious genius that ever lit the world, and sealed by his martyrdom, is now officially represented by men of vulgar talents, of vulgar aspirations, — to be rich, respectable, and fat, — and of vulgar lives. Hunkers of the Church claim exclusively to represent the martyr of the Cross. A sad sight!

Yet still religion is a great power amongst men, spite of these disadvantages. It was never so great before; for in the progressive development of mankind the higher faculties acquire continually a greater and greater influence. If Christianity means what was true and good in the teaching and character of Jesus, then there was never so much of it in the world. Spite of the defalcation and opposition of the churches, there is a continual growth in all those four forms of piety. Under the direction of able men, all those fragments of religion are made ready in their several places. In the department of mind, see how much has been done in this last hundred years; man has nearly doubled the intellectual property of the seventeenth century. The early history of mankind is better understood now than by the nations who lived it. What discoveries of science in all that relates to the heavens, to the earth and its inhabitants, mineral, vegetable, animal, human! In the philosophy of man, how much has been done to understand his nature and his history! In practical affairs, see what wonders have been wrought in a hundred years; look at England, France, Germany, and America, and see the power of the scientific head over the world of matter, the human power gained by better political organization of the tribes of men.

In the department of conscience, see what a love of justice develops itself in all Christendom; see the results of this for the last hundred years; in the reform of laws, of constitutions, in the great political, social, and domestic revolutions of our time. Men have clearer ideas of justice; they would have a church without a bishop, a State without a king, society without a lord, and a family without a slave. From this troublesome conscience comes the uneasiness of the Christian world. A revolution is a nation's act of penitence, of resolution, and of prayer,

— its agony and bloody sweat. See what a love of freedom there is shaking the institutions of the aged world. Tyrannies totter before the invisible hand of Justice, which, to the terror of the oppressors, writes, "Weighed, and found wanting." So the despot trembles for his guilty throne; the slave-driver begins to fear the God of the man he has kidnapped and enthralled. See the attempts making by the people to break down monopolies, to promote freedom of intercourse between all nations of the earth. See woman assert her native rights, long held in abeyance by the superior vigor of the manly arm.

In all that pertains to the affections, there has been a great advance. Love travels beyond the narrow bounds of England and of Christendom. See the efforts making to free the slave; to elevate the poor, — removing the causes of poverty by the charity that alleviates and the justice that cures; to heal the drunkard of his fiery thirst; to reform the criminals whom once we only hung. The gallows must come down, the dungeon be a school for piety, not the den of vengeance and of rage. Great pains begin to be taken with the deaf and dumb, the blind, the insane; even the idiot must be taught. Philanthropic men, who are freedom to the slave, feet to the lame, eyes to the blind, and hearing to the deaf, would be also understanding to the fool. In what is idly called "an age of faith," the town council of

Grenoble set archers at the gates, to draw upon strange beggars and shoot them down before the city walls. Look, now, at the New England provision for the destitute,—for the support of their bodies and the culture of their minds.

No Church leads off in these movements; ecclesiastical men take small interest therein; but they come from the three partial forms of piety, the intellectual, the moral, and the affectional. We need to have these all united with a conscious love of God. What hinders? The old ecclesiastical idea of God, as finite, imperfect in wisdom, in justice, and in love, still blocks the way. The God wholly external to the world of matter, acting by fits and starts, is not God enough for science, which requires a uniform, infinite force, with constant modes of action. The capricious Deity, wholly external to the human spirit,—jealous, partial, loving Jacob and hating Esau, revengeful, blasting with endless hell all but a fraction of his family,—this is not God enough for the scientific moralist, and the philanthropist running over with love. They want a God immanent in matter, immanent in spirit, yet infinite, and so transcending both,—the God of infinite perfection, infinite power, wisdom, justice, love, and self-fidelity. This idea is a stranger to the Christian, as to the Hebrew and Mohammedan church; and so stout men turn off therefrom, or else are driven away with hated names. One day these men will welcome the true idea of God, and have a conscious trust and love of Him to match their science, their justice, and their love of men; will become the prophets and apostles of the Absolute Religion, finding it wide enough for all truth, all justice, and all love, yea, for an absolute faith in God, in his motives, means, and ends. Then all this science of the nineteenth century, all this practical energy, this wide command over Nature, this power to organize the world of matter and yoke it to the will of man, this love of freedom and power to combine vast masses in productive industry; then all this wide literature of modern times, glittering with many-colored riches, and spread abroad so swift; then all this morality which clamors for the native right of men, this wide philanthropy, laying down its life to bless mankind, — all this shall join with the natural emotions of the soul, welcoming the Infinite God. It shall all unite into one religion; each part thereof "may call the farthest brother." Then what a work will religion achieve in the affairs of men! What institutions will it build, what welfare will it produce on earth, what men bring forth! Even now the several means are working for this one great end, only not visibly, not with the consciousness of men.

I do not complain of the "decline of piety." I

thank God for its increase. I see what has been done, but I look also to what remains to do. I am sure that mankind will do it. God is a master workman; He made man well, — for an end worthy of God, provided with means quite adequate to that end. No man, not an Isaiah or a Jesus, ever dares prophesy so high but man fulfils the oracle, and then goes dreaming his prophecy anew, and fulfilling it as he goes on. If you have a true idea of justice, a true sentiment of philanthropy or of faith in God, which men have not yet welcomed, if you can state your idea in speech, then mankind will stop and realize your idea, — make your abstract thought their concrete thing. Kings are nothing, armies fall before you. The idea sways them in its flight as the wind of summer bows the unripe corn of June.

This religion will build temples, not of stone only, but temples of living stones, temples of men, families, communities, nations, and a world. We want no monarchies in the name of God; we do want a democracy in that name, a democracy which rests on human nature, and, respecting that, reënacts the natural laws of God, the Constitution of the Universe, in the common statutes and written laws of the land.

We need this religion for its general and its special purposes; need it as subjective piety in each of these fragmentary forms, as joined into a totality of religious consciousness; we need it as morality, keeping the natural laws of God for the body and the spirit, in the individual, domestic, social, national, and general human or cosmic form, the divine sentiment becoming the human act. We need this to heal the vices of modern society, to revolutionize this modern feudalism of gold, and join the rich and poor, the employer and the employed, in one bond of human fellowship; we need it to break down the wall between class and class, nation and nation, race and race,—to join all classes into one nation, all nations into one great human family. Science alone is not adequate to achieve this; calculations of interest cannot effect it; political economy will not check the iron hand of power, nor relax the grasp of the oppressor from his victim's throat. Only religion, deep, wide spread, and true, can achieve this work.

Already it is going forward, not under the guidance of one great man with ideas to direct the march, and mind to plan the structure of the future age, but under many men, who know each his little speciality, all their several parts, while the Infinite Architect foresees and so provides for all. Much has been done in this century, now only half spent; much more is a-doing. But the greatest of its works is one which men do not talk about, nor see: it is the silent development of the several parts of a complete piety, one day to be united into a consciousness of the Absolute Religion, and to be the parent of a new church and new State, with communities and families such as the world has hitherto not seen.

We notice the material works of our time, the industrial activity, the rapid increase of wealth in either England, Old or New. Foolish men deplore this, and would go back to the time when an ignorant peasantry, clad in sheep-skins, full of blind, instinctive faith in God, and following only as they were led by men, built up the cathedrals of Upsala and Strasburg. In the order of development, the material comes first; even the excessive lust of gain, now turning the heads of Old England and the New, is part of the cure of the former unnatural mistake. Gross poverty is on its way to the grave. The natural man is before the spiritual man. We are laying a basis for a spiritual structure which no man has genius yet to plan. Years ago there were crowds of men at work in Lebanon, cutting down the algum, the cedar, and the fir, squaring into ashlar, boring, chiselling, mortising, tenoning, all manner of beams; some were rafting it along the coast to Joppa, and yet others teaming it up to Jerusalem. What sweat of horses was there, what lowing of oxen and complaint from the camels! Thousands of men were quarrying stone at Moriah for the foundation of the work. Yet only one man comprehended it all; the lumberers felling the cedar and sycamore, the carpenters and the muleteers, understood each their special work, no more. But the son of the Danite woman planned all this stone and timber into a temple, which, by the labor of many and the consciousness of a few, rose up on the mountain of Jerusalem, the wonder and the pride of all the land. So the great work, the humanization of man, is going forward. The girl that weaves muslins at Brussels, the captain of the emigrant ship sailing "past bleak Mozambique," hungry for Australian gold, the chemist who annihilates pain with a gas and teaches lightning to read and write, the philosopher who tells us the mighty faculties which lie hid in labyrinthine man, and the philanthropic maiden who in the dirt of a worldly city lives love which some theologians think is too much for God, — all of these, and thousands more, are getting together and preparing the materials for the great temple of man, whose builder and maker is God. You and I shall pass away, but mankind is the true son of God that abideth ever, to whom the Father says continually, "Come up higher."

I see the silent growth of religion in men. I see that the spiritual elements are a larger fraction of human consciousness than ever before; that there is more of truth, of justice, of love, and faith in God than was ever in the world. As we know and observe the natural laws of man, the constitution of the universe, the more, so will this religion continue to increase, and the results thereof appear in common life, in the individual, domestic, social, national, and universal human form.

Some men say they cannot love, or even know, God, except in the form of man. God as the Infinite seems to them abstract, and they cannot lay hold on Him until a man fills their corporeal eye and arms, and the affections cling thereto and are blest. So they love Christ, — not the Jesus of history, but the Christ of the Christian mythology, — an imaginary being, an ideal incarnation of God in man. Let them help themselves with this crutch of the fancy, as boys use sticks to leap a ditch or spring a wall; yet let them remember that the real historical incarnation of God is in mankind, not in one person, but all, and human history is a continual transfiguration. As the Divine seems nearest when human, and men have loved to believe in the union of God and man, so religion is loveliest when it assumes the form of common life, — when daily work is a daily sacrament, and life itself a psalm of gratitude and prayer of aspiration.

It is Palm Sunday to-day, and men in churches

remember what is written of the peasant from Galilee who rode into Jerusalem amid multitudes of earnest men not merely waiting for consolation, but going to meet it half-way, who yet knew not what they did, nor whom they welcomed. As that man went to the capital of a nation which knew him not, so in our time Religion rides her ass-colt into village and town, welcome to many a weary, toiling heart, but ignored and pelted by the successors of such as "took counsel against Jesus, to put him to death." How little do we know! But he that keeps the integrity of his own consciousness, and is faithful to himself day by day, is also faithful to God for eternity, and helps to restore the integrity of the world of men.

The religious actions of old times it is now easy to understand. They left their monuments, their pyramids, and temples which they built, the memory of the wars they fought against their brothers in the dear name of Jesus, or of Allah the Only. But the religious action of this age, not in the old form, —it will take the next generation to understand that.

My friends, this is a young nation, new as yet; you and I can do something to mould its destiny. There are millions before us. They will fulfil our prophecy, the truer the fairer. Our sentiment of religion, our ideas thereof, if true, shall bless them in their deepest, dearest life. They will rejoice if we shall break the yokes from off their necks, and rend asunder the old traditionary veil which hides from them their Father's face. All of your piety, partial or total, shall go down to gladden the faces of your children, and to bless their souls for ever and for ever.

VI.

OF THE CULTURE OF THE RELIGIOUS POWERS.

LET US GO ON UNTO PERFECTION. — Heb. vi. 1.

THE highest product of a nation is its men; of you and me is our character, the life which we make out of our time. Our reputation is what we come to be thought of, our character what we come to be. In this character the most important element is the religious, for it is to be the guide and director of all the rest, the foundation-element of human excellence.

In general our character is the result of three factors, namely, of our Nature, both that which is human, and which we have as men in common with all mankind, and that which is individual, and which we have as Sarah or George, in distinction from all men; next, of the Educational Forces about us; and, finally, of our own Will, which we exercise, and so determine the use we make of the two other factors; for it is for us to determine whether we will lie flat before natural instincts and educational forces, or modify their action upon us.

What is true in general of all culture is true in special of religious education. Religious character is the result of these three factors.

I suppose every earnest man, who knows what religion is, desires to become a religious man, to do the most of religious duty, have the most of religious rights, and enjoy the most of religious welfare; to give the most for God, and receive the most from Him. It does not always appear so, yet really is. At the bottom of our hearts we all wish for that. We have been misled by blind guides, who did not always mean to deceive us; we have often gone astray, led off by our instinctive passion in youth, our voluntary calculation in manhood, yet never meaning to deceive ourselves. But there is none of us who does not desire to be a religious man, — at least, I never met one who confessed it, or of whom I thought it true. But of course, they desire it with various degrees of will.

Writers often divide men into two classes, saints and sinners. I like not the division. The best men are bad enough in their own eyes. I hope God is better pleased with men than we are with ourselves, there are so many things in us all which are there against our consent, — evil tenants whom we cannot get rid of as yet. That smoky chimney of an ill-temper is a torment to poor Mr. Fiery, which he has not had courage or strength to remove in fifty winters. To "see ourselves as others see us," would often minister to pride and conceit; how many naughty things, actions and emotions too, I know of myself, which no calumniator ever casts in my teeth. Yet take the worst men whom you can find, — men that rob on the highway with open violence, pirates on the sea, the more dangerous thieves who devour widows' houses and plunder the unprotected in a manner thoroughly legal, respectable, and "Christian," men that steal from the poor; — take the tormentors of the Spanish Inquisition, assassins and murderers from New York and Naples, nay, the family of commissioners who in Boston are willing to kidnap their fellow-citizens for ten dollars a head, and bind them and their posterity for the perennial torture of American slavery; — even these men would curl and shudder at the thought of being without consciousness of God in the world; of living without any religion, and dying without any religion. I know some think religion is rather uncomfortable to live by, but the worst of men, as the best, thinks it is a good thing to die with. Men repent of many things on a death-bed;

when the storm blows, all the dead bodies are stirred in the bosom of the sea, and no one is then sorry for his efforts to become a religious man. Many a man, who lives in the violation of his personal, domestic, social, national, and general human duties, doubtless contrives to think he is a religious man, and if in the name of Mammon he robs the widow of a pound, he gives a penny to the orphan in the name of God, and thinks he serves each without much offending the other. Thus, kidnappers in these times are "exemplary members" of "Christian churches" where philanthropy gets roundly rated by the minister from week to week, and call themselves "miserable offenders" with the devoutest air. This is not all sham. The men want to keep on good terms with God, and take this as the cheapest, as well as the most respectable way. Louis the Fifteenth had a private chapel dedicated to the "Blessed Virgin" in the midst of his house of debauchery, where he and his poor victims were said to be "very devout after the Church fashion." Slave-traders and kidnappers take pains to repel all calumny from their "religious" reputation, and do not practise their craft till "divines" assure them it is patriarchal and even "Christian." I mention these things to show that men who are commonly thought eminently atrocious in their conduct and character, yet would not willingly be without religion. I shall take it for granted that all men wish to acquire a religious character.

I take it this is the Idea of a religious character. It is, first, to be faithful to ourselves, to rule body and spirit, each by the natural law thereof; to use, develop, and enjoy all the faculties, each in its just proportions, all in harmonious action, developed to the greatest degree which is possible under our circumstances; to have such an abiding consciousness of God, that you will have the fourfold form of piety, so often dwelt on before, and be inwardly blameless, harmonious, and holy.

It is, next, to be faithful to your fellow men; to do for them what is right, from right motives and for right ends; to love them as yourself; to be useful to them to the extent of your power; to live in such harmony with them that you shall rejoice in their joys, and all be mutually blessed with the bliss of each other.

It is also to be faithful to God; to know of Him, to have a realizing sense of his Infinite power, wisdom, justice, goodness, and holiness, and so a perfect love of God, a perfect trust in Him, a delight in the Infinite Being of God; to love him intellectually in the love of truth, morally as justice, affectionally as love, and totally as the Infinite God, Father and

Mother too of all this world; so to love God that you have no desire to transcend his law or violate your duty to yourself, your brother, or your God; so to love Him that there shall be no fear of God, none for yourself, none for mankind, but a perfect confidence and an absolute love shall take the place of every fear. In short, it is to serve God by the normal use, development, and enjoyment of every faculty of the spirit, every limb of the body, and every mode of power which we possess.

I think such is the ideal of a religious character; that there is no one who would not confess a desire to be religious in that sense, for it is to be a perfect man; no one who would not make some sacrifice for this end; most men would make a great one, some would leave father and mother, and lay down their own lives, to secure it.

What are some of the means to this end, to this grace and this glory? There are four great public educational forces, namely, the industrial, political, literary, and ecclesiastical action of the people, represented by the Business, the State, the Press, and the Church.* These have a general influence in the for-

* See Speeches, Addresses, and Occasional Sermons, by Theodore Parker, Boston, 1852, Vol. I. p. 407 *et seq.*, where these educational forces are dwelt on at length.

mation of the character, and so a special influence in the formation of the religious character; but as they cannot be trusted for the general work of forming the character, no more can they for this special function. They are less reliable in religion than in any other matter whatever. By these forces the whole community is a teacher of religion to all persons born therein; but it can only teach the mode and degree of religion it has itself learned and possessed, not that which it has not learned and does not possess. Not only can it not teach a religion higher than its own, but it hinders you in your attempt to learn a new and better mode of religion.

For several things we may trust these public educational forces in religion.

They teach you in the general popular fear of God, and a certain outward reverence which comes of that; the popular sacraments of our time, — to give your bodily presence in a meeting-house, perhaps to join a sectarian church, and profess great reverence for the Bible.

They will teach you the popular part of your practical duties, — personal, domestic, social, ecclesiastical, and political. But of course they can teach you only the popular part.

They may be relied on to teach the majority of men certain great truths, which are the common property of Christendom, such as the existence of a

God, the immortality of the soul, the certainty of a kind of retribution, and the like. Then each sect has certain truths of its own which it will commonly teach. Thus the Catholics will learn to reverence the Roman Church; the Protestants to venerate the Bible; the Calvinists to believe in the Trinity; and the Unitarians in the Oneness of God. All the sects will teach a certain decorum, the observance of Sunday, — to honor the popular virtues, to shun the unpopular vices.

The educational forces tend to produce this effect. You send your boys to the public schools of Boston, they learn the disciplines taught there, — to read, write, and calculate. What is not taught they do not learn. In Saxony the children learn German; Dutch, in Holland. In the same way the majority of men learn the common religion of the community, and profess it practically in their markets, their houses, their halls of legislature, their courts, and their jails. The commercial newspapers, the proceedings of Congress, the speeches of public men, — these are a part of the national profession of faith, and show what is the actual object of worship, and what the practical creed of the nation.

But for any eminence of religion you must look elsewhere; for any excellence of the sentiment, any superiority of the idea, any newness in the form of religion. These educational forces will teach you evanescent principles which seem to suit your present and partial interests, not eternal principles, which really suit your universal and everlasting interests. In Jerusalem these forces might educate a Gamaliel, — never a Jesus.

Charles River flows two miles an hour; chips and straws on its surface, therefore, if there be no wind, will float with that velocity. But if a man in a boat wishes to go ten miles an hour, he must row eight miles more than the stream will carry him. So we are all in the dull current of the popular religion, and may trust it to drift us as fast as it flows itself; we may rise with its flood, and be stranded and left dry when it ebbs out before some popular wickedness which blows from off the shore. The religious educational forces of a commercial town, — you see in the newspapers what religion they will teach you, — in the streets what men they would make.

These educational forces tend to make average Christians, and their influence is of great value to the community, — like the discipline of a camp. But to be eminent religious men, you must depend on very different helps. Let us look at some of them.

There are religious men who, by the religious genius they were born to, and the religious use they have made thereof, have risen far above the average of Christians. Such men are the first help; and a most important one they are. It is a fortunate thing when such an one stands in a church whither the public current drives in the people, and to the strength of his nature adds the strength of position. But it is not often that such a man stands in a pulpit. The common ecclesiastical training tends to produce dull and ordinary men, with little individual life, little zeal, and only the inspiration of a sect. However, if a man of religious genius, by some human accident, gets into a pulpit, he is in great danger of preaching himself out of it. Still there are such men, a few of them, stationed along the line of the human march; cities set on a hill, which no cloud of obloquy can wholly hide from sight. Nay, they are great beacons on the shore of the world, — light-houses on the headlands of the coast, sending their guidance far out to sea, to warn the mariner of his whereabouts, and welcome him to port and peace. Street-lamps there must be for the thoroughfares of the town, shop-lights also for the grocer and the apothecary; nay, hand-lights which are made to be carried from room to room and set down anywhere, and numerous they will ever be, each having its own function. This arrangement takes place in the ecclesiastical as well as in municipal affairs, for each sect has its street-lamps and its shop-lights to guide men to its particular huckstery of salvation, and little hand-lights to take into corners where the salesmen and the showmen are all ready with their wares. But the great Faros of Genoa, and Eddystone light-houses of religion must always be few and far between; the world is not yet rich enough in spirit to afford many of this sort.

Yet even in these men you seldom find the wholeness of religion. One has the sentiments thereof; he will kindle your religious feelings, your reverence, your devotion, your trust, and your love of God.

Another has only its ideas; new thoughts about religion, new truths, which he presents to the minds of men. Analytic, he destroys the ancient errors of theological systems; thrashes the creeds of the churches with the stout flail of philosophy, and sifts them as wheat, winnowing with a rough wind, great clouds of chaff blow off before his mighty vans. Synthetic, he takes the old truth which stood the critical thrashing and is now winnowed clean; he joins therewith new truth shot down from God, and welcomed into loving arms; and out of his large storehouse this scribe, well instructed unto the kingdom of heaven, brings forth things new and old, to serve as bread for the living, and seed-corn to generations not born as yet.

A third, with no eminence of feelings commonly called religious, — none of theological ideas, — will have yet an eminence of justice, and teach personal and social morality as no other man. He may turn to a single speciality of morals, and demand temperance, chastity, the reform of penal law, the reconstruction of society, the elevation of woman, and the education of the whole mass of men; or he may turn to general philanthropy, the universality of moral excellence, — it all comes from the same root, and with grateful welcome should be received.

Each of these teachers will do real service to your souls, — quickening the feelings, imparting ideas, and organizing the results of religion in moral acts. I know a great outcry has been made in all the churches against moral reformers, against men who would apply pure religion to common life, in the special or the universal form. You all know what clamor is always raised against a man who would abolish a vice from human society, or establish a new virtue. Every wolf is interested in the wilderness, and hates the axe and the plough of the settler, and would devour his child if he dared. So every nuisance in society has its supporters, whose property is invested therein. Paul found it so at Ephesus, Telemachus at Rome, and Garrison in America. I doubt not the men of Ephesus thought religion good in all matters except the making of silver shrines for Diana; "there it makes men mad." Men cry out against the advance of morality:

"Preach us religion; preach us Christianity, Christ and him crucified, and not this infidel matter of ending particular sins, and abounding in special virtues. Preach us the exceeding sinfulness of sin, 'original sin' 'which brought death into the world and all our woe;' preach the beauty of holiness, and the like of that, and let alone the actual sins of society, of the shop and the church and the State; — be silent about drunkenness and lust, about war, slavery, and the thousand forms of avarice which we rejoice in. Is it not enough, O Preacher, that we give you of our purse and our corporeal presence, that we weekly confess ourselves 'miserable offenders,' with 'no health in us,' and fast, perhaps, twice in our lives, but you must convict us of being idolaters also; yea, drunkards, gluttons, impure in youth and avaricious in manhood, — once a Voluptuary, and now a Hunker! Go to now, and preach us the blessedness of the righteous, Christ and him crucified!" When money speaks, the Church obeys, and the pulpit preaches for doctrine the commandments of the pews.

But it is these very moral reformers, who, in our time, have done more than all others to promote the feeling of piety which the churches profess so much to covet. The new ground of religion which the churches occupy is always won for them by men whom the churches hated. In the last thirty years these "pestilent moral reformers" of New England, I think, have done more to promote love of God, and faith in Him, than all the other preachers of all the churches. Justice is a part of piety; and such is the instinctive love of wholeness in man, that all attempts to promote justice amongst men lead ultimately to the love of God as God.

In every community you will find a man who thus represents some portion of religion, — often, perhaps, thinking that part is the whole, because it is all that he knows; here and there we find such an one in the pulpit. But now and then there comes a man who unites these three functions of piety into one great glory of religion; is eminent in feelings, ideas, and actions not the less. Each of those partial men may help us much, teaching his doctrine, kindling our feelings, giving example of his deed, and laying out religious work for us, spreading his pattern before society. Each of these may help us to a partial improvement. But when a man comes who unites them all, he will give us a new start, an inspiration which no other man can give; not partial, but total.

There are always some such men in the world; the seed of the prophets never dies out. It comes up in Israel and in Attica; here a prophet teaching truth as divine inspiration, there a philosopher with his human discovery. So the Herb of Grace springs up in corners where once old houses stood, or wherever the winds have borne the seed; and, cropped by the oxen, and trodden with their feet, it grows ever fresh and ever new. When Scribes and Pharisees become idolaters at Jerusalem, and the sheep without a shepherd

> "Look up and are not fed,
> But, swollen with wind and the rank mist they draw,
> Rot inwardly and foul contagion spread,"

the spirit of God comes newly down on some carpenter's son at Nazareth, whose lightning terrifies the non-conducting Scribe; the new encounters the perishable old, and all heaven rings with the thunder of the collision. Now and then such a person comes to stand betwixt the living and the dead. "Bury that," quoth he, "it is hopelessly dead, past all resurrection. This must be healed, tended, and made whole." He is a physician to churches sick of sin, as well as with it; burying the dead, he heals also the sick, and quickens the sound into new and healthy life. But the owners of swine that perish must needs cry out at the loss.

Yet such a man is not understood in his own generation. A man with a single eminent faculty is soon seen through and comprehended. This man is good for nothing but practice; that, only for thought. One is a sentimentalist; another, a traveller. But when a genius comes eminent in many and most heterogeneous faculties, men do not see through nor comprehend him in a short time. If he has in himself all the excellence of all the men in the metropolis, — why, it will take many a great city to comprehend him. The young maiden in the story, for the first time hearing her clerical lover preach, wondered that those lips could pray as sweetly as they kissed, but could not comprehend the twofold sacrament, the mystery of this double function of a single mouth. Anybody can see that corn grows in this field, and kale in that; the roughest clown knows this, but it takes a great many wise men to describe the botany of a whole continent. So is it ever. Here is a religious man, — writing on purely internal emotions of piety, of love of God, of faith in Him, of rest for the soul, the foretaste of heaven. He penetrates the deeps of religious joy, its peace enters his soul, his morning prayer is a psalm deeper than David's, with a beauty more various than the poetic wreath which the shepherd-king gathered from the hill-sides of Jordan or the gardens of Mount Zion. Straightway men say: "This man is a sentimentalist; he is a mystic, all contemplation, all feeling, — poetical, dreamy, — his light is moonshine." But erelong our sentimentalist writes of philosophy, and his keen eye sees mines of wisdom not quarried heretofore, and he brings a power of unsunned gold to light. Other men say: "O, this man is nothing but a philosopher, a mere thinker, a mighty head, but with no more heart than Chimborazo or Thomas Hobbes." Yet presently some great sin breaks out, and rolls its desolating flood over the land, uprooting field and town, and our philosopher goes out to resist the ruin. He denounces the evil, attacks the institution which thus deceives men. Straightway men call out: "Iconoclast! Boanerges! John Knox! destroyer!" and the like. Alas me! men do not know that the same sun gathers the dews which water the forget-me-not, drooping at noonday, and drives through the sky the irresistible storm that shatters the forest in its thunderous march, and piles the ruins of a mountain in an Alpine avalanche. The same soul which thundered its forked lightning on Scribes and Pharisees, hypocrites, poured out poetic parables from his golden urn, spreading forth the sunshine of the beatitudes upon friend and foe, and, half in heaven, breathed language wholly thence, — "Father, forgive them, for they know not what they do."

It is a great thing once in our days to meet with a man of religious genius largely developed into lovely life. He stirs the feelings infinite within us, and we go off quite other than we came. He has not put his soul into our bosom; he has done better, — has waked our soul in our own bosom. Men may go leagues long to listen to such a man, and come back well paid. He gives us seeds of future life for our little garden. So the husbandman journeys far to get a new root or a new seed, to fill his ground with beauty or his home with bread. After we have listened to the life of such a man, the world does not seem so low, nor man so mean; heaven looks nearer, yet higher too; humanity is more rich; if wrong appear yet more shameful, the wrongdoer is not so hopeless. After that I can endure trouble; my constant cross is not so heavy; the unwonted is less difficult to bear. Tears are not so scalding to an eye which has looked through them into the serene face of a great-souled man. Men seem friendlier, and God is exceeding dear. The magistrates of Jerusalem marvelled at the conduct of Peter and John, heedful of the higher law of God, spite of bonds and imprisonment and politicians; but they "took knowledge of them, that they had been with Jesus," and the marvel had its explanation. What a dull, stupid thing is a candle! Touch it with fire, and then look! We are all of us capable of being lit when some Prometheus comes down with the spark of God in his right hand. The word of Jesus touched the dull fishermen of Galilee, and they flamed into martyrs and apostles.

It is a great thing to meet such a man once in your lifetime, to be cheered and comforted in your sad wayfaring, and filled with new vigor and new faith in the Father of all. After that we thank God, and take courage and fare on our happier way. So a company of pilgrims journeying in the wilderness, dry, foot-sore, and hot, the water all spent in their goat-skins, their camels weary and sick, come to a grove of twelve palm-trees, and an unexpected spring of pure water wells up in the desert. Strightway their weariness is all forgot, their limping camels have become whole once more. Staying their thirst, they fill their bottles also with the cool refreshment, rest in the shadow from the noonday's heat, and then with freshened life, the soreness gone from every bone, pursue their noiseless and their happy march. Even so, says the Old Testament story, God sent his angel down in the wilderness to feed Elias with the bread of heaven, and in the strength thereof the prophet went his forty days, nor hungered not. I suppose some of us have had this experience, and in our time of bewilderment, of scorching desolation, and of sorrow, have come upon our well of water and twelve palm-trees in the sand, and so have marched all joyful through the wilderness. Elias left all the angels of God for you and me, — the friendlier for his acquaintance.

There is a continual need of men of this stamp. We live in the midst of religious machinery. Many mechanics at piety, often only apprentices and slow to learn, are turning the various ecclesiastical mills, and the creak of the motion is thought "the voice of God." You put into the hopper a crowd of persons, young and old, and soon they are ground out into the common run of Christians, sacked up, and stored away for safe-keeping in the appropriate bins of the great ecclesiastical establishment, and labelled with their party names. You look about in what is dryly called "the religious world." What a mass of machinery is there, of dead timber, not green trees! what a jar and discord of iron clattering upon iron! Action is of machinery, not of life, and it is green new life that you want. So men grow dull in their churches. What a weariness is an ordinary meeting on one of the fifty-two ordinary Sundays of the year! What a dreary thing is an ordinary sermon of an ordinary minister! He does not wish to preach it; the audience does not wish to hear it. So he makes a feint of preaching, they a feint of hearing him preach. But he preaches not; they hear not. He is dull as the cushion he beats, they as the cushions they cover. A body of men met in a church for nothing, and about nothing, and to hear nobody, is to me a ghastly spectacle. Did you ever see cattle in a cold day in the country crowd together in an enclosure, the ground frozen under their feet, and no hay spread upon it,—huddling together for warmth, hungry, but inactive, because penned up, and waiting with the heavy, slumberous patience of oxen till some man should come and shake down to them a truss of clean bright hay, still redolent of clover and honeysuckle? That is a cheerful sight; and when the farmer comes and hews their winter food out of the stack, what life is in these slumberous oxen! their venerable eyes are full of light, because they see their food. Ah me! how many a herd of men is stall-hungered in the churches, not getting even the hay of religion, only a little chaff swept off from old thrashing-floors whence the corn which great men beat out of its husk was long since gathered up to feed and bless mankind! Churches are built of stone. I have often thought pulpits should be cushioned with husks.

Of all melancholy social sights that one sees, few are so sad as a body of men got together to convert mankind to sectarianism by ecclesiastical machinery, —men dead as timber, cut down, dead and dry! Out of wire, muslin, thread, starch, gum, and sundry chemicals, French milliners make by dozens what they call roses, lilies of the valley, forget-me-nots, and the like. Scentless and seedless abortions are they, and no more. What a difference between the flower the lover gathers by the brookside for his maiden's breast, and the thing which the milliner makes with her scissors; between the forget-me-not of the meadow and the forget-me-not of the shop! Such an odds is there betwixt religious men and Christians manufactured in a mill.

In the factories of England you find men busy all their life in making each the twenty-sixth part of a watch. They can do nothing else, and become almost as much machines as the grindstone which sharpens their drill, or the rammage which carries their file. Much of our ecclesiastical machinery tends to make men into mere fixtures in a mill. So there must be a continual accession of new religious life from without into the churches to keep Christians living. Men of religious genius it is who bring it in. Without them "religion" in cities would become mere traditional theology, and "life in God" would be sitting in a meeting-house, and the baptism in water from an aqueduct taken for the communion of the Holy Ghost. Blessed be God that there are such men not smothered in the surplice of the priest, but still alive in God, and God alive in them!

In old towns all the water that fills the wells is dead water,—dead and dirty too; the rinsings of the streets, the soakings of stables, the slop of markets, the wash and offscouring of the town; even the filterings of the graveyard settle therein, and the child is fed with its grandsire's bones. Men would perish if left alone, dying of their drink. So, far off in the hills, above the level of the town, they seek some mountain lake, and furnish a pathway that its crystal beauty may come to town. There the living water leaps up in public fountains, it washes the streets, it satisfies the blameless cattle, it runs into every house to cleanse and purify and bless, and men are glad as the Hebrews when Moses smote the fabled rock. So comes religious genius unto men: some mountain of a man stands up tall, and all winter long takes the snows of heaven on his shoulders, all summer through receives the cold rain into his bosom; both become springs of living water at his feet. Then the proprietors of fetid wells and subterranean tanks, which they call "Bethesda," though often troubled by other than angels, and whence they retail their "salvation" a pennyworth at a time,— they cry out with sneer and scoff and scorn against our new-born saint. "Shall Christ come out of Galilee?" quoth they. "Art thou greater than our father Jacob, who gave us this well, and drank thereof himself, and his children, and his cattle? Who are you?" Thus, the man of forms has ever his calumny against the man of God.

Religious teachers there will ever be,— a few organizers, many an administrator of organizations; but inventors in religion are always few. These are the greatest external helps to the manhood of religion. All great teaching is the teacher's inspiration;

this is truer in religion than in aught besides, for here all is life, and nothing a trick of mechanism. Let us take all the good that we can gain from the rare men of religious genius, but never submit and make even them our lords; teachers ever, let them never be masters.

Then there are religious books, such as waken the soul by their direct action,—stirring us to piety, stirring us to morality,—books in which men of great religious growth have garnered up the experience of their life. Some of them are total,—for all religion; some partial,—for the several specialities thereof. These books are sacks of corn carried from land to land, to be sown, and bear manifold their golden fruit. There are not many such in the world. There are few masterpieces of poetry in all the earth; a boy's school-bag would hold them all, from Greece and Rome, Italy, Germany, England. The masterpieces of piety in literature are the rarest of all. In a mineralogist's cabinet what bushels there are of quartz, mica, hornblende, slate, and coal; and common minerals by heaps; reptiles and fishes done in stone; only here and there an emerald; and diamonds are exceeding rare. So is it with gems of holy thought. Some psalms are there from the Bible, though seldom a whole one that is true to the soul of man,—now and then an oracle from a Hebrew prophet, full of faith in God, a warrior of piety, — which keep their place in the cabinet of religion, though two or three thousand years have passed by since their authors ceased to be mortal. But the most quickening of all religious literature is still found in the first three Gospels of the New Testament, — in those dear beatitudes, in occasional flowers of religion, — parable and speech. The beatitudes will outlast the pyramids. Yet the New Testament and its choicest texts must be read with the caution of a free-born man. Even in the words of Jesus of Nazareth much is merely Hebrew, — marked with the limitations of the nation and the man.

Other religious books there are precious to the heart of man. Some of the works of Augustine, of Thomas à Kempis, of Fénelon, of Jeremy Taylor, of John Bunyan, of William Law, have proved exceeding dear to pious men throughout the Christian world. In a much narrower circle of readers, Buckminster, Channing, and Ware have comforted the souls of men. Herbert and Watts have here and there a "gem of purest ray serene," and now and then a flower blooms into beauty in the desert air of liturgies, breviaries, and collections of hymns. The religious influence of Wordsworth's poetry has been truly great. With no large poetic genius, often hemmed in by the narrowness of his traditionary creed and the puerile littleness of men about him, he had yet an exceeding love of God, which ran over into love of men, and beautified his every day; and many a poor girl, many a sad boy, has been cheered and lifted up in soul and sense by the brave piety in his sonnets and in his lyric sweeps of lofty song. A writer of our own time, with large genius and unfaltering piety, adorning a little village of New England with his fragrant life, has sent a great religious influence to many a house in field and town, and youths and maids rejoice in his electric touch. I will leave it to posterity to name his name,—the most original, as well as religious, of American writers.

But the great vice of what is called "religious literature" is this. It is the work of narrow-minded men, sectarians, and often bigots, who cannot see beyond their own little partisan chapel; men who know little of any thing, less of man, and least of all of real religion. What criticism do such men make on noble men? The criticism of an oyster on a thrush; nay, sometimes, of a toad "ugly and venomous," with no "jewel in its head," upon a nightingale. Literature of that character is a curse. In the name of God it misleads common men from religion, and it makes powerful men hate religion itself; at least hate its name. It bows weak men down till they tremble and fear all their mortal life. I lack words to express my detestation of this trash, — concocted of sectarian cant and superstitious fear. I tremble when I think of the darkness it spreads over human life, of the disease which it inoculates mankind withal, and the craven dread it writes out upon the face of its worshippers. Look at the history of the Athanasian Creed and the Westminster Catechism. They have done more, it seems to me, to retard the religious development of Christendom, than all the ribald works of confessed infidels, from Lucian, the king of scoffers, down to our own days. The American Tract Society, with the best intentions in the world, it seems to me is doing more damage to the nation than all the sellers of intoxicating drink and all the prostitutes in the land!

Some books on religious matters are the work of able men, men well disciplined, but yet contaminated with false views of God, of man, and of the relation between the two; with false views of life, of death, and of the next, eternal world. Such men were Baxter and Edwards and many more, — Protestant and Catholic, Christian, Hebrew, Buddhist, and Mahometan. All these books should be read with caution and distrust. Still a wise man, with a religious spirit, in the religious literature of the world, from Confucius to Emerson, may find much to help his growth.

After the attainment of manlier years in piety, other works, not intentionally religious, will help a man greatly. Books of science, which show the thought of God writ in the world of matter; books of history, which reveal the same mind in the development of the human race, slow, but as constant and as normal as the growth of a cedar or the disclosing of an egg; Newton and Laplace, Descartes and Kant, indirectly, through their science, stir devout souls to deeper devotion. A thoughtful man dissolves the matter of the universe, leaving only its forces; dissolves away the phenomena of human history, leaving only immortal spirit; he studies the law, the mode of action, of these forces, and this spirit, which make up the material and the human world; and I see not how he can fail to be filled with reverence, with trust, with boundless love of the Infinite God who devised these laws of matter and of mind, and thereby bears up this marvellous universe of things and men. Science also has its New Testament. The beatitudes of philosophy are profoundly touching; in the exact laws of matter and of mind the great Author of the world continually says, "Come unto me, all ye that labor and are heavy laden, and I will give you rest."

The study of Nature is another great help to the

cultivation of religion. Familiarity with the grass and the trees teaches us deeper lessons of love and trust than we can glean from the writings of Fenelon and Augustine. What lessons did Socrates, Jesus, and Luther learn from the great Bible of God, ever open before mankind! It is only indirectly that He speaks in the sights of a city, — the brick garden with diœcious fops for flowers. But in the country all is full of God, and the eternal flowers of heaven seem to shed sweet influence on the perishable blossoms of the earth. Nature is full of religious lessons to a thoughtful man. The great sermon of Jesus was preached on a mountain, which preached to him as he to the people, and his figures of speech were first natural figures of fact. But the religious use to be made of natural objects would require a sermon of itself.

The great reliance for religious growth must not be on any thing external; not on the great and living souls whom God sends, rarely, to the earth, to water the dry ground with their eloquence, and warm it with their human love; nor must it be on the choicest gems of religious thought, wherein saints and sages have garnered up their life and left it for us. We cannot rely on the beauty or the power of outward Nature to charm our wandering soul to obedience and trust in God. These things may jostle us by the elbow when we read, warn us of wandering, or of sloth, and open the gate, but we must rely on ourselves for entering in. By the aid of others and our own action we must form the ideal of a religious man, of what he ought to be and do, under our peculiar circumstances. To form this personal ideal, and fit ourselves thereto, requires an act of great earnestness on our part. It is not a thing to be done in an idle hour. It demands the greatest activity of the mightiest mode of mind. But what a difference there is between men in earnestness of character! Do you understand the "religion" of a frivolous man? With him it is all a trifle; the fashion of his religion is of less concern than the fashion of his hat or of the latchet of his shoes. He asks not for truth, for justice, for love, — asks not for God, cares not. The great sacrament of religious life is to him less valuable than a flask of Rhenish wine broke on a jester's head. The specific levity of these men appears in their relation to religion. The fool hath said in his heart, "There is no God." Quoth the fop in his waistcoat, "What if there be none? What is that to me? Let us dance and be silly!" Did you ever see a frivolous man and maid in love, — so they called it? I have: it was like putting on a new garment of uncertain fit; and the giving and the taking of what was called a "heart" was like buying a quantity of poison weed to turn to empty smoke. They were "fearfully and wonderfully made for each other." So have I seen a silly man give a bad coin to a beggar in the streets.

I know there are those whose practical religion is only decency. They have no experience of religion, but the hiring of a seat in a church where pew and pulpit both invite to sleep, — whose only sacrifice is their pew-tax; their single sacrament but bodily presence in a church. There are meeting-houses full of such men, which ecclesiastical upholsterers have furnished with pulpit, and pew, and priest, objects of pity to men with human hearts!

When an earnest young man offers a woman his heart and his life and his love, asking her for her heart and her life and her love, it is no easy hour to man or maid. The thought of it takes the rose out of the young cheek, gives a new lustre to the eye which has a deeper and mysterious look, and a terrible throbbing to the heart. For so much depends upon a word that forms or else misshapes so much in life, and soul and sense are clamoring for their right. The past comes up to help create the future, and all creation is new before the lover's eye, and all

> "The floor of heaven
> Is thick inlaid with patines of bright gold."

So is it in some great hour when an earnest man holds communion with himself, seeking to give and take with God, and asks: "What ought I in my life to be and do?" Depend upon it, only to the vulgarest of men is it a common hour. I will not say that every earnest man has his one enamored hour of betrothing himself to religion. Some have this sudden experience, and give themselves to piety as they espouse a bride found when not looked for, and welcomed with a great swelling of the heart and prophetic bloomings of the yearning soul. Others go hand in hand therewith as brother and sister, through all their early days in amiable amity which sin has never broke and seldom jarred; and so the wedlock of religion is as the acquaintance which began in babyhood, was friendship next at home and school, and slowly under tranquil skies grew up and blossomed out at last to love. This is the common way,—an ascent without a sudden leap. If bred as religious children, you grow up religious men. But under the easiest of discipline, I think, every earnest man has his time of trial and of questioning, when he asks himself, "Shall I serve the soul by a life of piety; or shall I only serve the flesh, listing in the popular armada of worldliness to do battle in that leprous host? That, I say, is a time of trial.

Let us suppose some earnest man forms the true ideal of religion, — of his duty to himself, his brother, and his God. He is next to observe and attend to himself, making his prayer a practice, and his ideal dream an actual day of life. Here he is to watch and scan himself, to see what causes help, and what hinder him in his religious growth. We have different dispositions, all of us; what tempts one, is nothing to another man; every heart knows only its own bitterness, not also that of another. Let me know my weak points and my strong ones; forewarned, I shall be then forearmed. This man in the period of passion is led off by the lusts of the body; that in the period of calculation is brought into yet greater peril by his ambition, — his love of riches, place, and the respect of men. The Devil rings a dollar in one man's ear; he dreams of money every day. Some sensual lust catches another, as flies with poisoned sweet. To speak mythologically, the Devil has different baits to lure his diverse prey. Love of applause strips this man of his conscience, his affection, and his self-respect, of his regard for God, and drives him naked through a dirty world. Let a man know in what guise the tempter comes, and when, and he will not suffer his honor to be broken through. For this purpose, in the earlier period of life, or later when placed in positions of new peril, it is well to ask at the close of every day, "What have I done that is wrong, — what have I said, or thought, or felt? What that is right?" It is well thus to orient yourself before your Idea and your God, and see if there be any evil thing in you. This is needful until the man has gained complete possession of every limb of his body and of each faculty of his spirit, and can use them each after its own law in his particular position. Then he will do right with as little trouble as he walks about his daily work. His life will sanctify itself.

Do you know how artists make their great pictures? First, they form the idea. It is a work of sweat and watching. The man assembles all the shapes of beauty and of power which he has ever seen, or thought, or fancied, or felt. They flash along before his quickened eye, wildered and wandering now. New forms of beauty spring into life at the bidding of his imagination, — so flowers at touch of spring. Erelong he has his idea, composite, gathered from many a form of partial beauty, and yet one; a new creation never seen before. Thus in his seething mind Phidias smelts the several beauty of five hundred Spartan maids into his one Pallas-Athena, born of *his* head this time, a grand eclecticism of loveliness. So Michael devised his awful form of God creating in the Vatican; and Raphael his dear Cecilia, sweetest of pictured saints, — so fair, she drew the angels down to see her sing, and ears were turned to eyes. Now the artist has formed his idea. But that is not all. Next, he must make the idea that is in his mind a picture in the eyes of men; his personal fiction must become a popular fact. So he toils over this new work for many a weary day, and week, and month, and year, with penitential brush oft painting out what once amiss he painted in, — for even art has its error, the painter's sin, and so its remorse; the artist is made wiser by his own defeat. At last his work stands there complete, — the holy queen of art. Genius is the father, of a heavenly line; but the mortal mother, that is Industry.

Now as an artist, like Phidias, Angelo, or Raphael, must hold a great act of imagination to form his idea, and then industriously toil, often wiping out in remorse what he drew in passion or in ignorance; so the man who would be religious must hold his creative act of prayer, to set the great example to himself, and then industriously toil to make it daily life, shaping his actual, not from the chance of circumstance, but from the ideal purpose of his soul.

There is no great growth in manly piety without fire to conceive, and then painstaking to reproduce the idea, — without the act of prayer, the act of industry. The act of prayer, — that is the one great vital means of religious growth; the resolute desire and the unconquerable will to be the image of a perfect man; the comparison of your actual day with your ideal dream; the rising forth, borne up on mighty pens, to fly towards the far heaven of religious joy. Fast as you learn a truth, moral, affectional, or religious, apply the special truth to daily life, and you increase your piety. So the best school for religion is the daily work of common life, with its daily discipline of personal, domestic, and social duties, — the daily work in field or shop, market or house, "the charities that soothe and heal and bless."

Nothing great is ever done without industry. Sloth sinks the idle boy to stupid ignorance, and vain to him are schools, and books, and all the appliances of the instructor's art. It is industry in religion which makes the man a saint. What zeal is there for money, — what diligence in learning to be a lawyer, a fiddler, or a smith! The same industry to be also religious men, — what noble images of God it would make us! ay, what blessed men. Even in the special qualities of fiddler, lawyer, smith, we should be more; for general manhood is the stuff we make into tradesmen of each special craft, and the gold which was fine in the ingot is fine also in the medal and the coin.

You have seen a skilful gardener about his work. He saves the slips of his pear-trees, prunings from his currant-bush; he watches for the sunny hours in spring to air his passion-flower and orange-tree. How nicely he shields his dahlias from the wind, his melons from the frost! Patiently he hoards cuttings from a rose-bush, and the stone of a peach; choice fruit in another's orchard next year is grafted on his crabbed stock, which in three years rejoices in alien flowers and apples not its own. Are we not gardeners, all of us, to fill our time with greener life, with fragrant beauty, and rich, timely fruit? There are bright, cheery morning hours good for putting in the seed; moments of sunnier delight, when some success not looked for, the finding of a friend, husband, or wife, the advent of a child, mellows the hours. Then nurse the tender plant of piety; one day its bloom will adorn your gloomy hour, and be a brightness in many a winter day which now you reck not of.

There are days of sadness when it rains sorrow on you, — when you mourn the loss of friends, their sad defeat in mortal life, or worse still, the failure of yourself, your wanderings from the way of life, or prostrate fall therein. Use, then, O man, these hours for penitence, if need be, and vigorous resolve. Water the choicest, tender plants; one day the little seedling you have planted with your tears shall be a broad tree, and under its arms you will screen your head from the windy storm and the tempest; — yes, find for your bones a quiet grave at last.

Do you commit a sin, an intentional violation of the law of God, you may make even that help you in your religious growth. He who never hungered knows not the worth of bread; who never suffered, nor sorrowed, nor went desolate and alone, knows not the full value of human sympathy and human love. I have sometimes thought that a man who had never sinned nor broke the integrity of his consciousness, nor, by wandering, disturbed the continuity of his march towards perfection, — that he could not know the power of religion to fortify the soul. But there are no such men. We learn to walk by stumbling at the first; and spiritual experience is also bought by errors of the soul. Penitence is but the cry of the child hurt in his fall. Shame on us that we affect the pain so oft, and only learn to whine an unnatural contrition! Sure I am that the grief of a soul, self-wounded, the sting of self-reproach, the torment of remorse for errors of passion, for sins of calculation, may quicken any man in his course to manhood, till he runs and is not weary. The mariner learns wisdom from each miscarriage of his ship, and fronts the seas anew to triumph over wind and wave.

Some of you are young men and maidens. You look forward to be husbands and wives, to be fathers and mothers, some day. Some of you seek to be rich, some honored. Is it not well to seek to have for yourself a noble, manly character, to be religious men and women, with a liberal development of mind and conscience, heart and soul? You will meet with losses, trials, disappointments, in your business, in your friends and families, and in yourselves; many a joy will also smile on you. You may use the sunny sky and its falling weather alike to help your religious growth. Your time, young men, what life and manhood you may make of that.

Some of you are old men, your heads white with manifold experience, and life is writ in storied hieroglyphics on cheek and brow. Venerable faces! I hope I learn from you. I hardly dare essay to teach men before whom time has unrolled his lengthened scroll, men far before me in experience of life. But let me ask you, if, while you have been doing your work, — have been gathering riches, and tasting the joys of time, — been son, husband, father, friend, — you have also greatened, deepened, heightened your manly character, and gained the greatest riches, — the wealth of a religious soul, incorruptible and undefiled, the joys that cannot fade away?

For old or young, there is no real and lasting human blessedness without this. It is the sole sufficient and assured defence against the sorrows of the world, the disappointments and the griefs of life, the pains of unrequited righteousness and hopes that went astray. It is a never-failing fountain of delight.

> "There are briers besetting every path,
> That call for patient care;
> There is a cross in every lot,
> And an earnest need for prayer;
> But the lowly heart that trusts in Thee
> Is happy everywhere."

VII.

OF CONSCIOUS RELIGION AS A SOURCE OF STRENGTH.

THE LORD IS THE STRENGTH OF MY LIFE. — Ps. xxvii. 1.

THERE are original differences of spiritual strength. I mean of intellectual, moral, affectional, and religious power; these depend on what may be called the natural spiritual constitution of the individual. One man is born with a strong spiritual constitution, another with a weak one! So one will be great, and the other little. It is no shame in this case, no merit in that. Surely it is no more merit to be born to genius than to gold, to mental more than to material strength; no more merit to be born to moral, affectional, and religious strength than to mere intellectual genius. But it is a great convenience to be born to this large estate of spiritual wealth, a very great advantage to possess the highest form of human power, — eminence of intellect, of conscience, of the affections, of the soul.

There is a primitive intellectual difference amongst men which is ineffaceable from the man's mortal being, as the primary qualities are ineffaceable from the atoms of matter. It will appear in all the life of the man. Even great wickedness will not wholly destroy this primeval loftiness of mind. Few men were ever better born in respect to intellect than Francis Bacon and Thomas Wentworth, — "the great Lord Verulam" and "the great Earl of Strafford:" few men ever gave larger proof of superior intellect, even in its highest forms of development, of general force and manly vigor of mind; few ever used great natural ability, great personal attainments, and great political place, for purposes so selfish, mean, and base. Few ever fell more completely. Yet, spite of that misdirection and abuse, the marks of greatness and strength appear in them both to the very last. Bacon was still "the wisest, brightest," if also "the meanest of mankind." I know a great man may ruin himself; stumbling is as easy for a mammoth as a mouse, and much more conspicuous; but even in his fall his greatness will be visible. The ruin of a colossus is gigantic, — its fragments are on a grand scale. You read the size of the ship in the timbers of the wreck, fastened with mighty bolts. The Tuscan bard is true to nature as to poetry in painting his odious potentates magnificently mighty even in hell. Satan fallen seems still "not less than archangel ruined"!

I do not deny this natural and ineffaceable difference between men in reference to their strength of character, their quantity of being. I am not going to say that conscious piety will make a great man out of a little one; that it would give to George the Third the strength of Charlemagne or Napoleon. No training will make the shrub-oak a tree-oak; no agriculture swell a cape to a continent. But I do mean to say, that religion, conscious piety, will increase the actual strength of the great and of the little; that through want of religious culture the possibility of strength is diminished in both the little and the great.

Not only does religion greaten the quantity of power, it betters its quality at the same time. So it both enlarges a man's general power for himself or his brother, and enhances the mode of that power, thus giving him a greater power of usefulness and a greater power of welfare, more force to delight, more force to enjoy. This is true of religion taken in its wide sense, — a life in harmony with myself, in concord with my brother, in unity with my God; true of religion in its highest form, the conscious worship of the Infinite God by the normal use of every faculty of the spirit, every limb of the body, and every portion of material or social power.

Without this conscious religious development, it seems to me that no strength or greatness is admirably human ; and with it, no smallness of opportunity, no littleness of gift, is contemptible or low. I reverence great powers, given or got; but I reverence much more the faithful use of powers either large or little.

Strength of character appears in two general modes of power, accordingly as it is tried by one or other of two tests. It is power to do, or power to bear. One is active, and the other passive, but both are only diverse modes of the same thing. The hard anvil can bear the blows of the hard hammer which smites it, because there is the same solidity in the nether anvil which bears up, as in the upper hammer which bears down. It takes as much solidity to bear the blow as to give it; only one is solidity active, the other merely passive.

Religion increases the general strength and volume of character. The reason is plain: Religion is keeping the natural law of human nature in its threefold mode of action, — in relation to myself, to my brother, and to my God; the coördination of my will with the will of God, with the ideal of my nature. So it is action according to my nature, not against it; it is the agreement of my finite will with the Infinite Will which controls the universe and provides for each portion thereof.

Now, to use a thing against its nature, to abuse it, is ultimately to fail of the natural end thereof, and waste the natural means provided for the attainment of the end. A boat is useful to journey with by sea, a chaise to journey with by land; use each for its purpose, you enjoy the means and achieve the end. But put off to sea in your chaise, or put on to land in your boat, you miss the end,—you lose also the means. This is true of the natural, as of the artificial instruments of man; of his limbs, as of his land-carriages or sea-carriages. Hands are to work with, feet to walk on; the feet would make a poor figure in working, the hands an ill figure in essaying to walk. The same rule holds good in respect to spiritual faculties as in bodily organs. Passion is not designed to rule conscience, but to serve; conscience not to serve passion, but to rule. If passion rule and conscience serve, the end is not reached, you are in a state of general discord with yourself, your brother, and your God; the means also fail and perish; conscience becomes weak, the passion itself dies from the plethora of its indulgence; the whole man grows less and less, till he becomes the smallest thing he is capable of dwindling into. But if conscience rule and passion serve, all goes well; you reach the end, — welfare in general, harmony with yourself, concord with your brother, and unity with your God; you keep the means, — conscience and passion are each in position, and at their proper function; the faculties enlarge until they reach their entire measure of possible growth, and the whole man becomes the greatest he is capable of being here and now.

You see this strength of character, which naturally results from religion, not only in its general forms, but in its special modes. Look a moment at the passive power, the power to endure suffering. See the fact in the endurance of the terrible artificial torments that are used to put down new forms of religion, or extinguish the old. While men believe in the divinity of matter, they try suspected persons by exposure to the elements, — walking over redhot ploughshares, holding fire in the naked hand, or plunging into water. All new forms of religion must pass through the same ordeal, and run the gauntlet betwixt bishops, priests, inquisitors; between scribes, Pharisees, and hypocrites. See how faithfully the trial has been borne. Men naturally shrink from pain; the stout man dreads the toothache, he curls at the mention of the rheumatism, and shivers at the idea of an ague; how suddenly he drops a piece of burning paper which would tease his hand for a minute! But let a man have religion wakened in his heart, and be convinced that it is of God, let others attempt to drive it out of him, and how ready is he to bear all that malice can devise or tyranny inflict! The thumb-screws and the racks, the whip, the gallows, and the stake, — the religious man has strength to bear all these; and Cranmer holds his right arm, erring now no more, in the flame, till the hand drops off in the scalding heat. You know the persecutions of Peter and Paul, the martyrdom of Stephen, the trials of early Christians, — Ignatius, Polycarp, Justin, Irenæus, and the rest. They all went out to preach the form of religion themselves had practised, and enjoyed in their own souls. What could they offer men as an inducement to conversion? The common argument at this day, — respectability, a comfortable life and an honorable death, the praise of men? Could Origen and Cyprian tell the young maiden: "Come to our church, and you will be sure to get a nice husband, as dainty fine as any patrician in Ephesus or Carthage?" Could they promise "a fashionable company in prayer," and a rich wife to the young man who joined their church? It was not exactly so; nay, it was considerably different. They could offer their converts hunger, and nakedness, and peril, and prison, and the sword; ay, and the scorn of relatives and the contemporaneous jeer of a cruel world. But "the word of God grew and prevailed." The nice voluptuary, the dainty woman, too delicate to set foot upon the ground, became converted, and then they could defy the axe of the headsman and the tormentor's rack. Unabashed they stood before wild beasts; ay, they looked in the face of the marshals and commissioners and district judges of those times,—men who perverted law and spit on justice with blasphemous expectoration,—and yet the religious soul did not fear!

In the Catholic Church this is Saint Victorian's Day. Here is the short of his story. He was an African nobleman of Adrumetum, governor of Carthage with the Roman title of Proconsul, the wealthiest man in the province of Africa. He was a Catholic; but Huneric, the king of the Vandals in Africa, was an Arian, and in the year four hundred and eighty began to persecute the Catholics. He commanded Victorian to continue the persecution, offering him great wealth and the highest honors. It was his legal obligation to obey the king. "Tell the king that I trust in Christ," said the Catholic proconsul; "the king may condemn me to the flames, to wild beasts, to any tortures, I shall never renounce the Church." He was put to the most tormenting tortures, and bore them like a man. Others met a similar death with the same steadiness of soul. Even the executioners felt the effect of such heroism of endurance. "Nobody," said they, "embraces our religion now; everybody follows the example of the martyrs."

The Catholic Church tried the same weapons against heretics that had been first found wanting when turned against the early Christians. The tyrant, with the instinct of Pharaoh, seeks to destroy the male children, the masculine intellect, conscience, affections, soul. Then a new race of Pauls and Justins springs up; a new Ignatius, Polycarp, and Victorian, start into life. The Church may burn Arnaldo da Brescia, Savonarola, Huss; — what profits it? The religion which the tyrant persecutes makes the victim stronger than the victor; then it steals into the heart of the people, and as the wind scatters the martyr's ashes far and wide, so the spectacle or the fame of his fidelity spreads abroad the sentiment of that religion which made him strong. The persecuting Nile wafts Moses into the king's court, and the new religion is within the walls.

You know how the Puritans were treated in England, the Covenanters in Scotland; you know how they bore trial. You have heard of John Graham, commonly called Lord Claverhouse. He lived about two hundred years ago in England and Scotland, one of that brood of monsters which still disgrace mankind, and, as vipers and rattlesnakes, seem born to centralize and incarnate the poison of the world. An original tormentor, if there had never been any cruelty he would have invented it, of his own head. Had he lived in New England in this time, he would doubtless have been a United States commissioner under the Fugitive Slave Bill, perhaps a judge or a marshal; at any rate, a slave-hunter, a kidnapper in some form; and of course he would now be as much honored in this city as he then was in Edinburgh and London, and perhaps as well paid. Well, Lord Claverhouse had a commission to root out the Covenanters with fire and sword, and went to that work with the zeal of an American kidnapper. By means of his marshals he one day caught a Scotch girl, a Covenanter. She was young, only eighteen; — she was comely to look upon. Her name was Margaret. Graham ordered her to be tied to a stake in the sea at low-water, and left to drown slowly at the advance of the tide. It was done: and his creatures — there were enough of them in Scotland, as of their descendants here, — his commissioners, his marshals, and his attorneys — sat down on the shore to watch the end of poor Margaret. It was an end not to be forgotten. In a clear, sweet voice she sung hymns to God till the waves of the sea broke over her head and floated her pious soul to her God and his heaven. Had Scotland been a Catholic country there would have been another SAINT Margaret, known as the

> "Genius of the shore
> In her large recompense, who would be good
> To all that wander in that perilous flood."

You all know what strength of endurance religion gave to Bunyan and Fox, and their compeers the Quakers, in Boston as well as England; to the Mormons in Missouri, and in all quarters of Christendom. Religion made these men formidably strong. The axe of the tormentor was as idle to stay them as the gallows to stop a sunbeam. This power of endurance is general, of all forms of religion. It does not depend on what is Jewish in Judaism, or Christian in Christianity, but on what is religious in religion, what is human in man.

But that is only a spasmodic form of heroism,—the reaction of human nature against unnatural evil. You see religion producing the same strength to endure sufferings which are not arbitrarily imposed by cruel men. The stories of martyrdom only bring out in unusual forms the silent heroism which works unheeded in society every day. The strength is always there; oppression, which makes wise men mad, in making religious men martyrs, only finds and reveals the heroism; it does not make it, more than the stone-cutter makes the marble which he hews into the form his thought requires. The heroism is always there. So there is always enough electricity in the air above this town to blast it to atoms and burn it to cinders. Not a babe could be born without it; not a snow-drop bloom; yet no one heeds the silent force. Let two different streams of air, one warm, the other cold, meet here, the lightning tells of the reserved power which hung all day above our heads.

I love now and then to look on the strength of endurance which religion gives the most heroic martyrs. Even in these times the example is needed. Though the fagot is only ashes now, and the axe's edge is blunt, there are other forms of martyrdom, bloodless yet not less cruel in motive and effect. But I love best to see this same strength in lovelier forms, enduring the common ills of life, — poverty, sickness, disappointment, the loss of friends, the withering of the fondest hopes of mortal men. One is occasional lightning, thundering and grand, but transient; the other is daily sunshine which makes no noisy stir on any day, but throughout the year is constant, creative, and exceeding beautiful.

Did you never see a young woman with the finest faculties, every hope of mortal success crushed in her heart; see her endure it all, the slow torture which eats away the mortal from the immortal, with a spirit still unruffled, — with a calm cheerfulness and a strong trust in God? We all have seen such things, — the loveliest forms of martyrdom.

Did you never see a young man with large faculties, fitting him to shine among the loftiest stars of this our human heaven, in the name of duty forego his own intellectual culture for the sake of a mother, a sister, or a father dependent upon his toil, and be a drudge when he might else have been a shining light; and by the grace of religion do it so that in all of what he counted drudgery he was kinglier than a king? Did you never see the wife, the daughter, or the son of a drunkard sustained by their religion to bear sorrows to which Nebuchadnezzar's sevenfold-heated furnace were a rose-garden, — bear it and not complain, — grow sweeter in that bitterness? There are many such examples all about us, and holy souls go through that misery of torture clean as sunlight through the pestilential air of a town stricken with plague. So the pagan poets tell a story of the fountain Arethusa, which, for many a league, ran through the salt and bitter sea, all the way from Peloponnesus to Trinacria, and then came up pure, sweet, and sparkling water, far off in Ortygia, spreading greenness and growth in the valley where the anemone and asphodel paid back their beauty to the stream which gave them life.

Such are daily examples of the fortitude and strength to suffer which religion gives. When we look carelessly on men in their work or their play, busy in the streets or thoughtful in a church, we think little of the amount of religion there is in these human.hearts; but when you need it in times of great trial, then it comes up in the broad streets and little lanes of life. Disappointment is a bitter root, and sorrow is a bitter flower, and suffering is a bitter fruit, but the religious soul makes medicine thereof, and is strengthened even by the poisons of life. So out of a brewer's dregs and a distiller's waste in a city have I seen the bee suck sweetest honey for present joy, and lay it up for winter's use. Yea, the strong man in the fable, while hungering, found honey in the lion's bones he once had slain; got delight from the destroyer, and meat out of the eater's mouth.

Why is it that the religious man has this power to suffer and endure? Religion is the normal mode of life for man, and when he uses his faculties according to their natural law, they act harmoniously, and all grow strong. Besides this, the religious man has a confidence in his God; he knows there is the Infinite One, who has foreseen all and provided for all, — provided a recompense for all the unavoidable suffering of his children here. If you know that it is a part of the purpose of the Infinite Father that you must suffer to accomplish your own development, or the development of mankind, yet understand that the suffering must needs be a good for you, — then you will not fear. "The flesh may quiver as the pincers tear," but you quiver not; the will is firm, and firm is the unconquerable trust. "Be still, O flesh, and burn!" says the martyr to the molecules of dust that form his chariot of time, and the three holy children of the Hebrew tale sing psalms in their fiery furnace, a Fourth with them; and Stephen in his stoning thinks that he sees his God, and to Paul in his prison there comes a great, cheering light; — yes, to Bunyan, and Fox, and Latimer, and John Rogers, in their torments; to the poor maiden stifled by the slowly strangling sea; to her whose crystal urn of love is shattered at her feet; to the young man who sees the college of his dream fade off into a barn; and the mother, wife, or child who sees the father of the family bloat, deform, and uglify himself into the drunkard, and, falling into the grave, crush underneath his lumbering weight all of their mortal hopes. Religion gives them all a strength to suffer, and be blessed by the trials they endure. There are times when nothing outward is left but suffering. Then it is a great thing to have the stomach for it, the faith in God which disenchants the soul of pain. Did not Jesus, in the Gospel, have his agony and his bloody sweat, — the last act of that great tragedy? did not religion come, an angel, to strengthen him, and all alone, deserted, forsaken, he could say, "I am not alone, for the Father is with me?"

"The darts of anguish fix not where the seat
Of suffering hath been thoroughly fortified
By acquiescence in the Will supreme,
For time and for eternity, by Faith,
Faith absolute in God, including Hope,
And the defence that lies in boundless love
Of His perfection; with habitual dread
Of aught unworthily conceived, endured
Impatiently, ill done or left undone,
To the dishonor of His holy Name.
Soul of our souls and safeguard of the world!
Sustain, thou only canst, the sick of heart.
Restore their languid spirits, and recall
Their lost affections unto Thee and Thine.
"Come labor, when the worn-out frame requires
Perpetual sabbath; come disease and want,
And sad exclusion through decay of sense;
But leave me unabated trust in Thee; —
And let Thy favor to the end of life
Sustain me with ability to seek
Repose and hope among eternal things,
Father of earth and heaven! and I am rich,
And will possess my portion in content."

See this same strength in another form, — the power to do. Religion not only gives the feminine capacity to suffer, but the masculine capability to do. The religious man can do more than another without religion, who is his equal in other respects; because he masters and concentrates his faculties, making them work in harmony with each other, in concord with mankind, in unity with God; and because he knows there is a God who works with him, and so arranges the forces of the universe, that every wrong shall be righted, and the ultimate well-being of each be made sure of for ever. Besides, he has a higher inspiration and loftier motive, which strengthen, refine, and ennoble him. Adam Clarke tells us how much more of mere intellectual labor he could perform after his conversion than before. Ignatius Loyola makes the same confession. They each attribute it to the technical peculiarity of their sectarianism, to Methodism or Catholicism, to Christianity; but the fact is universal, and applies to religion under all forms. It is easily explained by the greater harmony of the faculties, and by the higher motive which animates the man, the more certain trust which inspires him. An earnest youth in love with an earnest maid, — his love returned, — gets more power of character from the ardor of her affection and the strength of his passion; and when the soul of man rises up in its great act of love to become one with God, you need not marvel if the man is strong. "I can do all things," says Paul, "through Christ who strengtheneth me." Buddhists and Hebrews and Mohammedans say the same of their religion.

Then religion helps a man to two positive things, — first, to a desire of the right; next, to a progressive knowledge and practice of the right. Justice is always power; whoso has that commands the world. A fool in the right way, says the proverb, can beat a wise man in the wrong. The civilized man has an advantage over the savage, in his knowledge of Nature. He can make the forces of the universe toil for him: the wind drives his ship; the water turns his mill, spins, and weaves for him; lightning runs his errands; steam carries the new lord of Nature over land or ocean without rest. He that knows justice, and does it, has the same advantage over all that do it not. He sets his mill on the rock, and the river of God for ever turns his wheels.

The practice of the right in the common affairs of life is called Honesty. An honest man is one who knows, loves, and does right because it is right. Is there any thing but this total integrity which I call religion, that can be trusted to keep a man honest in small things and great things, in things private and things public? I know nothing else with this power. True it is said, "Honesty is the best policy;" and as all men love the best policy, they will be honest for that reason. But to follow the best policy is a very different thing from being honest; the love of justice and the love of personal profit or pleasure are quite different. But is honesty the best policy? Policy is means to achieve a special end. If the end you seek be the common object of desire, — if it be material pleasure in your period of passion, or material profit in your period of ambition, — if you seek for money, for ease, honor, power over men, and their approbation, — then honesty is not the best policy; is means from it, not to it. Honesty of thought and speech is the worst policy for a minister's clerical reputation. Charity impairs an estate; unpopular excellence is the ruin of a man's respectability. It is good policy to lie in the popular way; to steal after the respectable fashion. The hard creditor is surest of his debt; the cruel landlord does not lose his rent; the severe master is uniformly served the best; who gives little and with a grudge finds often the most of obvious gratitude. He that destroys the perishing is more honored in Christendom than he who comes to save the lost. The slave-hunter is a popular Christian in the American Church, and gets his pay in money and ecclesiastical reputation. The honesty of Jesus brought him to the bar of Herod and Pilate; their best policy nailed him to the cross. Was it good policy in Paul to turn Christian? His honesty brought him to weariness and painfulness, to cold and nakedness, to stripes and imprisonment, to a hateful reputation on the earth. Honesty the best policy for personal selfishness! Ask the "Holy Alliance." Honesty is the means to self-respect, to growth in manly qualities, to high human welfare, — a means to the kingdom of heaven. When men claim that honesty is the best policy, is it this which they mean?

I will not say a man cannot be honest without a distinct consciousness of his relation to God; but I must say, that consciousness of God is a great help to honesty in the business of a shop, or the business of a nation; and without religion, unconscious if no more, it seems to me honesty is not possible.

By reminding me of my relation to the universe, religion helps counteract the tendency to selfishness. Self-love is natural and indispensable; it keeps the man whole, — is the centripetal power, representing the natural cohesion of all the faculties. Without that, the man would drop to pieces, as it were, and be dissolved in the mass of men, as a lump of clay in the ocean. Selfishness is the abnormal excess of this self-love. It takes various forms. In the period of passion, it commonly shows itself as intemperate love of sensual pleasure ; in the period of ambition, as intemperate love of money, of power, rank, or renown. There are as many modes of selfishness as there are propensities which may go to excess. Self-love belongs to the natural harmony of the faculties, and is a means of strength. Selfishness comes from the tyranny of some one appetite, which subordinates the other faculties of man, and is a cause of weakness, a disqualification for my duties to myself, to my brother, and my God. Now the effort to become religious, working in you a love of man and of God, a desire of harmony with yourself, of concord with man and unity with Him, diminishes selfishness, develops your instinctive self-love into conscious self-respect, into faithfulness to yourself, and so enlarges continually the little ring of your character, and makes you strong to bear the crosses and do the duties of daily life.

Much of a man's ability consists in his power to concentrate his energies for a purpose ; in power to deny some private selfish lust — of material pleasure or profit — for the sake of public love. I know of naught but religion that can be trusted to promote this power of self-denial, which is indispensable to a manly man. There can be no great general power without this ; no strong character that lies deep in the sea, and holds on its way through sunshine and through storm, and unabashed by tempests, comes safe to port. I suppose you all know men and women, who now are not capable of any large self-denial, — the babies of mere selfish instinct. It is painful to look on such, domineered over by their propensities. Compared to noble-hearted men and women, they are as the mushroom and the toadstool to the oak, under whose shade the fungus springs up in a rainy night to blacken and perish in a day. Self-denial is indispensable to a strong character, and the loftiest kind thereof comes only of a religious stock, — from consciousness of obligation and dependence upon God.

In youth the seductions of passion lead us easily astray; in manhood there are the more dangerous seductions of ambition, when lust of pleasure gives way to lust of profit; and in old age the man is often the victim of the propensities he delicately nursed in earlier life, and dwindles down into the dotage of a hunker or a libertine. It is easy to yield now to this, and then to that, but both mislead us to our partial and general loss, to weakness of power and poverty of achievement, to shipwreck of this great argosy of mortal life. How many do you see slain by lust of pleasure! How many more by lust of power, — pecuniary, social, or political power! Religious self-denial would have kept them strong and beautiful and safe.

Religion gives a man courage. I do not mean the courage which comes of tough muscles and rigid nerves, — of a stomach which never surrenders. That also is a good thing, the hardihood of the flesh; let me do it no injustice. But I mean the higher, moral courage, which can look danger and death in the face unawed and undismayed; the courage that can encounter loss of ease, of wealth, of friends, of your own good name; the courage that can face a world full of howling and of scorn, — ay, of loathing and of hate; can see all this with a smile, and, suffering it all, can still toil on, conscious of the result, yet fearless still. I do not mean the courage that hates, that smites, that kills, but the calm courage that loves and heals and blesses such as smite and hate and kill; the courage that dares resist evil, popular, powerful, anointed evil, yet does it with good, and knows it shall thereby overcome. That is not a common quality. I think it never comes without religion. It belongs to all great forms of religious excellence; it is not specifically Hebrew or Christian, but generically human and of religion under all forms.

Without this courage a man looks little and mean, especially a man otherwise great, — with great intellect, and great culture, and occupying a great place. You see all about you how little such men are worth; too cowardly to brave a temporary defeat, they are swiftly brought to permanent ruin. Look over the long array of brilliant names in American, English, universal history, and see what lofty men, born to a large estate of intellect, and disciplined to manifold and brilliant mental power, for lack of courage to be true amid the false, and upright amid the grovelling, have laid their proud foreheads in the dust, and mean men have triumphed over the mighty!

Did you never read here in your Old Testament, here in your New Testament, here in your Apocrypha, how religion gave men, yea, and women too, this courage, and said to them, "Be strong and very courageous; turn not to the right hand, neither to the left," — and made heroes out of Jeremiah and Elias? Did you never read of the strength of courage, the courage of conscience, which religion gave to the "unlearned and ignorant men," who, from peasants that trembled before a Hebrew Rabbi's copious beard, became apostles to stand before the wrath of kings and not quake, to found churches by their prayers, and to feed them with their blood? You know, we all know, what courage conscious religion gave to our fathers. Their corporal courage grew more firmly knit, as men learned by bitter blows who crossed swords with them on the battle field; but their moral courage grew giant high. You know how they dwelt here, amid what suffering, yet with what patience; how they toiled to build up these houses, these churches, and the institutions of the State.

With this honesty, this self-denial, there comes a total energy of character which nothing else can give. You see what strength religion gives; what energy and continual persistence in their cause it gave to men like the Apostles, like the martyrs and great saints of the Christian Church, of the Hebrew, the Mohammedan, and the Pagan Church. You may see this energy in a rough form in the soldiers of the English revolution, in the "Ironsides" of Cromwell; in the stern and unflinching endurance of the Puritans of either England, the Old or the New, who both did and suffered what is possible to mortal flesh only when it is sustained by a religious faith. But you see it in forms far more beautiful, as represented by the missionaries who carry the glad tidings of their faith to other lands, and endure the sorrows of persecution with the longsuffering and loving-kindness we worship in the good God. This is not peculiar to Christianity. The Buddhists had their missionaries hundreds of years before Jesus of Nazareth first saw the light. They seem to have been the first that ever went abroad, not to conquer, but convert; not to get power, or wealth, or even wisdom, but to carry the power of the mind, the riches of conscience and the affections, and the wisdom of the soul; and in them you find the total energy which religious conviction gives to manly character in its hour of peril. But why go abroad to look for this? Our own streets exhibit the same thing in the form of the philanthropist. The Sister of Charity treads the miserable alleys of Naples and of Rome; the Catholic Visitor of the Poor winds along in the sloughs and slums of St. Giles's Parish in Protestant London, despised and hated by the well-endowed clergy, whose church aisles are never trodden save by wealthy feet; and in the mire of the street, in the reeking squalidness of the cellars, where misery burrows with crime, he labors for their bodies and their souls. In our own Boston do I not know feeble-bodied and delicate women, who with their feet write out the gospel of loving-kindness and tender mercy on the mud or the snow of the kennels of this city,—women of wise intellect and nice culture, who, like that great philanthropist, come to seek and to save that which is lost!

Look at the reformers of America at this day;—some of them men of large abilities, of commensurate culture, of easy estate, once respected, flattered, and courted too by their associates, but now despised for their justice and their charity, hated for the eminent affection which makes them look after the welfare of the criminal, the drunkard, the pauper, the outcast, and the slave, and feared for the power with which they assert the rights of man against the wrongs which avarice inflicts. See the total energy which marks these men, whose life is a long profession of religion, — their creed writ all over the land, and their history a slow martyrdom, — and you may see the vigor which comes of religious conviction. These are the nobler forms of energy. The soldier destroys, at best defends, while the philanthropist creates.

Last of all these forms of strength, religion gives the power of self-reliance; reliance on your mind for truth, on your conscience for justice, on your heart for love, on your soul for faith, and through all these reliance on the Infinite God. Then you will keep the integrity of your own nature spite of the mightiest men, spite of a multitude of millions, spite of States and churches and traditions, and a worldly world filled with covetousness and priestcraft. You will say to them all, "Stand by, and let alone; I must be true to myself, and thereby true to my God."

I think nothing but religion can give any man this strength to do and to suffer; that without this, the men of greatest gift and greatest attainment too, do not live out half the glory of their days, nor reach half their stature. Look over the list of the world's great failures, and see why Alexander, Cæsar, and Napoleon came each to such an untimely and vulgar end! Had they added religion to their attainments and their conquests, what empires of welfare would they not hold in fee, and give us to enjoy! Without it, the greatest man is a failure. With it, the smallest is a triumph. He adds to his character; he enjoys his strength; he delights while he rejoices, growing to more vigorous manliness; and when the fragrant petals of the spirit burst asunder and crowd off this outer husk of the body, and bloom into glorious humanity, what a strong and flamelike flower shall blossom there for everlasting life.

There are various forms of strength. Wealth is power; office is power; beauty is power; knowledge is power. Religion too is power. This is the power of powers, for it concentrates, moves, and directs aright the force of money, of office, of beauty, and of knowledge. Do men understand this? They often act and live as if they knew it not. Look at our "strong men," not only mighty by position in office or on money, but mighty by nature. In what are they strong? In a knowledge of the passions and prejudices of men; of the interests and expedients and honors of the day; in a knowledge of men's selfishness and their willingness to sin; in experienced skill to use the means for certain selfish, low, and ignoble ends, organizing a contrivance against mankind; in power of speech and act to make the better seem the worse, and wrong assume the guise of right. It is in this that our "great men" are chiefly great. They are weak in a knowledge of what in man is noble, even when he errs; they know nothing of justice; they care little for love. They know the animal that is in us, not the human, far less the godlike. Mighty in cunning, they are weak in knowledge of the true, the just, the good, the holy, and the ever-beautiful. They look up at the mountains and mock at God. So they are impotent to know the expedient of eternity, what profits now and profits for ever and ever. Blame them not too much; the educational forces of society breed up such men, as college lads all learn to cipher and to scan.

In the long run of the ages see how the religious man distances the unreligious. The memory of him who seeks to inaugurate cunning into the state for his own behoof, is erelong gibbeted before the world, and his lie is cast out with scorn and hate; and the treason of the traitor to mankind is remembered only with a curse; while the wisdom of the wise, the justice of the upright, the love of the affectionate, and the piety of holy-hearted men, incarnated in the institutions of the State, live and will for ever live, long after Rome and America have gone to the ground. Tyrants have a short breath, their fame a sudden ending; and the power of the ungodly, like the lamp of the wicked, shall soon be put out; their counsel is carried, but it is carried headlong. He that seeks only the praise of men gets that but for a day; while the religious man, who seeks only to be faithful to himself and his God, and represent on earth the absolute true and just, all heedless of the applause of men, lives, and will for ever live, in the admiration of mankind, and in "the pure eyes and perfect witness of all-judging Jove." Champollion painfully deciphers the names of the Egyptian kings who built the pyramids and swayed millions of men. For three thousand years that lettered Muse, the sculptured stone, in silence kept the secret of their name. But the fugitive slave, a bondsman of that king, with religion in his heart, has writ his power on all the continents, and dotted the name of Moses on every green or snow-clad isle of either sea. That name shall still endure when the last stones of the last pyramid become gas and exhale to heaven. The peasant of Galilee has embosomed his own name in the religion of mankind, and the world will keep it for ever. Foolish men! building your temple of fame on the expedients of to-day, and of selfishness and cunning and eloquent falsehood! That shall stand, — will it? On the frozen bosom of a northern lake go, build your palace of ice. Colonnade and capital, how they glitter in the light when the northern dawn is red about the pole, or the colder moon looks on your house of frost! "This will endure. Why carve out the granite, and painfully build upon the rock?" Ah me! at the touch of March, the ice-temple and its ice-foundation take the leap of Niagara; and in April the skiff of the fisherman finds no vestige of all that pomp and pride. But the temple of granite, — where is that? Ask Moses, ask Jesus, ask mankind, what power it is that lasts from age to age, when selfish ambition melts in the stream of time.

Well, we are all here for a great work, not merely to grow up and eat and drink, to have estates called after us and children born in our name. We are all here to be men; to do the most of human duty possible for us, and so to have the most of human right and enjoy the most of human welfare. Religion is a good thing in itself; it is the betrothed bride of the spirit of man, to be loved for her own sweet sake; not a servant, to be taken for use alone. But it is the means to this end, — to strength of character, enlarging the little and greatening the great.

You and I shall have enough to suffer, most of us; enough to do. We shall have our travail, our temptation, perhaps our agony, but our triumph too.

O smooth-faced youths and maids! your cheek and brow yet innocent of stain, do you believe you shall pass through life and suffer naught? Trial will come on you; — you shall have your agony and bloody sweat. Seek in the beginning for the strength which religion brings you, and you shall indeed be strong, powerful to suffer, and mighty also to do. I will not say your efforts will keep you from every error, every sin. When a boy, I might have thought so; as a man, I know better, by observation and my own experience too. Sin is an experiment that fails; a stumble, not upright walking. Expect such mishaps, errors of the mind, errors of the conscience, errors of the affections, errors of the soul. What pine-tree never lost a limb? The best mathematician now and then misses a figure, must rub out his work and start anew. The greatest poet must often mend a line, and will write faulty verses in the heat of song. Milton has many a scraggy line, and even good Homer sometimes nods. What defects are there in the proud works of Raphael and Angelo! Is there no failure in Mozart? In such a mighty work as this of life, such a complication of forces within, of circumstances without, such imperfect guidance as the world can furnish in this work, I should expect to miss the way sometimes, and with painful feet, and heart stung by self-reproach, or grief, or shame, retread the way shamefaced and sad. The field that is ploughed all over by Remorse, driving his team that breathe fire, yields not a faint harvest to the great Reaper's hand. Trust in God will do two things. It will keep you from many an error; nobody knows how great a gain this is, till he has tried. Then it will help you after you have wandered from the way. Fallen, you will not despair, but rise the wiser and the stronger for the fall. Do you look for strength to your brave young hearts, and streams of life to issue thence? Here you shall find it, and with freshened life pass on your way. Religion is the Moses to smite the rock in the wilderness.

O bearded men, and women that have kept and hoarded much in your experienced hearts! you also seek for power to bear your crosses and to do your work. Religion will be the strength of your life, — you may do all things through this. When the last act of the mortal drama draws towards a close, you will look joyfully to the end, not with fear, but with a triumphant joy.

There are two great things which make up the obvious part of life,—to do, to suffer. Behind both as cause, and before each as result, is one thing greater, — to BE. Religion is true Being, normal life in yourself, in Nature, in men, and in God.

VIII.

OF CONSCIOUS RELIGION AS A SOURCE OF JOY.

I WILL GO UNTO GOD, MY EXCEEDING JOY. — Ps. xliii. 4.

JOY is not often mentioned in religious books. It is sometimes thought to have no place in religion; at least none here and now. The joy of the religious man is thought to be chiefly in the future. Religion is painted with a sad countenance. Artists sometimes mix joyous colors in their representations thereof, but theologians almost never. With them, religion is gloomy, severe, and grim. This is eminently the case in New England. The Puritans as a class were devoutly religious in their way, but they were sad men; they had many fast-days and few times of rejoicing. Even Sunday, which to the rest of Christendom was an occasion of festivity, was to them a day of grimness and of fearing the Lord; a weariness to the old men, and an intolerable burden to the children. Look at the pictures of those men, so bony and gaunt and grim; of the women, so austere and unloving in their look. The unjoyous characteristics of Puritanism still cleave to us, and color our mode of religion at this day, and, spite of ourselves, taint our general philosophy and view of life.

The Catholic Church is less serious, less in earnest with religion, than the Church of the Puritans, — less moral and reliant on God than the Protestant Church in general, — so it seems to me; but even there little room is left for joy. Their richest music is a *Miserere*, not an *Exultemus* or a *Te Deum.* The joyous chanting of Christmas, of Easter, and of Pentecost is inferior to the sad wail of Palm-Sunday and Good-Friday. The *Stabat Mater* and the *Dies Iræ* are the most characteristic hymns of the Catholic Church. The paintings and statues are chiefly monuments of woe, — saints in their torments, Jesus in his passion; his *stations* are stations of affliction, and the *via sacra* of his life is painted as a long *via dolorosa;* God is represented as a Thunderer, distinguished chiefly by self-esteem and destructiveness.

Take the Christian Church as a whole, from its first day to this, study all expressions of the religious feeling and thought of Christendom, in literature, painting, and music, it is strangely deficient in joy. Religion is unnatural self-denial; morality is symbolized by a celibate monk, eating parched pease and a water-cress; piety, by a joyless nun. The saints of the Christian Church, Catholic and Protestant, are either stern, heroic men, who went first and foremost on a field of battle, to peril their lives, men whose heroism was of iron, — and they have never been extolled above their merit, — or else weeping men, sentimental, sickly, sad, sorrowful, and afraid. Most preachers would rather send away their audience weeping, than with a resolute, a cheerful, and a joyous heart. Yet nothing is easier to start from a multitude than a tear. Cotton Mather, in his life of his kinsman, Nathaniel, a pious clergyman who died young, mentions as his crowning merit the fulness of his fastings, the abundant mortifications he needlessly imposed upon himself, his tear-stained face. Smiles are strange phenomena in a church; sadness and tears are therein at home.

Even the less earnest sects of America, calling themselves "Liberal Christians," whose ship of souls does not lie very deep in the sea of life, seem to think joy is not very nearly related to religion. The piety of a round-faced and joyous man is always a little suspected. The Cross is still the popular symbol of Christianity, and the type of the saint is a man of sorrows and acquainted with grief, having no form or comeliness. Sermons of joy you seldom hear; the voice of the pulpit is mainly a whine; its flowers are nightshade, and its psalms a *Miserere.*

Everybody knows what joy is, — a certain sense of gladness and of pleasure, a contentment and a satisfaction, sometimes noisily breaking into transient surges of rapture, sometimes rolling with the tranquil swell of calm delight. It is a state which comes upon any particular faculty, when that finds its natural gratification. So there may be a partial joy of any one faculty, or a total joy of the whole man, all the faculties normally developed and normally gratified. If religion be the service of God by the normal development, use, and enjoyment of every limb of the body, every faculty of the spirit, and every power acquired over matter or man, then it is plain that religion must always aim at, and under favorable circumstances will achieve, a complete and total joy for all men.

There is no man wholly destitute of some partial and transient joy; for if all the conditions needful to the welfare of each faculty of mind, or to each appetite, were wanting, then, part by part, the man would perish and disappear. On the other hand, no man, I think, has ever had a complete, total, and permanent enjoyment of every part of his nature. That is the ideal to which we tend, but one not capable of complete attainment in a progressive being. For if the ideal of yesterday has become the actual of to-day, to-morrow we are seized with manly disquiet and unrest, and soar up towards another ideal.

We have all more or less of joy, the quantity and quality differing amazingly amongst men. There are as many forms of joy as there are propensities which hunger and thirst after their satisfaction. What a difference in the source whence men derive their customary delight.

Here is a man whose whole joy seems to come from his body; not from its nobler senses, offering him the pleasures of the ear and the eye, but from the lower parts of the flesh, imbruted now to passions which seem base when made to minister the chief delight to man. We could not think highly of one who knew no joy above the pleasure of eating and drinking, or of any other merely animal satisfaction. Such joys cannot raise man far. If one had his chief delight in fine robes, the taste would rather degrade him. Yet these two appetites, for finery in food and finery in dress, have doubtless done their part to civilize mankind. It is surely better for the race to rejoice in all the sumptuous delicacies of art, than to feed precariously on wild acorns which the wind shakes down. The foolish fondness for gay apparel has served a purpose.

Nay, so marvellous is the economy of God in his engineering of the world, that no drop of waste water runs over the dam of the universe; and as the atom which now sparkles in the rainbow, the next minute shall feed a fainting rose, so even these sensual desires have helped to uplift mankind from mere subordination to the material world.

There is another man whose chief joy is not merely bodily, but yet resides in his selfish appetites, in his lust of money, or lust of power. I pass by the joy of the miser, of the ambitious politician, of the pirate and the kidnapper. They are so well known amongst us that you can easily estimate their worth.

Now and then we find men whose happiness comes almost wholly from pure and lofty springs, from the high senses of the body or the high faculties of the spirit,—joys of the mind, of the conscience, of the affections, of the soul. Difference of quality is more important than difference in mere bulk; an hour of love is worth an age of lust. We all look with some reverence on such as seek the higher quality of joy.

You are pleased to see birds feeding their wide-mouthed little ones; sheep and oxen intent upon their grassy bread; reapers under a hedge enjoying their mid-day meal, reposing on sheaves of corn new cut. All this is nature; the element of necessity consecrates the meal. Artistic pictures of such scenes are always attractive. But pictures or descriptions of feasts — where the design is not to satisfy a natural want, but where eating and drinking are made a luxurious art, the end of life, and man seems only an appendage to the table — are never wholly pleasing. You feel a little ashamed of the quality of such delight. Even the marvellous pencil of Paul of Verona here fails to please. But a picture of men finding a joy in the higher senses, still more in thought, in the common, everyday duties of life, in works of benevolence or justice, in the delight of love, in contemplation, or in prayer, — this can touch us all. We like the quality of such delight, and love to look on men in such a mood of joy. I need only refer to the most admired paintings of the great masters, Dutch or Italian, and to the poetry which chronicles the mortal modes of high delight. The spiritual element must subordinate the material, in order to make the sensual joy welcome to a nice eye. In the Saint Cecilia of Raphael, in Titian's Marriage at Cana, in Leonardo's Last Supper, it is the preponderance of spiritual over sensuous emotion that charms the eye. So is it in all poetry, from the feeding of the five thousand to the sweet story of Lorenzo and Jessica, and the moonlight scene of their love whereby "heaven is thick inlaid with patines of bright gold."

The joy of a New England miser, gloating over extortions which even the law would cough at, the delight of a tyrant clutching at power, of a Boston kidnapper griping some trembling slave, or counting out the price of blood which a wicked government bribes him withal, — that would hardly be acceptable even here and to-day,* though painted with the most angelic power and skill. It would be a painted satire, not a pictured praise; the portrait of a devil's joy can be no man's delight.

Everybody knows the joy of the senses. The higher faculties have a corresponding joy. As there is a scale of faculties ascending from the sense of touch and taste, the first developed and most widely spread in the world of living things, up to affection, rejoicing to delight, and to the religious emotions which consciously connect us with the Infinite God; so there is a corresponding scale of joys, delight rising above delight, from the baby fed by his mother's breast to the most experienced man, enlarged by science and by art, filled with a tranquil trust in the infinite protection of the all-bounteous God. The higher the faculty, the more transcendent is its joy.

---

* This sermon was preached April 6, 1851, presently after the kidnapping of Mr. Sims, in Boston, and before his "trial" was completed.

The partial and transient joy of any faculty comes from the fractional and brief fulfilment of the conditions of its nature; the complete and permanent joy of the whole man comes from a total and continuous supply of the conditions of the entire nature of man.

Now, for this complete and lasting joy, these conditions must be thus fulfilled for me as an individual, for my family, for my neighborhood, for the nation, and for the world, else my joy is not complete; for though I can in thought for a moment abstract myself from the family, society, nation, and from all mankind, it is but for a moment. Practically I am bound up with all the world; an integer indeed, but a fraction of mankind. I cannot enjoy my daily bread because of the hunger of the men I fain would feed. I am not wholly and long delighted with a book relating some new wonder of science, or offering me some jewelled diadem of literary art, because, I think straightway of the thousand brother men in this town to whom even the old wonders of science and the ancient diadems of literary art are all unknown. The morsel that I eat alone is not sweet, because the fatherless has not eaten it with me. Yet we all desire this complete joy; we are not content without it; I feel it belongs to me, to all men, as individuals and as fractions of society. When mankind comes of age, he must enter on this estate. The very desire thereof shows it is a part of the Divine plan of the world, for each natural desire has the means to satisfy it put somewhere in the universe, and there is a mutual attraction between the two, which at last must meet. Natural desire is the prophecy of satisfaction.

Look over the bountiful distribution of joy in the world. It abounds in the lower walks of creation. The young fish, you shall even now find on the shallow beaches of some sheltered Atlantic bay, how happy they are! Voiceless, dwelling in the cold unsocial element of water, moving with the flapping of the sea, and never still amid the ocean waves' immeasurable laugh, — how delighted are these little children of God! Their life seems one continuous holiday, the shoal waters a play-ground. Their food is plenteous as the water itself. Society is abundant, and of the most unimpeachable respectability. They have their little child's games which last all day. No one is hungry, ill-mannered, ill-dressed, dyspeptic, love-lorn, or melancholy. They fear no hell. These cold, white-fleshed, and bloodless little atomies seem ever full of joy as they can hold; wise without study, learned enough with no book or school, and well cared for amid their own neglect. They recollect no past, they provide for no future, the great God of the ocean their only memory or forethought. These little, short-lived minnows are to me a sermon eloquent; they are a psalm to God, above the loftiest hymnings of Theban Pindar, or of the Hebrew king.

On the land, see the joy of the insects just now coming into life. The new-born butterfly, who begins his summer life to-day, how joyous he is in his claret-colored robe, so daintily set off with a silver edge! No Pharisee, enlarging the borders of his garments, getting greetings in the markets and the uppermost seat at feasts, and called of men "Rabbi," is ever so brimful of glee as our little silver-bordered fly. He has a low seat in the universe, for he is only a butterfly; but to him it is good as the uppermost; and in the sunny, sheltered spots in the woods, with brown leaves about him, and the promise of violets and five-fingers by and by, the great sun gently greets him, and the dear God continually says to this son of a worm, "Come up higher!"

The adventurous birds that have just come to visit us, how delighted they are, and of a bright morning how they tell their joy! each robin and blackbird waking, not with a dry mouth and a parched tongue, but with a bosom full of morning psalms to gladden the day with "their sweet jargoning." What a cheap luxury they pick up in the fields; and in a clear sunrise and a warm sky find a delight which makes the pomp of Nebuchadnezzar seem ridiculous!

Even the reptiles, the cold snake, the bunchy and calumniated toad, the frog, now newly wakened from his hybernating sleep, have a joy in their existence which is complete and seems perfect. How that long symbol of "the old enemy" basks delighted in the sun! In the idle days which in childhood I once had, I have seen, as I thought, the gospel of God's love written in the life of this reptile, for whom Christians have such a mythological hatred, but whom the good God blesses with a new, shining skin every year, — written more clearly than even Nazarene Jesus could tell the tale. No wonder! it was the dear God who wrote His gospel in that scroll. How joyously the frogs welcome in the spring, which knocks at the icy door of their dwelling, and rouses them to new life! What delight have they in their thin, piping notes at this time, and in the hoarse thunders wherewith they will shake the bog in weeks to come; in their wooing and their marriage song!

The young of all animals are full of delight. God baptizes his new-born children of the air, the land, the sea, with joy; admits them to full communion in his great church, where He that taketh thought for oxen suffers no sparrow to fall to the ground without his fatherly love. A new lamb, or calf, or colt, just opening its eyes on the old world, is happy as fabled Adam in his Eden. With what sportings, and friskings, and frolickings do all young animals celebrate their Advent and Epiphany in the world of time! As they grow older, they have a wider and a wiser joy, — the delight of the passions and the affections, to apply the language of men to the consciousness of the cattle. It takes the form, not of rude leapings, but of quiet cheerfulness. The matronly cow, ruminating beside her playful and hornless little one, is a type of quiet joy and entire satisfaction, — all her nature clothed in well-befitting happiness.

Even animals that we think austere and sad, — the lonely hawk, the solitary jay, who loves New England winters, and the innumerable shellfish, — have their personal and domestic joy, well known to their intimate acquaintances. The toad whom we vilify as ugly, and even call venomous, malicious, and spiteful, is a kind neighbor, and seems as contented as the day is long. So is it with the spider, who is not the malignant kidnapper that he is thought, but has a little, harmless world of joy. A stream of welfare flows from end to end of their little life, — not very broad, not very deep, but wide and deep enough to bathe their every limb, and bring contentment and satisfaction to each want.

Did not the same God who pours out the light from yonder golden sun, and holds all the stars in his leash of love, make and watch over the smallest of these creatures? Nay, He who leaves not forsaken Jesus alone never deserts the spider and the toad.

Wait a few weeks and go into the fields, of a warm day, at morning, noon, or night, and all creation is a-hum with happiness, the young and old, the reptile, insect, beast, and fowls of heaven, rejoice in their brave delight. All about us is full of joy, fuller than we notice. Take a handful of water from the rotting timbers of a wharf; little polyps are therein, medusæ and the like, with few senses, few faculties; but they all swim in a tide of joy, and it seems as if the world was made for them alone; for them the tide ebbs and flows, for them the winter goes, the summer comes, and the universe subsists for them alone.

Some men tell us that, at the other extreme of the scale, those vast bodies, the suns and satellites, have also a consciousness and a delight; that "in reason's ear they all rejoice." But that is poetry. Not in reason's, but fancy's ear do they rejoice. The rest is fact, plain prose.

All animate creatures in their natural condition have, it is true, their woes; but they are brief in time, little in quantity, and soon forgot. When you look microscopically and telescopically at the natural suffering in the world of animals, you find it is just enough to tie the girdle, and hold the little creature together, and keep him from violating his own individual being; or else to unite the tribe and keep them from violating their social being. So it seems only the girdle of the individual of the flock, and no more an evil, when thus looked at, than the bruises we get in our essays to walk. Suffering marks the outer limit of the narrow margin of oscillation left for the caprice of the individual animal or man,— the pain a warning to mark the bound.

A similar joy appears in young children well born and well nurtured. But the human power of error, though still not greater in proportion to our greater nature, is so much more, and man so little subordinate to his instincts, that we have wandered far from the true road of material happiness. So the new-born child comes trailing the errors of his ancestry behind him at his birth. Still, the healthy child, wisely cared for, though tethered with such a brittle chain of being, is no exception to the general rule of joy. He

"Is a dew-drop which the morn brings forth,
Not formed to undergo unkindly shocks,
Or to be trailed along the soiling earth;—
A gem that glitters while it lives,
And no forewarning gives,
But at the touch of wrong, without a strife,
Slips in a moment out of life."

In the world of adult men there is much less of this joy; it is not a great river that with mighty stream runs round and round the world of human consciousness, all ignorant of ebb. Our faces are care-stricken, not many joyous; most of them look as if they had met and felt the peltings of the storm, and only hoped for the rainbow. The songs of the people are mostly sad; only the savage in tropic climes — subordinate to nature, there a gentle mistress — is blithe and gay as the monkeys and the parrots in his native grove of Africa; and there his joy is only jollity, the joy of saucy flesh.

There are two chief causes for this lack of joy with men. This is one: —

I. We have not yet fulfilled the necessary material conditions thereof. The individual has not kept the natural law, and hence has some schism in the flesh from his intemperance or want; some schism in the spirit from lack of harmony within; or there is some schism between him and the world of matter, he not in unison with things around; he has a miserable body, that goes stooping and feeble, must be waited for and waited on, and, like the rulers of the Gentiles, exercises authority over him; or he lacks development of spiritual powers; or else is poor, and needs material supplies.

Or if the special individual is right in all these

things, and so might have his personal joy, the mass of men in your neighborhood, your nation, or the world, are deficient in all these, in body, mind, and estate, and with your individual joy there comes a social grief, and so the worm in the bud robs your blossom of half its fragrant bloom, and hinders all its fruit. Man is social not less than personal; sympathy is national, even human, reaching out to the ends of the earth; and if the hungry cry of those who have reaped down the world's harvest smite your ear, why, your bread turns sour, and is bread of affliction. The rich scholar, with abundant time, in his well-stored library, has the less joy in his own books while he remembers there are nobler souls that starve for the crumbs which fall from his table, or drudge at some ungrateful toil not meant for them. The healthy doctor, well fed and nicely clad, cannot so steel his heart against the ignorance and want and pain he daily sees, that his health and table and science, and rosy girls, shall give him the same delight which would come thereof in a world free from such society of suffering.

> "The clouds that gather round the setting sun
> Do take a sober coloring from an eye
> That hath kept watch o'er man's mortality."

Now the pain which comes from this source, this lack of mind, body, and estate on the part of the special individual, or of the race, is all legitimate and merciful; I would not have it less. There is never too much suffering of this sort in the world, only enough to teach mankind to live in harmony with Nature, in concord with each other, in unity with God. Here, as in the animals, this pain is but the girdle round the loins of you or me to keep the individual whole; or about the waist of mankind, to keep us all united in one brotherhood. Here, as there, suffering marks the limit of our margin of oscillation, warns against trespass, and says, "Pause and forbear."

Yet we are all seeking for this joy. Each man needs it; knows he needs it, yet needs it deeper than he knows. So is it with mankind: the common heart by which we live cries to God for satisfaction of our every need, and for our natural joy. The need thereof stirs the self-love of men to toil, the sight of pain quickens the nobler man to rouse his sluggish brother to end it all. The sad experience of the world shows this, — that man must find his joy, not in subordinating himself to matter, or to the instincts of the flesh, as the beasts find theirs, or of the weak to the strong, but in subordinating matter to mind, instinct to conscious reason, and then coördinating all men into one family of religious love.

II. Here is the other cause. Much of this lack

of joy comes from false notions of religion, — false ideas of God, of man, and of the relation between the two. We are bid to think it wicked to be joyous. In the common opinion of churches, a religious man must be a sad man, his tears become his meat. Men who in our day are eminent "leaders of the churches" are not joyous men; their faces are grim and austere, not marked with manly delight. Some men are sad at sight of the want, the pain, and the misdirection of men. It was unavoidable that Jesus of Nazareth should ofttimes be "exceeding sorrowful." He must indeed weep over Jerusalem. The Apostles, hunted from city to city, might be excused for sadness. For centuries the Christian Church had reason to be a sad Church. Persecution made our New England fathers stern and sour men, and their form of religion caught a stain from their history. I see why this is so, and blame no man for it. It was once unavoidable. But now it is a great mistake to renounce the natural joy of life; above all, to renounce it in the name of God. No doubt it takes the whole human race to represent in history the whole of Human Nature; but if the "Church," that is theological men, make a mock at joy, then the "world" will go to excess in the opposite extreme. Men in whom the religious and moral powers are not developed in proportion with the intellectual, the æsthetic, or the physical appetites, will try to possess this joy, and without religion. But nothing is long fruitful of delight when divorced from the consciousness of God; nothing thrives that is at enmity with God. Such joy is poor, heartless, and unsatisfying. Men in churches set up a Magdalen, a nun, a monk, a hermit, or a priest, as a representative of religion. Men out of churches want joy; they will flee off where they can find it, and leave religion behind them. Yet joy without religion is but a poor, wandering Hagar, her little water spent, her bread all gone, and no angel to marshal the way to the well where she shall drink and feed her fainting child, and say, THOU, GOD, SEEST ME!

There is little joy in the ecclesiastical consciousness of religion. Writers and preachers of Christianity commonly dwell on the dark side of human nature. They tell us of our weakness, not of our ability to be and to do. They mourn and scold over human folly, human sin, human depravity, often leaving untold the noble deeds of man and his nobler powers. "Man is a worm," say they.

They do the same with God. They paint him as a king, not as a father; and as a king who rules by low and selfish means, for low and selfish ends, from low and selfish motives, and with a most melancholy result of his ruling. According to the common opinion of the Christian churches, God's is the most unsuccessful despotism that has ever been set agoing, leading to the eternal ruin of the immense majority of his subjects, as the result of the absolute selfishness of the theological deity. In the theology called Christian the most conspicuous characteristics of God are great force, great self-esteem, and immense destructiveness. He is painted as cruel, revengeful, and without mercy,—the grimmest of the gods. The heathen devils all glower at us through the mask of the theological God. The Mexicans worshipped an idea of God, to which they sacrificed hundreds of captives and criminals. Christian divines tell us of a God that will not kill, but torment in hell the greater portion of his children, and will feed fat his "glory" with the damnation of mankind, the everlasting sacrifice of each ruined soul! If men think that man is a worm, and God has lifted the heavenly heel to give him a squelch which shall last for ever, the relation between God and man is certainly not pleasant for us to think of.

God is thought a hard creditor, man a poor debtor; "religion" is the sum he is to pay; so he puts that down grudgingly, and with the stingiest fist. Or else God is painted as a grim and awful judge, man a poor, trembling culprit, shivering before his own conscience, and slinking down for fear of the vengeance of the awful judge, hell gaping underneath his feet. Does any one doubt this? Let him read the Book of Revelation, or the writings of John Calvin, of Baxter, or Edwards or even of Jeremy Taylor. The theological God is mainly a great devil, and as the theological devil hates "believers," whom he seeks to devour, so the theological God hates "unbelievers," and seeks successfully to devour them, gnawed upon eternally in hell. In general, theological books represent God as terrible. They make religion a melancholy sort of thing, unnatural to man, which he would escape from if he dared, or if he could. It is seldom spoken of as a thing good in itself, but valuable to promote order on the earth, and help men to get "saved" and obtain a share of eternal happiness. It is not a joy, but a burthen, which some men are to be well and eternally paid for bearing in the heat of the mortal day. Yes, to the majority of men it is represented as of no use at all in their present or future condition; for if a man has not Christianity enough to purchase a share in heaven, his religion is a useless load, — only a torment on earth, and of no value at all in the next life! What is the use of religion to men in eternal torment? So, by the showing of the most respectable theologians, religion can bring no joy, save to the "elect," who are but a poor fraction of mankind, and commonly exhibit little of it here.

The general tone of writings called religious is sad and melancholy. Religion adorns her brow with yellow leaves smitten by the frost, not with rosebuds and violets. The leading men in the more serious churches are earnest persons, self-denying, but grim, unlovely, and joyless men. Look through the ecclesiastial literature of the Christian world, — it is chiefly of this sad complexion. The branches of the theological tree are rough and thorny, not well laden with leaves, and of blossoms it has few that are attractive. It was natural enough that the Christians, when persecuted and trodden down, should weep and wail in their literature. In the first three centuries they do so; — in every period of persecution. The dark shades of the New England forest lowered over New England theology, and Want and War knit their ugly brows in the meeting-houses of the day. But the same thing continued, and it lasts still. Now it is the habit of Christendom, though sometimes it seems only a trick.

In what is called Christian literature nothing surprises you more than the absence of joy. There is much of the terror of religion, little of its delights. Look over the list of sermons of South,

Edwards, Chalmers, Hopkins, Emmons, even of Jeremy Taylor, and you find few sermons on the joys of religion. The same is true of Massillon, of Bourdaloue, and Bossuet. The popular ecclesiastical notion of religion is not to be represented as a wife and mother, cheerful, contented, and happy in her work, but as a reluctant nun, abstracted, idle, tearful, and with a profound melancholy; not the melancholy which comes from seeing actual evils we know not how to cure,—the sadness of one strong to wish and will, but feeble to achieve;—no, the more incurable sadness which comes from a distrust of Nature and of God, and from the habit of worrying about the soul,—the melancholy of fear; not the melancholy which looks sadly on misery and crime, which wept out its "O Jerusalem! Jerusalem!" but the sadness which whines in a corner, and chews its own lips from sheer distrust.

The writers who dwell on the joys of religion too often have very inadequate ideas thereof. For they all, from Augustine to Chalmers, start with the idea that God is imperfect, and not wholly to be trusted. Accordingly they seek and obtain but a very one-sided development of their nature, thinking they must sacrifice so much of it; and hence have not that strength of religious character, nor that wholeness thereof, which is necessary to complete manly joy in religion.

Such being the case, fear of God predominates over love of Him; trust of God is only special under such and such circumstances, not universal under all circumstances; and religious joy is thin, and poor, and cold.

You find mention of religious joy in some of the great Christian writers, especially among the mystics, in Tauler and Kempis, Scougal, Fenelon, William Law, and Jacob Behme, not to mention others. Even Bunyan has his delectable mountains, and though in the other world, the light therefrom shines serene and joyous along the paths of mortal life. But in most, if not in all, of these writers, religious joy is deemed an artificial privilege, reserved by God's decree for only a few, purchased by unnatural modes of life, and miraculously bestowed. Even in greathearted Martin Luther, one of the most joyous of men, it is not a right which belongs to human nature, and comes naturally from the normal action of the faculties of man; it is the result of "divine grace," not of human nature. Thus this religious joy of the churches is often hampered and restricted, and the man must be belittled before he is capable thereof. In the ecclesiastical saint there is always something sneaking; some manly quality is left out, or driven out, some unmanly quality forced in. I believe this has been so in all ages of Christianity, and in all Christian sects at this day. Study the character and history of the saints of the Catholic and Protestant churches. Look at their mode of life, their sources and forms of joy. You see it is so. They must turn Human Nature out of doors before the Divine Nature can come in. So the heavenly bridegroom, adorned for his wife, comes to a house swept and garnished indeed, but cheerless, empty, and cold, only theological furniture left in, the bride herself swept out. Look at the marbles of antiquity, — at the face of pagan Plato, of Aristotle, "the master of such as know," — or at the faces of modern philosophers, and compare them with the actual or ideal countenance of Christian saints, — with Saint Francis, with Saint Thomas, with Ignatius Loyola, with the ideal Magdalens and Madonnas of art, or with the dark, sad, and woe-stained faces of the leading clergy of the predominant sects, — and you see at once the absence of natural delight.

Religion is often separated from common life. So a sharp distinction is made between the "flesh" and the "spirit." The flesh is all sinful, all that belongs to it thought poor, and mean, and low; to taste the joys of piety, the senses must be fettered and put in jail, and then, where theology has made a solitude, it proclaims peace. On the one side is the "world," on the other "religion;" and there is a great gulf fixed between the two, which neither

Dives, nor Lazarus, nor yet Abraham, can pass over. Here all the delight is in "things temporal;" there the delight is only in "things eternal." Worldly men have their delight in the things of this world, and no more; heavenly men, only in the joys of the next life; and they who have the worst time here shall have the best hereafter. Religion is thought out of place at a ball, at a theatre, at any amusement; dancing is thought more than half a sin. Religion loves funerals, is seldom at a wedding, — only to sadden the scene, — for woman is bid to be ashamed of natural human love, and man of being loved. "We are conceived in sin," quoth theology; "the 'God-man' was born with no human father."

It seems commonly thought that the joys of religion are inconsistent with active daily life. Men who have written thereof are chiefly ascetic and romantic persons of retired lives, of shy habits; they prefer thought to work, passive contemplation to active meditation, and dreamy sentimentalism to all other and manlier joys. The natural result of this ecstasy, not the normal activity of the whole man, but irregular, extravagant, and insane action of a few noble powers. Hence those writings are not wholesome; the air they exhale is close and unhealthy, for such pietism is the sickness of the soul, not its soundness and its health.

I believe what I say will apply to almost the whole class of writers on sentimental religion, — to the mystical writers of the Brahminic, Buddhistic, Christian, and Mahometan sects. He must be a whole man who writes a sound book on a theme so deep as the religious joys of man, — his delight in Nature, in man, and in God. But the false ideas of the popular theory corrupt the faculties of noble and great men. So, in the writings of Law and Fenelon, of Taylor and Henry More, you find this unhealthiness pervading what they do and say. There is much you sympathize in, but much also which offends a nice taste, and revolts the reason, the affections, and all the high faculties of a sound man. You may see the excess of this unhealthiness in the works of St. Bridget or of St. Theresa, in Molinos and Swedenborg, even in Taylor, in Fenelon, and Augustine; in the dreams and fancied revelations of monks and nuns, when nature clamored for her rights, or in the sermons and prayers of ascetic clergymen, whom a false idea of God and religion has driven to depravity of body and sickness of the soul.

We may see the effects of this false idea on the conduct and character of active men in a Methodist camp-meeting; or in a form yet more painful, in the pinched faces, and narrow, unnatural foreheads of men and women early caught and imprisoned in some of the popular forms of fear of God. I have sometimes shuddered to hear such men talk of their joy of religion, — a joy unnatural and shameful, which delighted in the contemplation of torment as the portion of mankind.

Read the life of St. Hugh, an Archbishop of Lyons. See in what his joys of religion consisted. If any one spoke of news in his presence, he checked them, saying, "This life is all given us for weeping and penance, not for idle discourses." It was his "constant prayer that God would extinguish in his heart all attachment to creatures, that His pure love might reign in all his affections." "His love of heavenly things made all temporal affairs seem burdensome and tedious." "Women he would never look in the face, so that he knew not the features of his own mother." He continually recited the Psalter and the Lord's Prayer; the latter on one occasion "three hundred times in a single night!"

In saying all this, I do not wish to blame men. I would rather write an apology for the religious errors of Pagans or Christians, than a satire thereon. I only mention the fact. It is not a strange one, for we find analogous errors in the history of every department of human affairs. What dreams of astrologers and alchemists came before the cool, sober thought of chemists and astronomers! The mistakes in religion are not greater in proportion to the strength of the religious faculty and the greatness of the interest at stake, than the mistakes in agriculture or politics. The theology of Boston is not much worse than its "law and order" just now; and they who in pulpits, administer the popular theology, are not much more mistaken than they who, in courts and jails, administer the public law. But in religion these mistaken notions have been so common, that the very name of religious joy is associated with superstition, bigotry, extravagance, madness. You attend a meeting "for conference and prayer," and you come away a little disgusted, with more pity than sympathy for the earnest men who have so mistaken the nature of God, of man, and of the relation between the two; who have so erred as to the beginning of religion, its processes and its result. You pass thence to a meeting of philosophical men met for science, or philanthropic men met for benevolence, and what a change! Both are equally earnest; but in the one all is hot, unnatural, restricted, and presided over by fear; in the other all is cool, all is free, and there is no fear.

In consequence of this abuse, men often slight the sentiment of religion, and deny the real and sober joy which it naturally affords. This is a great loss, for, setting aside the extravagance, the claim to miraculous communion with God, putting aside all ecstasy, as only the insanity of religious action, it is true that, in its widest sense and in its highest form, religion is a source of the deepest and noblest joys of man. Let us put away the childish things and look at the real joys of manly religion itself.

A true form of religion does not interfere with any natural delight of man. True religion is normal life, not of one faculty alone, but of all in due coördination. The human consciousness of the Infinite God will show itself, not merely in belief, or prayer and thanksgiving, but by the legitimate action of every limb of the body and every faculty of the spirit. Then all the legitimate appetites have their place. Do you want the natural gratification of the body? Religion bids you seek it in the natural and legitimate way, not in a manner unnatural and against the body's law. It counts the body sacred, as well as the soul, and knows that a holy spirit demands a holy flesh. Thus it enhances even the delights of the body, by keeping every sense in its place. The actual commandments of God written on every fibre of human flesh, are not less authoritative than the Ten which Jehovah is said to have written on stone at Sinai.

Do you seek the active business of life? This religion will bid you pursue your calling, hand-craft or head-craft, and buy and sell and get gain, the Golden Rule your standard measure, and all your daily work a sacrament whereby you communicate with man and God. Do you want riches, honor, fame, the applause of men? This religion tells you to subordinate the low aim to the high; to keep self-love in its natural channel; to preserve the integrity of your own spirit; and then, if you will and can, to get riches, power, honor, fame, and the applause of men, by honestly earning them all, so that you shall be the manlier, and mankind the richer, for all that you do and enjoy. Then the approbation of your own soul and the sense of concord with men and of unity with God, will add a certain wholeness to your delight in the work of your hands.

Do you desire the joys of the intellect working in any or all its manifold forms of action? The world is all before you where to choose, and Providence your guide. The law of God says, "Of every tree of the field shalt thou eat. Nothing that is natural shall harm thee. Put forth thy hand and try. Be not afraid that Truth or Search shall ever offend God, or harm the soul of man." Does a new truth threaten an old church? It will build up ten new ones in its stead. No man ever loved truth too much, or had too much of it, or was too diligent in the search therefor. To use the reason for reasonable things is a part of religion itself. Thus consciousness of God well developed in man gives greater joy to the natural delights of the intellect itself, which it helps to tranquillize and render strong.

You need the exercise of the moral faculties. This religion will bid you trust your own conscience, never to fear to ask thereof for the everlasting right, and be faithful thereto. Justice will not hurt you, nor offend God; and if your justice pull down the old kingdom, with its statutes of selfishness and laws of sin and death, it will build up a new and better state in its stead, the Commonwealth of Righteousness, where the eternal laws of God are reënacted into the codes of men, laws of love and life. No man ever loved justice too much, — his own rights, or the rights of men, — or was too faithful to his own conscience. Loyalty to that is fealty to God; and the consciousness of Him enhances the moral delight of moral men, as the intellectual joy of scientific and thoughtful men.

Do you seek the joy of the affections which cling to finite objects of attraction, to wife and child, brother and sister, parent and friend? Religion will tell you it is impossible to love these too much; that it is impossible to be too affectionate, or to be too wise or too just. No man can be too faithful to his own heart, nor have, in general, too much love. Love of the "creature" is part of the service we owe the Creator; one of the forms of love to God. Conscious piety will enhance the delight of mortal affections, and will greaten and beautify every form of love, — connubial, parental, and filial, friendly and philanthropic love.

Nay, all these — the love of truth and beauty, of justice and right, of men — are but parts of the great integral piety, the love of God, the Author of Truth, of Justice, and of Love. The normal delight in God's world, the animal joy in material things, the intellectual in truth and beauty, the moral in justice and right, the affectional delight in the persons of men, the satisfactions of labor of hand or head or heart, — all these are a part of our large delight in God, for religion is not one thing and life another, but the two are one. The normal and conscious worship of the Infinite God will enlarge every faculty, enhancing its quantity and quality of delight.

Let me dwell yet longer on this affectional delight. Last Sunday I spoke of the Increase of Power which comes of the religious use of the faculties. One form thereof I purposely passed by and left for this hour, — the ability to love other men. Religion, by producing harmony with yourself, concord with men, and unity with God, prevents the excess of self-love, enlarges the power of unselfish affection, increases the quantity of love, and so the man has a greater delight in the welfare of other men.

I will not say that this religion increases the powers of instinctive affection, except indirectly and in general, as it enlarges the man's whole quantity of being, and refines its quality. Yet much of the power of affection is not instinctive, but the result of conscious and voluntary action. It is not mere instinct which drives me unconsciously and bound to love a friend; I do it consciously, freely, because it suits the whole of me, not merely one impulsive part. The consciousness of my connection with God, of my obligation to God, of his Providence watching over all, — this, and the effort to keep every law He has written in my constitution, enlarges my capability to love men.

I pass by connubial love, wherein affection and passion blend each its several bloom, and there are still two other forms of conscious love. One is friendship, the other philanthropy.

In friendship I love a man for his good and

mine too. There is action on both sides; I take delight in him, but only on condition that he takes delight in me. I ask much of my friend, not only gratitude and justice, but forbearance and patience towards me; — yes, sacrifice of himself. I do this not selfishly, not wilfully. I love my friend for his character and his conduct, for what he is to me and I am to him. My friendship is limited, and does not reach out so far as justice, which has the range of the world. Who can claim friendship of any one? The New England kidnapper has a right to the philanthropy even of his victim; but he seems to have a right to the friendship only of pirates and men that would assassinate the liberty of mankind. But no man is wholly wicked and self-abandoned, and so has forfeited all claim to the friendship of the noblest; and such is the blessed wealth of the human heart, that it continually runs over with mercy for the merciless, and love for the unlovely.

In philanthropy I love a man for his sake, not at all for mine. I take the delight of justice and of charity in him, but do not ask him to take any delight in me. I ask nothing of him, not even gratitude, nor justice; perhaps expect neither. I love him because he is a man, and without regard to his character and conduct; and would feed and clothe and warm and bless the murderer, or even the Boston kidnapper. Philanthropy makes its sun rise on the evil and on the good, and sends its rain on the just and on the unjust. Its circle is measured by its power, not its will. It is not personal, limited in its application to Robert or Marion, but universal as justice, reaching to all, it joins the wayfaring Samaritan to his national enemy who had fallen among thieves.

Now I wish to say that religion enlarges a man's power of friendship and of philanthropy, and consequently enhances the delight of both. Look a moment at the joy of each.

The joy of friendship is a deep and beautiful delight. Here you receive as well as give, get not only from yourself, as your unconsciousness becomes conscious, and the seed you planted for the bread of another becomes a perfect flower for your own eye and bosom; but you receive from another self. This is one of the dearest joys; it is the mutuality of affection, your delight in another's person, and his delight in you; it is a reciprocity of persons. There are those we love not with instinctive passion, as man and wife; nor with instinctive affection, as parent and child; nor with the love of philanthropy; but with emotions of another class, with friendly love. It is delightful to do kind deeds for such, and receive kind deeds from them. Not that you need or they need the gift; but both the giving. You need to give to them, they to give to you. Their very presence is a still and silent joy. After long intimacy of this sort, you scarce need speech to communicate sympathy; the fellow-feeling has a language and tells its own tale. In loving a friend, I have all the joy of self-love without its limitation. I find my life extending into another being, his into me. So I multiply my existence. If I love one man in this way, and he love me, I have doubled my delight; if I love two, it is yet further enlarged. So I live in each friend I add to myself; his joys are mine and mine are his; there is a solidarity of affection between us, and his material delights give permanent happiness to me. As a man enlarges his industrial power by material instruments, the wind and the river joined to him by skilful thought, so he enlarges his means of happiness by each friend his affection joins to him. A man with a forty-friend power would be a millionaire at the treasury of love.

The joy of philanthropy is a high delight, worth all the exaltations of St. Hugh, and the ecstasies of St. Bridget and St. Theresa. Compare it with the rapture which Jonathan Edwards anticipates for the "elect" in heaven, looking down upon the damned, and seeing their misery, and making "heaven ring with the praises of God's justice towards the wicked, and his grace towards the saints!" Such is the odds betwixt the religion of nature and the theology of the Christian Church.

There is a great satisfaction in doing good to others, — to men that you never saw, nor will see, — who will never hear of you, but not the less be blessed by your bounty, — even in doing good to the unthankful and the unmerciful. You have helped a poor woman in Boston out of the want and wretchedness her drunken husband has brought on her, and filled her house withal; you have delivered a slave out of the claw of the kidnapper, the "barbarous and heathen kidnapper in Benguela," or the "Christian and honorable kidnapper in Boston," commissioned, and paid for the function; you have taken some child out of the peril of the streets, found him a home, and helped him grow up to be a self-respectful and useful man; — suppose the poor woman shall never know the name of her benefactor, nor the slave of his deliverer, nor the child of his saviour, — that you get no gratitude from the persons, no justice from the public; you are thought a fool for your charity, and a culprit for your justice, the government seeking to hang you; still the philanthropy has filled your bosom with violets and lilies, and you run over with the delight thereof. You would be ashamed to receive gratitude, or ask justice. "Father, forgive them!" was the appropriate benediction of one of the great masters of philanthropy. Do you look for reciprocal affection?

> "I have heard of hearts unkind, kind deeds
> With coldness still returning;
> Alas! the gratitude of men
> Hath oftener left me mourning."

The good Samaritan, leaving his "neighbor" who had fallen among thieves well cared for at the inn, jogs home on his mule with a heart that kings might envy; but when he comes again, if the man, healed by his nursing, offers thanks, — "Nay," says the Samaritan, "nay, now, be still and say nothing about it. It is all nothing; only human nature. I could not help it. You would do the same!" Such a man feeds his affection by such deeds of love, till he has the heart of God in his bosom, and a whole paradise of delight. Meantime the Priest and the Levite have hastened to the temple, and offered their sacrifice, tithed their mint, their anise, and their cumin, made broad their phylacteries and enlarged the borders of their garments, and dropped with brassy ring their shekels in the temple chest, shoving aside the poor widow with her two mites, which make a farthing; now they stand before the seven golden candlesticks and pray, "Father, I thank Thee that I am not like other men, who trust in good works and the light of nature; I give tithes of all that I possess. I thank Thee that I am one of Thine Elect, and shall have glory when this Samaritan goeth down to the pit."

I once knew a little boy in the country, whose father gave him a half-dime to help the sufferers at a fire in New Brunswick; the young lad dropped his mite into the box at church, — it was his earliest alms, — with a deep delight which sweetened his consciousness for weeks to come with the thought of the good that his five cents would do. What were all sweetmeats and dainties to this? Our little boy's mother had told him that the good God loved actions such as these, Himself dropping the sun and moon into the alms-box of the world; and the grave, sober father, who had earned the silver with serious sweat, his broadaxe ringing in the tough oak of New England, brushed a tear out of his eye at seeing the son's delight in helping men whom none of the family had ever seen.

Philanthropy begins small, and helps itself along, sometimes by love of sheep and oxen, and dogs and swine. Did not the great Jesus ride into the holy city "on the foal of an ass"? By and by our philanthropist goes out to widest circles, makes great sacrifice of comfort, of money, of reputation; his philanthropic power continually grows, and an inundation of delight fills up his mighty soul. The shillings which a poor girl pays for missionaries to Burmah and Guinea are shillings which bring more delight than all the gewgaws they could buy.

I have seen a man buy baskets of cherries in a foreign town, and throw them by handfuls to the little boys and girls in the streets wholly unknown to him. He doubtless got more joy from that, than if he had had the appetite of a miser, and stomach enough to eat up all the cherries in the valley of the Rhine. Men of wealth, who use money for philanthropy, to feed the poor, to build hospitals and asylums, schools and colleges, get more joy from this use thereof, than if they had the pecuniary swallow and stomach of a gigantic miser, and themselves eat up the schools and colleges, the hospitals and asylums, which others built. They who build widows' houses, not they who devour them, have the most joy thereof.

The man who devotes the larger wealth of the mind, reason, understanding, imagination, with all the treasures of culture and the graceful dignity of eloquence, to serve some noble cause, despised as yet, and sacrifices not money alone, but reputation, and takes shame as outward recompense for truth and justice and love, — think you that he has less delight than the worldly man well gifted, cultivated well, whose mind lies a prostitute to the opinion of the mob, and is tricked off with the ornaments of shame, and in office shines "the first of bartered jades"? Look about you in Boston, and answer, ye that know! Go to the men who sacrifice their intellect, their conscience, their affections, for place and a name, ask them what they have got in exchange for their soul? and then go to such as have left all for God and his law, and ask them of their reward.

Now religion enlarges this capacity for both friendship and philanthropy, and so the quantity of joy which comes thereof, the happiness of the affections.

This religion has delights peculiar to the religious faculty, the happiness of the Soul. I love the Infinite God as the ideal of all perfection,— beauty to the imagination, truth to the reason, justice to the conscience, the perfect person to the affections, the Infinite and Self-faithful God to the soul. With this there vanishes away all fear of God, all fear of ultimate evil for any thing that is. If this escape from fear of God were all, that alone were a great thing. How men hate fear! From the dreadful God of the popular theology, and its odious immortality, they flee to annihilation; and atheism itself seems a relief. But this religion which grows out of the idea of the Infinite God casts out all fear and the torment thereof. I am content to be afraid of some men, stronger and wickeder than I; I know they can hurt me; I know they wish it; I know they will. To them my truth is "error of the carnal reason;" my justice is "violation of the law" of men; my love, philanthropic or friendly, is "levying war"; my religion is "infidelity," — "sin against the Holy Ghost." I fear these men; they turn their swine into my garden to root up and tread down every little herb of grace, or plant that flowers for present or for future joy. These men may hang me, or assassinate me in the street. I will try to keep out of their wicked way. If they will hurt me, I must bear it as best I can. But the fear of such men will not disturb me much. Their power is only for a time. "Thus far, but no further," quoth Death to the tyrant; and I am free.

But to fear God whom I cannot escape, whom death cannot defend me from, that would indeed be most dreadful. Irreligion is the fear of God. It takes two forms. In atheism, the form of denial, you fear without naming the object of horror, perhaps calling it Chance or Fate; in superstition, the form of affirmation, you fear Him by name, believe and tremble. Superstition and atheism are fellow-trunks from the same root of bitterness. I would as soon worship in the wigwam of Odin and Thor, as in the temple of Fear called by a Hebrew or a Christian name.

With a knowledge of the Infinite God, and with a fair development of the religious faculties, you cease to fear, you love. As nocturnal darkness, or the gray mist of morn, is chased away before the rising sun, so dread and horror flee off before the footsteps of love. Instead of fear, a sense of complete and absolute trust in God comes in, gives you repose and peace, filling you with tranquillity and dear delight in God. Then I know not what a day shall bring forth; some knave may strip me of my house and home, an accident — my own or another's fault — deprive me of the respect of men, and death leave me destitute of every finite friend, the objects of instinctive or of voluntary love all scattered from before my eyes; some hireling of the government, for ten pieces of silver, may send me off a slave for all my mortal life; decay of sense may perplex me, wisdom shut out an eye and ear; and disease may rack my frame. Still I am not afraid. I know what eternity will be. I appeal from man to God. Forsaken, I am not alone, uncomforted, not comfortless. I fold my arms and smile at the ruin which time has made, the peace of God all radiant in my soul.

Let me look full in the face the evil which I meet in the personal tragedies of private life, in the social evils which darkly variegate this and all other great towns; let me see monstrous political sin, dooming one man to a throne because he has trod thousands down to wretchedness and dirt; nay, let me see such things as happen now in Boston. I know no sadder sight on all this globe of lands: for to-day a brother-man is held in a dungeon by the avarice of this city, which seeks to make him a slave, and he out of his jail sends round a petition to the clergymen of Boston, asking their prayers for his unalienable rights, — a prayer which they will refuse, for those "churches of Christ" are this day a "den of thieves," shambles for the sale of human flesh.* Let me look on all these things, still I am not dismayed. I know, I feel, I am sure of this, that the Infinite God has known it all, provided for it all; that as He is all-powerful, all-wise, all-just, all-loving, and all-holy too, no absolute evil shall ever come to any child of his, erring or sinned against. I will do all for the right: then, if I fail, the result abides with God; it is His to care for and not mine. Thus am I powerful to bear, as powerful to do. I know of no calamity, irresistible, sudden, seemingly total, but religion can abundantly defend the head and heart against its harm. So I can be calm. De-

* The prophecy was only too true, but here and there remembered his God.

feated, and unable to rise, I will "lie low in the hand of the Father," smiling with the delight of most triumphant trust.

> "These surface troubles come and go
> Like rufflings of the sea;
> The deeper depth is out of reach
> To all, my God, but Thee."

With this tranquillity of trust there comes a still, a peculiar and silent joy in God. You feel your delight in Him, and His in you. The man is not beside himself, he is self-possessed and cool. There is no ecstasy, no fancied "being swallowed up in God;" but there is a lasting inward sweetness and abiding joy. It will not come out in raptures; it will not pray all night, making much ado for nothing done; but it will fill the whole man with beatitudes, with delight in the Infinite God. There will be a calm and habitual peace, a light around the mortal brow, but a light which passes from glory to glory till it changes into perfect fulness of delicious joy. God gives to the loving in their sorrow or their sleep.

Let us undervalue no partial satisfaction, which may be had without the consciousness of God. If it be legitimate and natural to man, let it have its place and its joy. Religion is not every thing. But yet the happiness of this inner human world, the delight of loving God and absolutely trusting Him, is plainly the dearest of all delights. I love the world of sense, its beauty to the eye and ear; the natural luxury of taste and touch. It is indeed a glorious world, — the stars of earth, that gem the ground with dewy loveliness, the flowers of heaven, whose amaranthine bloom attracts alike the admiring gaze of clown or sage, and draws the lover's eye while the same spirit is blooming also in his and in another's heart. I love the world of science, — the deeper loveliness which the mind beholds in each eternal star, or the rathe violet of this April day. What a more wondrous wonder is the uniform force of Nature, whose constant modes of operation are all exact as mathematic law, and whence the great minds of Kepler, Newton, and Laplace gather the flowers of nature's art, and bind them up in handfuls for our lesser wits! I rejoice in the world of men, in the all-conquering toil which subordinates matter unto man, making the river, ocean, winds, to serve mankind; which bridles the lightning and rides it through the sky, and sails the stormiest seas unharmed. I rejoice in the statutes which reënact the eternal laws of God, and administer justice betwixt man and man. I delight in human love in all its forms, instinctive or voluntary, in friendship and philanthropy; the mutuality of persons is a dear and sacred joy to me. But the delight in God is yet more, — dearer than each of these; one we like not much to name. Add to it all these several delights, which get each a charm from this consciousness of God, and you taste and see the real happiness of religion.

Religion without joy, — it is no religion. Superstition, the fear of God, might well be sad. The devotees thereof seek their delight in violating the functions of the body and the spirit. In the theological garden the Tree of Life bears fruit indeed, a few fair apples, but out of reach, which no man can gather till death lift us on his shoulders, and then they are not apples for a mortal mouth. You turn off from the literature of this superstition, and look on sunny Nature, on the minnow in the sea, on the robin in the field, on the frog, the snake, the spider, and the toad, and smile at sight of their gladness in the world, and wish to share it yourself. You turn to the literature which makes a mock at all religion. You find enough of it in Greece and Rome at the decay of paganism, enough still in brilliant France at the dissolution of Christian mythology, in the last century and in this. There also is an attempt at joy, but the attempt is vain, and the little life of men is full of wine and uproar and scarlet women, is poor, unsatisfactory, and short, rounded with bitterness at the last. The chief tree in that garden blossoms bright enough, but it bears only apples of Sodom for a body without a soul, a here with no hereafter, in a world without a God. In such a place the brilliance of genius is only lightning, not light. In such company you almost long for the iron age of theology and the hard literature of the "divines," lean and old and sour, but yet teaching us of a Will above the poor caprice of men, of a Mind beyond this perishing intellect, of an Arm which made men tremble indeed, but also upheld the world. At least there is Duty in that grim creation, and self-denial for the sake of God.

Things should not be so. Sensuality is not adequate delight for men who look to immortality. Religion is not at enmity with joy. No: it is irreligion, — atheistic now and now superstitious. There is no tyranny in God. Man is not a worm, the world a vale of tears. Tears enough there are, and long will be, — the morning mist of the human day. We can wipe off some of them, can rend a little the cloud of ignorance and want and crime, and let in the gladdening light of life. Nay, grief and sorrow are the world's medicine, salutary as such, and not excessive for the ill they come to cure. But if we are to make them our daily food, and call that angels' bread, surely it is a mistake which the world of matter cries out upon, and human nature itself forbids.

The development of religion in man is the condition of the highest happiness. Temperance, the piety of the body, prepares that for the corporeal joys, the humble in their place, the highest also in their own; wisdom, the piety of mind, justice, the piety of conscience, and love, the piety of the affections, — the love of God with all our varied faculties, — these furnish us the complete spiritual joy which is the birthright of each man. It is the function of religion to minister this happiness, which comes of self-denial for the sake of God.

The joy of religion must be proportionate to the purity of the feeling, the completeness of the idea, and the perfection of the act. When all are as they should be, what a joy is there for man! No disappointment will have lasting power over you, no sorrow destroy your peace of soul. Even the remembrance of sins past by will be assuaged by the experience you thereby have, and by the new life which has grown over them. The sorrows of the world will not seem as death-pangs, but the birth-pains of new and holier life. The sins of mankind, the dreadful wars, the tyrannies of the strong over the weak, or of the many over the few, will be seen to be only the stumbling of this last child of God learning to walk, to use his limbs and possess himself of the world which waits to be mastered by man's wisdom, ruled by man's justice, directed by man's love, as part of the great human worship of the Infinite God. The Past, the Present, and the Future will appear working together for you and all mankind, — all made from the perfect motive of God, for a perfect end and as a perfect means. You will know that the providence of the Great Author of us all is so complete and universal, that every wrong that man has suffered which he could not escape, every sorrow he has borne that could not be resisted nor passed by, every duty we have done, had a purpose to serve in the infinite housekeeping of the universe, and is warrant for so much eternal blessedness in the world to come. You look on the base and wicked men who seem as worms in the mire of civilization, often delighting to bite and devour one another, and you remark that these also are children of God; that He loves each of them, and will suffer no ancient Judas, nor modern kidnapper of men, to perish; that there is no child of perdition in all the family of God, but He will lead home his sinner and his saint, and such as are sick with the leprosy of their wickedness, "the murrain of beasts," bowed down and not able to lift themselves up, He will carry in his arms!

The joys of the flesh are finite, and soon run through. Objects of passion are the dolls wherewith we learn to use our higher faculties, and through all our life the joy of religion, the delight in God, becomes more and more. All that ancient saints ever had thereof, the peace which the world could not give, the rest unto the soul, which Jesus spoke of,—all these are for you and me, here and now and to-day, if we will. Our own souls hunger for it, God offers it to us all. "Come and take," says the Father of the world.

"While Thou, O my God, art my Help and Defender,
No cares can o'erwhelm me, no terrors appall;
The wiles and the snares of this world will but render
More lively my hope in my God and my All.
And when Thou demandest the life Thou hast given,
With joy will I answer Thy merciful call;
And quit Thee on earth, but to find Thee in heaven,
My Portion for ever, my God, and my All."

IX.

OF CONVENTIONAL AND NATURAL SACRAMENTS.

I WILL HAVE MERCY, AND NOT SACRIFICE. — Matt. ix. 13.

NOTHING in human experience is so lovely as the consciousness of God; nothing so tranquillizing, elevating, beautifying. See it on a merely personal scale in a man, imagine it on a national scale in a great people, — the natural development of religion into its various forms is one of the most beautiful phenomena of the world. But, alas! men too often love to meddle a little with nature; not simply to develop, complete, and perfect what begun spontaneously, but to alter after individual caprice, so that the universal, eternal, and unchangeable force is made to take the form of their personal, temporary, and shifting caprice.

Thus in old gardens you may see pines, yew-trees, and oaks clipped into fantastic and unnatural forms, looking like any thing but trees, not works of nature, but tricks of skill. A fan, a pyramid, or a peacock is taken for the model of a tree, and the poor oak or yew is teased into some approach to that alien type. But the tree is always stinted, ugly, and short-lived under such treatment. Pliant nature assumes the form thrust on her, and then dies. So the savage, who has not yet learned to clothe his body, colors it with gall-nuts or ochre, tattooes his fancy upon his skin, mutilates the members, and hangs "barbaric pearl and gold" where nature left no need nor room for ornament. Civilized nations cut off the manly beard, and scrimp and screw the female form, warping, twisting, distorting, and wasting the dear handiwork of God. So we see men, as those trees, walking in a vain show far astray from the guidance of nature, looking as if "nature's journeymen had made them, and not made them well, they imitate humanity so abominably."

But man is not content to meddle with his body. He must try his hand on the soul, warping and twisting, tattooing and mutilating that also, coloring it with ochre and gall-nuts of more astringent bite, and hanging barbaric pendants thereon. Attempts are made to interfere with the religious faculty, and give it a conventional direction; to make it take on certain forms of human caprice, not human nature. Some monstrous fancy is adopted for the model man, and then common men are clipped, and pruned, and headed down, or bent in, and twisted into a resemblance to that type. Nay, men are thought to be religious, just as they conform to the unnatural abomination. "God likes none but the clipped spirit," quoth the priest. "No natural man for Him. Away with your whole men. Mutilation is the test of piety!"

If some Apelles or Michael Angelo could paint the religious condition of mankind, and represent by form and color to the eye all this mutilation, twisting, distorting, and tattooing of the invisible spirit, what a sight it would be,—these dwarfs and cripples, one-legged, one-eyed, one-handed, and half-headed, half-hearted men! what a harlequin-show there would be! what motley on men's shoulders! what caps and bells on reverend heads, and tattooing which would leave Australia far behind! What strange jewels are the fashionable theological opinions of Christendom! Surely such liveries were never invented before! In that picture men would look as striped as the Pope's guard. And if some Adamitic men and women were also represented, walking about in this varicolored paradise of theology, arrayed in the natural costume of religion, "when unadorned, adorned the most," how different they would seem! Truly that gibbeting of theological folly in a picture would be a more instructive

"Last Judgment" than even the great Michael ever thought of painting.

In all forms of religion hitherto there has been noticed, not merely the natural difference between right and wrong, good and evil, but also an artificial and conventional difference between things sacred and things profane. Some things are deemed common and laical; others are called holy and clerical. This conventional distinction begins early, extends wide, and will outlast you and me a great many years. Thus, what is now-a-days said under oath is officially thought a holy and clerical sort of truth; while what is said without oath, though equally correspondent with facts, is officially considered only a common and laical sort of truth. Some persons, as atheists and such as deny the immortality of the soul, are thought incapable of this clerical truth, and so not allowed to swear, or otherwise testify, in court.

In earlier ages of the world, and even now, this conventional distinction between laical and clerical, sacred and profane, applies to places, as groves, hill-tops, temples, and the like; to times, as new moons with one, full moons with another, Friday with the Turks, Saturday with the Jews, Sunday with the Christians; to things, as statues of saints and deities, the tools of public worship; to persons, and some are set apart from mankind as "the Lord's lot," and deemed holy; to actions, some of which are reckoned pleasing to God, not because they are naturally right, good, beautiful, or useful, but only as conventionally sacred; and to opinions, which for the same reason were pronounced revealed, and so holy and clerical.

The laws of the land, for a long time, observed this artificial distinction. Thus a blow struck in a church or temple brought a severer punishment on the offender than if given elsewhere. Even now in Boston it is lawful to "gamble," except on Saturday night and Sunday; and all common work on that day is penal. Formerly it was legally thought worse to steal church property than any other. To rob a beggar was a small thing; it was a great sin to steal from a meeting-house. To take a whole loaf from a baker's basket was a trifle, but to steal the consecrated wafer from the church-box brought the offender to the stake. Says Charlemagne, "Less mercy is to be shown to men who rob and steal from the church, than to common thieves." In New England, until lately, for striking a clergyman a man was punished twice as much as for striking a layman; not because a bishop is to be blameless, "no striker," and so less likely, and less able, to retaliate, but because he is a holy person. Not long ago there was no penalty in this State for disturbing a moral meeting, but a severe one for disturbing a religious meeting. Opinions connected with religion have had laws to defend them. It was once a capital crime to deny the Trinity, or the inspiration of the Song of Solomon, while a man might deny all the axioms of Euclid, all the conclusions of science, and the law let him alone. It seems that these artificial and foreign "sacred things" cannot take care of themselves so well as the indigenous "things of this world." Religion was thought to extend to certain places, times, things, persons, actions, and opinions, and the law gave them a peculiar protection; but religion was not thought to extend much further. So the law stopped there. About three hundred years ago, an Italian sculptor was burned alive, in Spain, for breaking a statue he had himself made, being angry because the customer would not pay the price for it. The statue was a graven image of the Virgin Mary. Had it been the image of his own mother, he might have ground it to powder if he liked, or he might have beat his own living wife, and had no fault found with him.

There was a deeper reason for this capricious distinction than we sometimes think. Religion ought to be the ruler in all the affairs of men; but before we come to the absolute religion, which will one day do this, men begin with certain particular things which they claim as divine. Religion is to have eminent domain over them, while over other things it has a joint jurisdiction with "the world." It was well that their idea of religion went as far as it did. In the Middle Ages, if a fugitive slave fled to the Catholic Church and got to the altar, his masters had no legal right to touch him but by permission of the priest. The bishop interfered, made terms with the masters, and then delivered him up or not as they promised well or ill. The spirit of religion was supposed to rule in the church, and to protect the outcast. Men counselled wiser than they knew. It was a good thing that religion, such a rude notion as men had of it, prevailed in that narrow spot. When the tyrant would not respect God in all space, it was well that he should tremble before the sanctuary of a stone altar in a meeting-house. He would not respect a man, let him learn by beginning with a priest. If a murderer or a traitor took refuge in the heathen temples, nobody could drive him away or disturb him, for only God had jurisdiction in the holy place. So was it with the Hebrew cities of refuge: without, the atrocity of the world prevailed; within was the humanity of religion. The great begins small.

I believe there is no nation acquainted with fire but makes this artificial distinction. It is the first feeble attempt of the religious faculty to assume power in the outward world; in due time it will extend its jurisdiction over all time and space, over all things, all thoughts, all men, all deeds.

It is curious to see how this faculty goes on enlarging its territory: one day religion watches over the beginning of human life; then over its end; next over its most eminent events, such as marriage, or the entrance upon an office, making a will, or giving testimony, all of which are connected with some act of religion. You see what it all points towards, — a coördination of all human faculties with the religious. Here is the great forest of human life, — a tangled brushwood, full of wild appetites and prowling calculations, — to be cleared up. Religion hews down a few trees, burns over a little spot, puts in a few choice seeds, and scares off therefrom the wild beasts of appetite, the cunning beasts of calculation. This is only the beginning of clearing up the whole forest. What pains the savage in New England took with his little patch of artichokes, beans, pumpkins, and corn! With his rude tools, how poorly he dug and watered it, and for what a stingy harvest! He often chose the worst spot, he knew no better, and got but small return, not knowing how to make bread out of the ground. His garden was a very little patch in the woods, and looked ridiculous beside the square leagues of wild woodland, a howling wilderness, that reached from the Kennebec to the Mississippi. But it was the first step towards cultivating the whole continent. So is it with the sacred things of the Hottentot and the Hebrew, the Caffre and the Christian. Let us not despise the rude commencement of great things.

To simplify the matter, let us consider only the Actions pronounced religious. Certain deeds are selected and declared sacred, not on account of their natural usefulness or beauty, but by some caprice. These are declared the "ordinances of religion," the "sacraments" thereof, — things which represent and express religion, — which it is pronounced religious to do, and irreligious not to do. If there is a national form of religion, then there is a national sacrament, established by authority; so a social sacrament for society, established, like the "law of honor,' by custom, the tacit consent of society. Thus is there a domestic sacrament for the family, and a personal ordinance of religion for the individual man. Accordingly, these conventional actions come to be thought the exclusive expression of religion, and therefore pleasing to God; they are not thought educational, means of growth, but final, the essential substance of religion. Some man is appointed to look after the performance of these actions, and it is thought desirable to get the greatest possible number of persons to participate in them; and he that turns many to these conventional sacraments is thought a great servant of God.

Look at some of these artificial sacraments. The Indians of New England left tobacco or the fat of the deer on the rocks, an offering to the Great Spirit. With them it was an "ordinance of religion," and stood for an act of piety and morality both. The clerical Powwows recommended the action to the people. What a time they had of it, those red savages here in the woods! It was thought impious not to perform the ritual act; but their religion did not forbid its votary to lie, to steal, to torture his foe with all conceivable cruelty.

Two thousand years ago our Teutonic fathers in the North of Europe worshipped a goddess named Hertha. They had a forest consecrated to her on an island; therein was a sacred image of her, which was, now and then, carried about the country, on a carriage drawn by cows, — the statue covered with cloth and hid from sight. War was suspended wherever the chariot came, and weapons of iron put out of sight. It was then washed in a certain lake; and, to shroud the whole in grim mystery, the priests who had performed the ritual act were drowned in the same lake. This was the great national sacrament of the people. It was wholly artificial, neither useful nor beautiful. The statue was an idol of wood; the cows who drew it were no better than other cows. There was nothing holy in the image, the grove, or the ceremony; the drowning of the priests was a cruel butchery.

As a sacrament, the New-Hollander cuts off the last joint of the little finger of his son's left hand; it is an offering to God, who has made the finger a joint too long for piety.

The Hebrews had their outward ordinances of religion, — two personal sacraments of universal obligation, binding on each man, — circumcision, and rest on the Sabbath. There were two more national sacraments, binding on the nation, — the formal worship of Jehovah, in Jerusalem, at stated times, and by a prescribed ritual; and the celebration of the three national festivals. These were the sacraments of religion. To eat the paschal lamb was a "virtue," to taste swine's flesh a "sin." It was a capital crime to heal a sick man on Saturday. All these were artificial. Circumcision was a bad thing in itself, and gets its appropriate hit in the New Testament. Rest on the seventh day was no better than on the first; no better than work on the second; and worship in Jerusalem, at that time, and by that form, no better than worship at Jericho, by another form, and at a different time. The three feasts were no better than the festivals of Easter and of Yule. Yet those things were made the tests of piety and of morality. Not to attend to them was deemed impiety against God. The Hebrew priest took great pains to interest the people in all this matter, to have the sacrifices offered, circumcision performed, the Sabbath and the feasts kept. He who hobbled the most in this lame way, and on these artificial crutches, was thought the greatest priest. What a reputation did puritanical Nehemiah get by his zeal in these trifles! But when Jesus of Nazareth came, his heart full of natural religion, he made way with most of these ordinances.

Amongst Christians in general there is one specific sacramental opinion, — that Jesus of Nazareth is the only Son of God. The opinion itself is of no value. You may admit all the excellence of Jesus, and copy it all, and yet never have the opinion. I do not find that the historical person, Jesus, had any such opinion at all. Nay, the opinion is an evil, for it leads men to take this noble man and prostrate their mind and conscience before his words; just as much as Jesus is elevated above the human is man sunk below it. But for ages, in the Church, this has been thought the one thing needful to make a man a Christian, to make him "pious" and acceptable to God, — the great internal ordinance and subjective sacrament of religion.

In the Catholic Church there is another sacramental opinion distinctive of that Christian sect, — the belief that the Roman Church is divine and infallible. The Protestants have also their distinctive, sacramental opinion, — that the Scriptures are divine and infallible.

The consistent Catholic tells you there is no salvation without the belief of his sacramental doctrine; consistent Protestants claim the same value for their Shibboleth. So a man is to be "saved," and "reconciled with God" by faith; a general faith, — the belief that Jesus of Nazareth is the only Son of God; a particular faith, — the belief in the divine and infallible Church, or the divine and infallible Scriptures.

Then the Catholics have certain additional outward sacraments, which are subsidiary, and called the "ordinances of religion," — such as baptism, confirmation, penance, extreme unction, and the like. The Protestants have likewise their additional outward sacraments subsidiary to the other, and which are their "ordinances of religion," — such as bodily presence at church, which is enjoined upon all, and is the great external artificial sacrament of the Protestants; baptism for a few; communion for a selecter few; and belief in all the doctrines of the special sect, — an internal sacrament which is actually enjoyed by only the smallest portion of the selectest few.

Now all of these are purely artificial sacraments. They are not good in themselves. Each of them has once had an educational value for mankind; some of them still have, to a portion of mankind. But they are not valued for their tendency to promote natural piety and natural morality, only as things good in themselves; not as means to the grace and helps to the glory of religion, but as religion itself. Ecclesiastically it is thought just as meritorious a thing to attend the preaching of a dull, ignorant, stupid fellow, who has nothing to teach and teaches it, as to listen to the eloquent piety of a Fenelon, Taylor, or Buckminster, or to the beautiful philanthropy of St. Roch, Oberlin, or Channing. Bodily presence in the church being the sacrament, it is of small consequence what bulk of dulness presses the pulpit while the sacrament goes on. There is a "real presence," if naught else be real. An indifferent man baptized with water is thought a much better "Christian" than a man full of piety and morality but without the elemental sprinkling.

If you ask a New England Powwow for proof of the religious character of a red man, he would have cited the offering of tobacco to the Great Spirit; a Teutonic priest would refer to the reverence of his countrymen for the ceremony just spoken of; a New-Hollander would dwell on the devotion of his neighbors, and show the little fingers cut off; a Hebrew would expatiate on the sacrament of circumcision, of Sabbath-keeping, of attendance upon the formal sacrifice at Jerusalem, the observance of the three feasts, and abstinence from swine's flesh; the Christian dwells on his distinctive sacramental opinion, that Jesus is the Son of Jehovah. Ask the Catholic priests for proof that Joseph is a Christian, they will tell you, "He believes in the divine and infallible Roman Church, and receives its sacraments;" ask the Protestant priests for a proof of their brother's piety, they will refer to his belief in the divine and infallible Scriptures, to his attendance at church, his baptism with water, his communion in wine and bread; and, if he is an eminent "saint," to his belief in all the technical opinions of his sect. True, they may all add other things which belong to real religion, but you will find that these artificial sacraments are the things relied on as proofs of religion, of Christianity, the signs of acceptableness with God, and of eternal bliss. The others are only "of works,"— these "of faith;" one of "natural religion," the next of "revealed religion;" morality is provisional, and the sacraments a finality.

Accordingly, great pains are taken to bring men to these results. If a minister does this to large numbers, he is called "an eminent servant of the

Lord," — that is, a great circumciser, a great sprinkler or plunger. Francis Xavier "converted" thousands of men to what he called Christianity; they took the sacrament of belief, and of baptism, — in due time the others; and Francis was made a saint. But it does not appear that he made them any better men, better sons, brothers, husbands, fathers, better neighbors and friends. He only brought them to the artificial sacrament. It is often the ambition of a Protestant minister to extend the jurisdiction of his artificial sacraments, to bring men to baptism and communion, not to industry, temperance, and bodily well-being; not to wisdom, justice, friendship, and philanthropy; not to an absolute love of God, a joyous, absolute faith in the Dear Mother of us all.

Let us do no injustice to those poor, leaky vessels of worship which we have borrowed from the Egyptians to whom we were once in bondage. They all have had their use. Man sets up his mythologies and his sacraments to suit his condition of soul at the time. You cannot name a ceremony connected with religion, howsoever absurd or wicked it may appear, but once it came out of the soul of some man who needed it; and it helped him at the time. The tobacco offered to Hobomock at Narragansett, the procession of Hertha in Pannonia, the ritual mutilation in New Holland, in Judea, or, still worse, in Phrygia and Crete, all once had their meaning. Nay, human sacrifice was once the highest act of worship which some dark-minded savage could comprehend, and in good faith the victim was made ready at Mexico or at Moriah. But the best of them are only educational, not final; and the sooner we can outgrow those childish things, the better.

Men often mock at such things. What mouths Arnobius and Augustine made at the heathen superstitions, taking their cue from pagan Lucian of Samosata, the prince of scoffers; they have given the face of Christendom an anti-Pagan twist which it keeps to this day. How Voltaire and his accomplished coadjutors repeated the mock, at the cost of the followers of Augustine and Arnobius! This is hardly wise, and not reverent. Those things are to be regarded as the work of children, who have their snow-houses in winter, their earth-houses in summer, their games and plays, — trifles to us, but serious things to the little folk; of great service in the education of the eye and hand, — nay, of the understanding itself. How the little boy cries because he cannot spin his top like the older brothers! He learns to spin it, and is delighted with its snoring hum; learning skill by that, he by and by goes on to higher acts of boyish life. So is it with these artificial sacraments. Xavier brought a new top to the men of India; Charlemagne slew the Saxons who would not accept his, — as rude boys force the little ones from old to new sports.

It is no evil to have some things of the sort; no more than it is for a boy to ride a stick before he can mount a horse; or for a little girl to fill her arms with a Nuremberg baby before she can manage human children. Only the evil is, that these things are thought the real and natural sacrament of religion; and so the end thereof is lost in the means. That often happens, and is fatal to religious growth. If the boy become a man, still kept to his wooden stick, counting it a real horse, better than all the trotters and pacers in Connecticut, if he had stables for sticks in place of steeds, and men to groom and tend his wooden hobby; if the girl, become a woman now, still hugged her doll from Nuremberg, making believe it was a child, — loved it better than sons and daughters, and left her own baby to dandle a lump of wood, counting a child only provisional, and the doll a finality, — then we should see the same error that was committed by Xavier and others, and repeated by clergymen and whole troops of Christians. I have seen assemblies of Christian divines, excellent and self-denying men, in earnest session and grave debate, who seemed to me only venerable boys riding cockhorse on their grandam's crutch.

The general Christian belief, that Jesus was the Son of God, is now no spiritual sacrament; the specific belief of the Catholic or Protestant at this day is worth no more. Nay, all these stand in the way of the human race, and hinder our march. So the outward Christian sacraments — baptism, confirmation, communion, confession, penance, and the rest — seem to me only stones of stumbling in the way of mankind; they are as far from the real ordinances of religion as dandling a doll is from the mother's holy duty.

The natural and real ordinance of religion is in general a manly life, all the man's faculties of body and spirit developed or developing in their natural and harmonious way, the body ruled by the spirit, its instincts all in their places, the mind active, the conscience, the affections, the soul, all at work in their natural way. Religion is the sacrament of religion; itself its ordinance. Piety and goodness are its substance, and all normal life its form. The love of God and the love of man, with all that belongs thereto, worship with every limb of the body, every faculty of the spirit, every power we possess over matter or men, — that is the sacramental substance of religion; a life obedient to the love of God and of man, — that is the sacramental form of religion. All else is means, provisional; this the end, a finality. Thus my business, my daily work with the hand, if an honest and manly work, is the ordinance of religion to my body; seeking and expressing truth and beauty is the ordinance of religion to my mind; doing justice to all about me is the moral ordinance of religion; loving men is the natural sacrament of the affections; holiness is the natural ordinance of the soul. Putting all together, — my internal consciousness of piety and goodness, my outward life which represents that, is the great natural sacrament, the one compendious and universal ordinance. Then my religion is not one thing, and my life another; the two are one. Thus religion is the sacrament of religion, morality the test of piety.

If you believe God limited to one spot, then that is counted specifically holy; and your religion draws or drives you thither. If you believe that religion demands only certain particular things, they will be thought sacramental, and the doing thereof the proof of religion. But when you know that God is infinite, is everywhere, then all space is holy ground; all days are holy time; all truth is God's word; all persons are subjects of religious duty, invested with unalienable religious rights, and claiming respect and love as fellow-children of the same dear God. Then, too, all work becomes sacred and venerable; common life, your highest or your humblest toil, is your element of daily communion with men, as your act of prayer is your communion with the Infinite God.

This is the history of all artificial sacraments. A man rises with more than the ordinary amount of religion; by the accident of his personal character, or by some circumstance or event in his history, he does some particular thing as an act of religion. To him it is such, and represents his feeling of penitence, or resolution, or gratitude, or faith in God. Other men wish to be as religious as he, and do the same thing, hoping to get thereby the same amount of religion. By and by the deed itself is mistaken for religion, repeated again and again. The feeling which first prompted it is all gone, the act becomes merely mechanical, and thus of no value.

Thousands of years ago some man of wicked ways resolved to break from them and start anew, converted by some saint. He calls the neighbors together at the side of the Euphrates, the Jordan, or the Nile, — elements which he deems divine, — and plunges in: "Thus I will wipe off all ancient sin," says he; "by this act I pledge myself to a new life, — this holy element is witness to my vow; let the saints bear record!" The penitence is real, the resolution is real, the act of self-baptism means something. By and by other penitent men do the same, from the same motive, struck by his example. Crowds look on from curiosity; a few idly imitate the form; then many from fashion. Soon it is all ceremony, and means nothing. It is the property of the priest; it is cherished still, and stands in place of religion. The single, momentary dispensation of water is thought of more religious importance than the daily dispensation of righteousness. Men go leagues long on pilgrimage, — to dip them in the sacred stream, and return washed, but not clean; baptized, but neither beautiful nor blameless. At length it is thought that baptism, the poor, outward act, atones for a life of conscious sin. Imperial Constantine, hypocritical and murderous, mourning that the Church will not twice baptize, is converted, but cunningly postpones his plunge till old age, that he may sin his fill, then dip and die clean and new.

So is it with all artificial forms. When they become antiquated, the attempt to revive them, to put new life therein, is always useless and unnatural; it is only a show, too often a cheat. At this day the routine of form is valued most by those who care only for the form, and tread the substance underneath their feet. Put the wig of dead men's hair on your bald head, it is only a barber's cap, not nature's graceful covering, and underneath, the hypocritic head lies bald and bare. Put it on your head if you will, but do not insist that little children and fair-haired maids shall shear off the the locks of nature, and hide their heads beneath your deceitful handiwork. The boy is grown up to manhood, he rides real horses; nay, owns, tames, and rears them for himself. How idle to ask him to mount again his hobby, or to ride cockhorse on his grandam's crutch once more! You may galvanize the corpse into momentary and convulsive action, not into life. You may baptize men by the thousand, plunging them in the Jordan and Euphrates, Indus, Ganges, and Irrawaddy, if you will, surpassing even Ignatius and Francis Xavier. Nay, such is the perfection of the arts, that, with steam and Cochituate to serve you, you might sprinkle men in battalions, yea, whole regiments at a dash. What boots it all? A drop of piety is worth all the Jordan, Euphrates, Indus, Ganges, Irrawaddy, — worth all the oceans which the good God ever made.

Men love dramatic scenes. Imagine, then, a troop of men — slave-traders, kidnappers, and their crew — come up for judgment at the throne of Christ. "Behold your evil deeds!" cries Jesus in their ears. "Dear Lord," say they, "speak not of that; we were all baptized, in manhood or in infancy, gave bodily presence at a church, enrolled our names among the priest's elect, believed the whole creed, and took the sacrament in every form. What wouldst thou more, dear Christ? Dost thou ask provisional morality of us? Are not these things ultimate, the finality of salvation?"

I always look with pain on any effort to put the piety of our times into the artificial sacraments of another and a ruder age. It is often attempted, sometimes with pure and holy feelings, with great self-denial; but it is always worthless. The new wine of religion must be put into new bottles. See what improvements are yearly made in science, in agriculture, weaving, ship-building, in medicine, in every art. Shall there be none in religion, none in the application of its great sentiments to daily life? Shall we improve only in our ploughs, not also in the forms of piety?

At this day great pains are taken to put religion into artificial sacraments, which, alas! have no connection with a manly life. I do not know of a score of ministers devoting their time and talents solely to the advancement of natural piety and natural morality. I know of hundreds who take continual pains to promote those artificial sacraments,—earnest, devout, and self-denying men. Why is this so? It is because they think the ceremony is religion; not religion's accidental furniture, but religion itself. It is painful to see such an amount of manly and earnest effort, of toil and self-denial and prayer, devoted to an end so little worth. The result is very painful, more so than the process itself.

We call ourselves a Christian people, a religious nation. Why? Are we a religious people because the heart of the nation is turned towards God and his holy law? The most prominent churches just now have practically told us, that there is no law of God above the statute politicians write on parchment in the Capitol; that Congress is higher than the Almighty, the President a finality; and that God must hide his head behind the Compromise! Is it because the highest talent of the nation, its ablest zeal, its stoutest heroism, is religious in its motive, religious in its aim, religious in its means, religious in its end? Nobody pretends that. A respectable man would be thought crazy, and called a "fanatic," who should care much for religion in any of its higher forms. Self-denial for popularity and for money or office,—that is common; it abounds in every street. Self-denial for religion,—is that so common? Are we called Christians because we value the character of Jesus of Nazareth, and wish to be like him? Is it the ambition of calculating fathers, that their sons be closely like the friend of publicans and sinners? Nay, is it the ambition of reverend and most Christian clergymen to be like him? — I mean, to think with the freedom he thought withal; to be just with such severe and beauteous righteousness; to love with such affection, — so strong, yet so tender, so beautiful, so wide, so womanly and deep? Is it to have faith in God like his absolute trust; a faith in God's person and his function too; a faith in truth, in justice, in holiness, and love; a faith in God as Cause and Providence, in man as the effect and child of God? Is it the end of laymen and clergymen to produce such a religion, — to build up and multiply Christians of that manly sort?

Compliance with forms is made the test of piety, its indispensable condition. These forms are commonly twofold: liturgical, — compliance with the ritual; dogmatical, — compliance with the creed. It is not shown that the rite has a universal, natural connection with piety; only that it was once historically connected with a pious man. Nobody thinks that circumcision, baptism, or taking the Lord's supper, has a natural and indispensable connection with piety; only it is maintained that these things have been practised by pious men, and so are imposed on others by their authority. It is not shown that the creed has its foundation in the nature of man, still less in the nature of God; only that it rested once in the consciousness of some pious man, and has also been imposed on us by authority. So, it is not shown that these tests have any natural connection with religion; only that they once had an historical connection; and that, of course, was either temporary, naturally ending with the stage of civilization which it belonged to, or even personal, peculiar to the man it begun with.

Yet it is remarkable how much those temporary or mere personal expedients are set up as indispensable conditions and exclusive tests of piety. The Catholic Church, on the whole, is an excellent institution; Christendom could no more do without it, than Europe dispense with monarchies; but the steadfast Catholic must say, "Out of the Church there is no piety, no religion beyond the Church's ritual and creed." The Protestant churches are, on the whole, an excellent institution; Christendom could no more dispense with them, than New England with her almshouses and jails; but the steadfast Protestant will say, "There can be no piety without accepting the Bible as the word of God, no saving religion without faith in the letter of Scripture." Not only has the Catholic his Shibboleth, and the Protestant his, but each sect its own. The Calvinist says, "There is no piety without a belief in the Trinity." The Unitarians say, "There is no piety without a belief in the miracles of the New Testament." The Jews require a knowledge of Moses; Mahometans, a reverence for their prophet; and Christians, in general, agree there is no "saving piety" without submissive reverence to Christ. The late Dr. Arnold, a most enlightened and religious man, declared that he had no knowledge of God except as manifested through Jesus Christ. Yet all the wide world over, everywhere, men know of God and worship Him,—the savage fearing, while the enlightened learns to love.

Since compliance with the ritual and the creed is made the sole and exclusive test of piety, religious teachers aim to produce this compliance in both kinds, and succeeding therein, are satisfied that piety dwells in their disciples' heart. But the ritual compliance may be purely artificial; not something which grows out of the man, but sticks on. The compliance with the doctrine may be apparent, and not real at all. The word belief is taken in a good many senses. It does not always mean a total experience of the doctrine, a realizing sense thereof; not always an intellectual conviction. They often are the best believers of the creed who have the least experience in the love of God, but little intellect, and have made no investigation of the matter credited. Belief often means only that the believer does not openly reject the doctrine he is said to hold. So the thing thus believed is not always a new branch growing out of the old bole; nor is it a foreign scion grafted in, and living out of the old stock, as much at home as if a native there, and bearing fruit after its better kind; it is merely stuck into the bark of the old tree,—nay, often not even that, but only lodged in the branches, — fruitless, leafless, lifeless, and dry as a stick, — a deformity, and without use.

In this way it comes to pass that compliance with the rite, and belief in a doctrine, which in some men were the result of a long life of piety and hard struggle, actually mean nothing at all. So that the ritual and the creed have no more effect in promoting the "convert's" piety and morality, than would belief in the multiplication-table and the habit of saying it over. You are surprised that the doctrines of Christ do not affect the Christian, and ceremonies which once revolutionized the heart they were born in, now leave the worshipper as cold as the stone beneath his knee. Be not astonished at the result. The marble does not feel the commandments which are graven there; the communion chalice never tastes the consecrated wine. The marble and metal are only mechanical in their action; it was not meant that they should taste or feel.

Then piety, as a sentiment, is taken as the whole of religion; its end is in itself. The tests, liturgical or dogmatic, show that piety is in the man; all he has next to do is to increase the quantity. The proof of that increase is a greatening of love for the form and for the doctrine; the habit of dawdling about the one and talking about the other. The sentiment of religion is allowed to continue a sentiment, and nothing more; soon it becomes less, a sentimentalism, a sickly sentiment which will never beget a deed.

It is a good thing to get up pious feeling; there is no danger we shall have too much of that. But the feeling should lead to a thought, the thought to a deed, else it is of small value; at any rate, it does not do all of its work for the individual, and nothing for any one beside. This religious sentimentality is called Mysticism or Pietism, in the bad sense of those two words. In most of the churches which have a serious purpose, and are not content with the mere routine of office, it is a part of the pastor's aim to produce piety, the love of God. That is right, for piety, in its wide sense, is the foundation of all manly excellence. But in general they seem to know only these liturgical and dogmatic tests of piety; hence they aim to have piety put in that conventional form, and reject with scorn all other and natural modes of expressing love to God.

It is a good thing to aim to produce piety, a great good: an evil, to limit in this way; a great evil, not to leave it free to take its natural form; a very great evil, to keep it indoors so long, that it becomes sick and good for nothing, not daring to go out at all.

It is remarkable how often ecclesiastical men make this mistake. They judge a man to be religious or otherwise, solely by this test. You hear strict ministers speak of a layman as an "amiable man," but "not pious." They do not know that amiableness is one form of natural piety, and that the more piety a man gets, the more amiable he becomes. The piety which they know has no connection with honesty, none with friendship, none with philanthropy; its only relations are with the ritual and creed. When the late John Quincy Adams died, his piety was one topic of commendation in most of the many sermons preached in memory of the man. What was the proof or sign of that piety? Scarcely any one found it in his integrity, which had not failed for many a year; or his faithful attendance on his political duty; or his unflinching love of liberty, and the noble war the aged champion fought for the unalienable rights of man. No! They found the test in the fact that he was a member of a church; that he went to meeting, and was more decorous than most men while there; that he daily read the Bible, and repeated each night a simple and beautiful little prayer, which mothers teach their babes of grace. No "regular minister," I think, found the proof of his piety in his zeal for man's welfare, in the cleanness of his life, and hands which never took a bribe. One, I remember, found a sign of that piety in the fact, that he never covered his reverend head till fairly out of church!

You remember the Orthodox judgment on Dr. Channing. Soon after his death, it was declared in a leading Trinitarian journal of America, that without doubt he had gone to the place of torment, to expiate the sin of denying the Deity of Christ. All the noble life of that great and good and loving man was not thought equal to the formal belief, that the Jesus of the Gospels is the Jehovah of the Psalms.

After ecclesiastical men produce their piety, they do not aim to set it to do the natural work of mankind. Morality is not thought to be the proof of piety, nor even the sign of it. They dam up the stream of human nature till they have got a sufficient head of piety, and then, instead of setting it to turn the useful mill of life, or even drawing it off to water the world's dry grounds, they let the waters run over the dam, promoting nothing but sectarian froth and noise; or, if it be allowed to turn the wheels, it must not grind sound corn for human bread, but chiefly rattle the clapper of the theologic mill.

The most serious sects in America now and then have a revival. The aim is to produce pietism; but commonly you do not find the subjects of a revival more disposed to morality after that than before; it is but seldom they are better sons or more loving lovers, partners or parents more faithful than before. It is only the ritual and the creed which they love the better. Intelligent men of the serious sects will tell you, such revivals do more harm than good, because the feelings are excited unnaturally, and then not directed to their appropriate, useful work.

The most important actual business of the clergy is, first, to keep up the present amount of morality. All sects agree in that work, and do a service by the attempt. For there are always sluggish men, slumberers, who need to be awaked, loiterers, who must be called out to, and hurried forward. Next, it is to produce piety, try it by these tests, and put it into these forms. All sects likewise agree in that, and therein they do good, and a great good. But after the piety is produced, it is not wholly natural piety, nor do they aim to apply it to the natural work thereof.

Such is the most important business of the pulpit, — almost its only business. Hence unpopular vices, vices below the average virtue of society, get abundantly preached at. And popular virtues, virtues up to the average of society, get abundantly praised. But popular vices go unwhipped, and unpopular virtues all unhonored pass the pulpit by. The great Dagon of the popular idolatry stands there in the market-place, to receive the servile and corrupting homage of the crowd, dashing the little ones to ruin at his feet; the popular priest is busy with his Philistine pietism, and never tells the people that it is an idol, and not God, which they adore. It is not his function to do that. Hence a man of more than the average excellence, more than the average wisdom, justice, philanthropy, or faith in God, and resolutely bent on promoting piety and morality in all their forms, is thought out of place in a sectarian pulpit; and is just as much out of place there, as a Unitarian would be in a Trinitarian pulpit, or a Calvinist in a Unitarian, — as much so as a weaver of broadcloth would be in a mill for making ribbons or gauze.

Hence, too, it comes to pass, that it is not thought fit to attack popular errors in the pulpit, nor speak of wide spread public sins; not even to expose the fault of your own denomination to itself. The sins of Unitarians may be aimed at only from Trinitarian pulpits. It is not lawful for a sect to be instructed by a friend. The sins of commerce must not be rebuked in a trading town. In time of war we must not plead for peace. The sins of politics the minister must never touch. Why not? Because they are "actual sins of the times," and his kingdom "is not of this world." Decorous ministers are ordained and appointed to apologize for respectable iniquity, and to eulogize every wicked but popular, great man. So long as the public sepulchres may not be cleansed, there must be priestly Pharisees to wash their outside white. The Northern priest is paid to consecrate the tyranny of capital, as the Southern to consecrate the despotism of the master over his negro slave. Men say you must not touch the actual sins of the times in a pulpit, — it would hurt men's feelings; and they must not be disquieted from their decorous, their solemn, their accustomed sleep. "You must preach the Gospel, young fanatic," quoth the world. And that means preaching the common doctrines so as to convict no man's conscience of any actual sin; then press out a little pietism, and decant it off into the old leathern bottles of the Church.

The late Mr. Polk affords a melancholy example of the effect of this mode of proceeding. On his death-bed, when a man ought to have nothing to do but to die, the poor man remembers that he has "not been baptized," wishes to know if there is any "hope" for him, receives the dispensation of water in the usual form, and is thought to die "a Christian!" What a sad sign of the state of religion amongst us! To him or to his advisers it did not seem to occur, that, if we live right, it is of small consequence how we die; that a life full of duties is the real baptism in the name of man and God, and the sign of the Holy Spirit. The churches never taught him so. But snivelling at the end is not a Christian and a manly death.

The effect of getting up the feeling of piety, and stopping with that, is like the effect of reading novels and nothing else. Thereby the feelings of benevolence, of piety, of hope, of joy, are excited, but lead to no acts; the character becomes enervated, the mind feeble, the conscience inert, the will impotent; the heart, long wont to weep at the novelist's unreal woes, at sorrows in silk and fine linen, is harder than Pharaoh's when a dirty Irish girl asks for a loaf in the name of God, or when a sable mother begs money wherewith to save her daughter from the seraglios of New Orleans. Self-denial for the sake of noble enterprise is quite impossible to such. All the great feelings naturally lead to commensurate deeds; to excite the feeling and leave undone the deed, is baneful in the extreme.

I do not say novels are not good reading and profitable; they are, just so far as they stimulate the intellect, the conscience, the affections, the soul, to healthful action, and set the man to work; but just so far as they make you content with mere feeling, and constrain the feeling to be nothing but feeling, they are pernicious. Such reading is mental dissipation. To excite the devotional feelings, to produce a great love of God, and not allow that to become work, is likewise dissipation, all the more pernicious, — dissipation of the conscience, of the soul. I do not say it comes in the name of self-indulgence, as the other; it is often begun in the name of self-denial, and achieved at great cost of self-denial too.

Profligacy of the religious sentiment, voluptuousness with God, is the most dangerous of luxuries. Novel-reading, after the fashion hinted at, is highly dangerous. How many youths and maidens are seriously hurt thereby! But as far as I can judge, in all Christendom there are more that suffer from this spiritual dissoluteness. I speak less to censure than to warn. I hate to see a man uncharitable, dishonest, selfish, mean, and sly, — "for ever standing on his guard and watching" unto fraud. I am sorry to hear of a woman given up to self-indulgence, accomplished, but without the highest grace, — womanly good works, — luxurious, indolent, "born to consume the corn," — that is bad enough. But when I learn that this hard man is a class leader, and has "the gift of prayer," is a famous hand at a conference, the builder of churches, a great defender of ecclesiastical doctrines and devotional forms, that he cries out upon every heresy, banning men in the name of God; when I hear that this luxurious woman delights in mystic devotion, and has a wantonness of prayer, — it makes me far more sad; and there is then no hope! The kidnapper at his court is a loathly thing; but the same kidnapper at his "communion!" — great God! and has thy Church become so low! Let us turn off our eyes and look away.

Hence it comes to pass, that much of all this ecclesiastic pains to produce piety is abortive; it ends in sickness and routine. Men who have the reputation of piety in a vulgar sense are the last men you would look to for any great good work. They will not oppose slavery and war and lust of land, — national sins that are popular; nor intemperance and excessive love of gold, — popular, personal, and social sins. They would not promote the public education of the people, and care not to raise woman to her natural equality with man. "It is no part of piety to do such things," say they; "we are not under the covenant of works, but of grace only. What care we for painful personal righteousness, which profiteth little, when only the imputed can save us, and that so swiftly!"

Nay, they hinder all these great works. The bitterest opposition to the elevation of all men is made in the name of devotion; so is the defence of slavery and war, and the flat degradation of woman. Here is a church, which at a public meeting solemnly instructs its minister elect not to preach on politics, or on the subjects of reform. They want him to "preach piety," "nothing but piety," "evangelical piety;" not a weekday piety but a Sabbath piety, which is up and at church once in seven days, — keeps her pew of a Sunday, but her bed all the week, — ghastly, lean, dyspeptic, coughing, bowed together, and in nowise able to lift up herself.

Hence "piety" gets a bad reputation amongst philanthropists, as it serves to hinder the development of humanity. Even amongst men of business a reputation for "piety" would make a new comer distrusted; the money-lender would look more carefully to his collateral security.

At Blenheim and at Windsor you will find clipped yew-trees, cut into the shape of hearts and diamonds, nay, of lions and eagles, looking like any thing but trees. So in Boston, in all New England, everywhere in Christendom, you find clipped men, their piety cut into various artificial forms, looking like any thing but men. The saints of the popular theology, what are they good for? For belief and routine, — for all of religion save only real piety and morality.

Persons of this stamp continually disappoint us. You expect manly work, and cannot get it done. Did you ever see little children play "Money?" They clasp their hands together and strike them gently on their knee; the elastic air compressed by this motion sounds like the jingling of small silver coin. You open the hand: there is nothing in it, — not small money enough to buy a last year's walnut or a blueberry. It was only the jingle of the money, — all of money but the money's worth. So is this unnatural form of piety; it has the jingle of godliness, and seems just as good as real piety, until you come to spend it; then it is good for nothing, — it will not pass anywhere amongst active men. A handful of it comes to nothing. Alas me! the children play at "Money," and call it sport; men grown play with a similar delusion, and call it the worship of God.

Now there is much of this false piety in the world, produced by this false notion, that there are only these two tests of piety. It leads to a great deal of mischief. Men are deceived who look to you for work; you yourself are deceived in hoping for peace, beauty, comfort, and gladness, from such a deception.

"So, floating down a languid stream,
The lily-leaves oft lilies seem,
Reflecting back the whitened beam
Of morning's slanting sun; —
But as I near and nearer came,
I missed the lily's fragrant flame, —
The gay deceit was done.
No snow-white lily blossomed fair,
There came no perfume on the air;
Only an idle leaf lay there,
And wantoned in the sun."

Under these circumstances, piety dies away till there is nothing left but the name and the form. There is the ritual, the belief, such as it is, but nothing else. It is the symbol of narrowness and bigotry, often of self-conceit, sometimes of envy and malice and all uncharitableness. It leads to no outward work, it produces no inward satisfaction, no harmony with yourself, no concord with your brother, no unity with God. It leads to no real and natural tranquillity, no income of the Holy Spirit, no access of new being, no rest in God. There is the form of godliness, and nothing of its power. Some earnest-minded men see this, and are disgusted with all that bears the name of religion. Do you wonder at this? Remove the cause, as well as blame the consequence.

If pains be taken to cultivate piety, and, as it grows up, if it be left to its own natural development, it will have its own form of manifestation. The feeling of love to God, the Infinite Object, will not continue a mere feeling. Directed to the Infinite Object, it will be directed also towards men, and become a deed. As you love God the more, you must also love men the more, and so must serve them better. Your prayer will not content you, though beautiful as David's loftiest Psalm; you must put it into a practice more lovely yet. Then your prayer will help you, your piety be a real motive, a perpetual blessing. It will increase continually, rising as prayer to come down again as practice, — will first raise "a mortal to the skies," then draw that angel down. So the water which rises in electric ecstasy to heaven, and gleams in the rising or descending sun, comes down as simple dew and rain, to quiet the dust in the common road, to cool the pavement of the heated town, to wash away the unhealthiness of city lanes, and nurse the common grass which feeds the horses and the kine.

At the beginning of your growth in piety, there is, doubtless, need of forms, of special time and place. There need not be another's form, or there may be, just as you like. The girl learning to write imitates carefully each mark on the copy, thinking of the rules for holding the pen. But as you grow, you think less of the form, of the substance more. So the pen becomes not a mere instrument, but almost a limb; the letters are formed even without a thought. Without the form, you have the effect thereof.

If there be piety in the heart, and it be allowed to live and grow and attain its manly form, it will quicken every noble faculty in man. Morality will not be dry, and charity will not be cold; the reason will not grovel with mere ideas, nor the understanding with calculations; the shaft of wit will lose its poison, merriment its levity, common life its tedium. Disappointment, sorrow, suffering, will not break the heart, which will find soothing and comfort in its saddest woe. The consciousness of error, that vexes oft the noble soul, will find some compensation for its grief. Remorse, which wounds men so sadly and so sore, will leave us the sweetest honey, gleaned up from the flowers we trod upon when we should have gathered their richness, and happily will sting us out of our offence.

The common test of Christianity is not the natural sacrament; it is only this poor conventional thing. Look at this. The land is full of Bibles. I am glad of it. I am no worshipper of the Bible, yet I reverence its wisdom, I honor its beauty of holiness, and love exceedingly the tranquil trust in God which its great authors had. Some of the best things that I have ever learned from man this book has taught me. Think of the great souls in this Hebrew Old Testament; of the two great men in the New, — Jesus, who made the great religious motion in the world's parliament, and Paul, who supported it! I am glad the Bible goes everywhere. But men take it for master, not for help; read it as a sacrament, not to get a wiser and a higher light. They worship its letter, and the better spirit of Moses, of Esaias, of the Holy Psalms, so old and yet so young, so everlasting in their beauteous faith in God, — the sublime spirit of one greater than the temple, and lord of the Sabbath, who scorned to put the new wine of God into the old and rotten bags of men — that is not in Christendom. O, no! men do not ask for that. The yeasty soul would rend asunder tradition's leathern bags. Worship of Bibles never made men write Bibles; it hinders us from living them. Worship no things for that; not the created, but, O Creator! let us worship Thee. Catholicism is worship of a church, instead of Gód; Protestantism is worship of a book. Both could not generate a Jesus or a Moses.

For proof of religion men appeal to our churches, built by the self-denial of hard-working men. They prove nothing, — nay, nothing at all. The polygamous Mormons far outdo the Christians in their zeal. The throng of men attending church is small proof of religion. Think of the vain things which lead men to this church or to that; of the vain thoughts which fill them there; of the vain words they hear, or which are only spoke, not even heard! What a small amount of real piety and real morality is needed to make up a popular "Christian!" Alas! we have set up an artificial sacrament; we comply with that, then call ourselves religious, — yea, Christians. We try ecclesiastic metal by its brassy look and brassy ring, then stamp it with the popular image of our idolatry, and it passes current in the shop, tribute fit for Cæsar. The humble publican of the parable, not daring to lift up his eyes to heaven; the poor widow, with her two mites that made a farthing; the outcast Samaritan, with his way-side benevolence to him that fell among the thieves, — might shame forth from the Christian Church each Pharisee who drops his minted and his jingling piety, with brassy noise, into the public chest. Render unto Cæsar the things that be Cæsar's.

The real test of religion is its natural sacrament, — is life. To know whom you worship, let me see you in your shop, let me overhear you in your trade; let me know how you rent your houses, how you get your money, how you keep it, or how it is spent. It is easy to pass the Sunday idle, idly lounging in the twilight of idle words, or basking in the sunshine of some strong man's most earnest speech. It is easy to repeat the words of David, or of Jesus, and to call it prayer. But the sacramental test of your religion is not your Sunday idly spent, not the words of David or of Jesus that you repeat; it is your weekday life, your works, and not your words. Tried by this natural test, the Americans are a heathen people, not religious; far, far from that. Compare us with the Chinese by the artificial standard of the missionary, we are immensely above them; by the natural sacrament of obedience to the law of God, how much is the Christian before the heathen man?

The national test of religion is the nation's justice, — justice to other states abroad, the strong, the weak, and justice to all sorts of men at home. The law-book is the nation's creed; the newspapers chant the actual liturgy and service of the day. What avails it that the priest calls us "Christian," while the newspapers and the Congress prove us infidel? The social sacrament of religion is justice to all about you in society,—is honesty in trade and work, is friendship and philanthropy; the religious strong must help the weak. The ecclesiastical sacrament of a church must be its effort to promote piety and goodness in its own members first, and then to spread it round the world. Care for the bodies and souls of men, that is the real sacrament and ordinance of religion for society, the Church and State.

For the individual man, for you and me, there are two great natural sacraments. One is inward and not directly seen, save by the eye of God and by your own,—the continual effort, the great life-long act of prayer to be a man, with a man's body and a man's spirit, doing a man's duties, having a man's rights, and thereby enjoying the welfare of a man. That is one,—the internal ordinance of religion. The other is like it,—the earnest attempt to embody this in outward life, to make the manly act of prayer a manly act of practice too. These are the only sacraments for the only worship of the only God. Let me undervalue no means of growth, no hope of glory; these are the ends of growth, the glory which men hope.

Is not all this true? You and I,—we all know it. There is but one religion, natural and revealed by nature, — by outward nature poorly and in hints, but by man's inward spirit copiously and at large. It is piety in your prayer; in your practice it is morality. But try the nations, society, the Church, persons, by this sacramental test, and what a spectacle we are! For the religion of the State, study the ends and actions of the State; study the religion of the Church by the doctrines and the practice of the Church; the religion of society, — read it in the great cities of the land. "Thy kingdom come, Thy will be done," prays the minister. Listen to the "Amen" of the courts and the market, responding all the week! The actual religion of mankind is always summed up in the most conspicuous men. Is that religion Christian? Spirit of the Crucified! how we take thy honored name in vain! Yet we did not mean to be led astray: the nations did not mean it; the cities meant it not; the churches prayed for better things; the chief men stumbled and fell. We have altogether mistaken the ordinance of religion, and must mend that.

The New England Indian insisted upon his poor, hungry sacrament; so did the barbarian German; so the Jew, the Catholic, the Protestant; and each sectarian has his Shibboleth of ritual and creed. How poor and puerile are all these things! How puerile and poor the idea of God asking such trifles of mortal man! We shall never mend matters till we take the real religious sacrament, scorning to be deluded longer by such idle shows.

Now it has come to such a pass, that men wish to limit all religion to their artificial sacraments. The natural ordinance of human piety must not be even commended in the church. You must not apply religion to politics; it makes men mad. There is no law of God above the written laws of men. You must not apply it to trade: business is business; religion is religion. Business has the week for his time, the world for his market-place; religion has her Sunday and her meeting-house; let each pursue his own affairs. So the minister must not expose the sins of trade nor the sins of politics. Then, too, public opinion must be equally free from the incursions of piety. "O Religion!" say men, "be busy with thy sacramental creeds, thy sacramental rites, thy crumb of bread, thy sip of wine, thy thimbleful of water sprinkled on a baby's face, but leave the state, the market and all men, to serve the Devil, and be lost." "Very well," says the priest, "I accept the condition. Come and take our blessed religion!"

I began by saying how beautiful is real piety; so let me end. I love to study this in the forms of the past, in the mystic forms of Thomas à Kempis and William Law, in Fenelon and Swedenborg, in John

Tauler, in St. Bernard and St. Victor, in Taylor and Herbert. But there it appears not in its fairest form. I love to see piety at its work better than in its play or its repose; in philanthropists better than in monks and nuns, who gave their lives to contemplation and to wordy prayer, and their bodies to be burned. I love piety embodied in a Gothic or Roman cathedral, an artistic prayer in stone, but better in a nation well fed, well housed, well clad, instructed well, a natural prayer in man or woman. I love the water touched by electric fire, and stealing upwards to the sky, lovely in the light of the uprising or slowly sinking sun. I love it not the less descending down as dew and rain, to still the dust in all the country roads, to cool the pavement in the heated town, to wash the city's dirtiest lane, and in the fields giving grass to the cattle, and bread to men. What is so fair as sentiment, is lovelier as life.

All the triumphs of ancient piety are for you and me; the lofty sentiment, the high resolve, the vision filled with justice, beauty, truth, and love. The great, ascending prayer, the manly consciousness of God, his income to your soul as justice, beauty, truth, and faith and love, — all these wait there for you, — happiness now and here; hereafter the certain blessedness which cannot pass away.

Piety is beautiful in all; to a great man it comes as age comes to the Parthenon or the Pyramids, making what was vast and high majestic, venerable, sublime, and to their beauty giving a solemn awe they never knew before. To men not great, to the commonest men, it also comes, bringing refinement and a loveliness of substance and of shape; so that in a vulgar ecclesiastic crowd they seem like sculptured gems or beryl and of emerald among the common pebbles of the sea.

Piety is beautiful in all relations of life. When your wooing, winsome soul shall wed the won to be your other and superior self, a conscious piety hallows and beautifies the matrimonial vow, — deepens and sanctifies connubial love. When a new soul is added to your household, — a new rose-bud to your bosom, — a bright, particular star dropped from the upper sphere and dazzling in your diadem, — your conscious love of God will give the heavenly visitant the truest, the most prophetic and most blessed baptismal welcome here. And when, out of the circle that twines you round with loving hearts beloved, some one is taken, born out of your family, not into it, a conscious piety will seem to send celestial baptism to the heaven-born soul. And when the mists of age gather about your eye, when the silver cord of life is loosed and the golden bowl at the fountain begins to break, with what a blessed triumph shall you close your mortal sense to this romantic moon and this majestic sun, to the stars of earth that bloom below, the starry flowers that burn above, to open your soul on glory which the eye has not seen, nor yet the heart of man been competent to dream!

"Thy sweetness hath betrayed Thee, Lord!
Dear Spirit! it is Thou;
Deeper and deeper in my heart
I feel Thee nestling now!

"Dear Comforter! Eternal Love!
Yes, Thou wilt stay with me,
If manly thoughts and loving ways
Build but a nest for Thee!"

X.

OF COMMUNION WITH GOD

THE COMMUNION OF THE HOLY GHOST BE WITH YOU ALL. — 2 Cor. xiii. 14.

SIMEON the Stylite lived on the top of the pillar at Antioch for seven-and-thirty-years, for the sake of being nearer to God and holding communion with Him. Some men shut themselves up in convents and nunneries under vows of perpetual asceticism, thinking that God will come into the soul the easier if the flesh be worn thin, the body looped and windowed with bad usage and unnatural hard fare. All the monasteries are designed to produce communion with God. "He dwells," say the priests, "not in the broad way and the green, but in the stillness of the cloister." All the churches in Christendom are built to promote access to Him in various forms. "This is the gate of heaven," says the priest, of his church. All the ritual services are for this end, — to draw God down to men, or draw men up to God; or to appease His "wrath." So also are the mosques of the Mahometans, the synagogues of the Jews, and all the temples of the world. The Pyramids of Egypt, the Parthenon at Athens, St. Peter's at Rome, the Mormon temple at Nauvoo,—all are but the arms of man artificially lengthened and reached out to grasp the Holy Ghost, enfold it to the human heart, and commune with it, soul to soul. The little hymn which a mother teaches her child, cradled on her knee, the solemn litany which England pays her thousand priests to chant each day in every cathedral of the land,—all are for the same end, to promote communion with God. For this the Quaker sits silent in his unadorned meeting-house waiting for the Spirit, lying low in the hand of God to receive His inspiration. For this you and I lift up our hearts in silent or unspoken prayer. The petition for this communion is common to the enlightened of all mankind. It may ascend equally from Catholic or Quaker, from bond and free, from Hebrew, Buddhist, Christian, Mahometan,—from all who have any considerable growth of soul.

I love to look at common life, business and politics, from the stand-point of religion, and hence am thought to be hard upon the sins of the State and the sins of business, trying all things by the higher law of God. But if religion is good for any thing, it is as a rule of conduct for daily life, in the business of the individual and the business of the nation. It is poor policy and bad business that cannot bear to be looked at in the light that lighteneth every man, and tried by the divine measure of all things. It is a poor clock that will not keep the time of the universe.

I love to look at philosophy — science and metaphysics — from the stand-point of religion, and see how the conclusions of the intellect square with the natural instincts of the heart and soul. Then I love to change places, and look at religion and all the spontaneous instincts of the soul, with the eye of the intellect, from the stand-point of philosophy. Hence I am thought to be hard upon the Church; amiable enough toward natural human religion, but cruel toward revealed, divine theology. Yet if the intellect is good for any thing, it is good to try the foundations of religion with. The mind is the eye of consciousness. It is a poor doctrine that cannot bear to be looked at in the dry light of reason. Let us look hard and dry at this notion of communion with God, and by reason severely ascertain if there be such a thing; what it is; how it is to be had; and what comes thereof.

There must be such a thing as communion between God and man. I mean, defining that provisionally, there must be a giving on God's part, and a taking on man's part. To state the matter thus is to make it evident, — since it follows from the nature of God; for from the necessity of his nature the Infinite Being must create and preserve the finite, and to the finite must, in its forms, give and communicate of his own kind. It is according to the infinite nature of God to do so; as according to the finite nature of light to shine, of fire to burn, of water to wet. It follows as well from the nature of man as finite and derivative. From the necessity of his nature, he must receive existence and the means of continuance. He must get all his primitive power, which he starts with, and all his materials for secondary and automatic growth, from the Primitive and Infinite Source. The mode of man's finite being is of necessity a receiving; of God's infinite being, of necessity a giving. You cannot conceive of any finite thing existing without God, the Infinite basis and ground thereof; nor of God existing without something. God is the necessary logical condition of a world, its necessitating cause; a world, the necessary logical condition of God, his necessitated consequence. Communion between the two is a mutual necessity of nature, on God's part and on man's part. I mean it is according to the infinite perfection of God's nature to create, and so objectify Himself, and then preserve and bless whatever He creates. So by His nature He creates, preserves, and gives. And it is according to the finite nature of man to take. So by his nature, soon as created, he depends and receives, and is preserved only by receiving from the Infinite Source.

That is the conclusion of modern metaphysical science. The stream of philosophy runs down from Aristotle to Hegel and Hickok, and breaks off with this conclusion; and I see not how it can be gainsaid. The statements are apodictic, self-evident at every step.

All that is painfully abstract; let me make it plainer if I can, — at least shoot one shaft more at the same mark from the other side. You start with yourself, with nothing but yourself. You are conscious of yourself; not of yourself perhaps as Substance, surely as Power to be, to do, to suffer. But you are conscious of yourself not as self-originated at all, or as self-sustained alone; only as dependent, — first for existence, ever since for support.

You take the primary ideas of consciousness which are inseparable from it, the atoms of self-consciousness; amongst them you find the idea of God. Carefully examined by the scrutinizing intellect, it is the idea of God as Infinite, — perfectly powerful, wise, just, loving, holy, — absolute being, with no limitation. It is this which made you, made all; sustains you, sustains all; made your body, not by a single act, but by a series of acts extending over millions of years, — for man's body is the resultant of all created things; made your spirit, — your mind, your conscience, your affections, your soul, your will; appointed for each its natural mode of action; set each at its several aim. Self-consciousness leads you to consciousness of God; at last to consciousness of Infinite God. He is the Primitive, whence you are the derivative. You must receive, or you could not be a finite man; and He must give, or He could not be the Infinite God. Hence the communion is unavoidable, an ontological fact.

God must be omnipresent in space. There can be no mote that peoples the sunbeams, no spot on an insect's wing, no little cell of life which the microscope discovers in the seed-sporule of a moss, and brings to light, but God is there, in the mote that peoples the sunbeams, in that spot on the insect's wing, in that cell of life the microscope discovers in the seed-sporule of a moss.

God must be also omnipresent in time. There is no second of time elapsing now, there has been none millions of years ago, before the oldest stars began to burn, but God was in that second of time.

Follow the eye of the great space-penetrating telescope at Cambridge into the vast halls of creation, to the furthest nebulous spot seen in Orion's belt, — a spot whose bigness no natural mind can adequately conceive, — and God is there. Follow the eye of the great sharply defining microscope at Berlin into some corner of creation, to that little dot, one of many millions that people an inch of stone, once animate with swarming life, a spot too small for mortal mind adequately to conceive, — and God is there.

Get you a metaphysic microscope of time to divide a second into its billionth part; God is in that. Get you a metaphysic telescope of time, to go back in millenniums as the glass in miles, and multiply the duration of a solar system by itself to get an immensity of time, — still God is there, in each elapsing second of that millennial stream of centuries; His Here conterminous with the all of space, his Now coeval with the all of time.

Through all this space, in all this time, His Being extends, "spreads undivided, operates unspent;" God in all his infinity, — perfectly powerful, perfectly wise, perfectly just, perfectly loving and holy. His being is an infinite activity, a creating, and so a giving of Himself to the world. The world's being is a becoming, a being created and continued. This is so in the nebula of Orion's belt, and in the seed-sporule of the smallest moss. It is so now, and was the same millions of millenniums ago.

All this is philosophy, the unavoidable conclusion of the human mind. It is not the opinion of Coleridge and Kant, but their science; not what they guess, but what they know.

In virtue of this immanence of God in matter, we say the world is a revelation of God; its existence a show of His. Some good books picture to us the shows of things, and report in print the whisper of God which men have heard in the material world. They say that God is a good optician, — for the eye is a telescope and a microscope, the two in one; that He is a good chemist also, ordering all things "by measure and number and weight;" that he is a good mechanic, — for the machinery of the world, old as it is, is yet "constructed after the most approved principles of modern science." All that is true, but the finite mechanic is not in his work; he wakes it and then withdraws. God is in His work, —

> "As full, as perfect in a hair as heart;"
> "Acts not by partial, but by general laws."

All nature works from within; the force that animates it is in every part. It was objected to Sir Isaac Newton's philosophy, that it makes the world all mechanism, which goes without external help, and so is a universe without a God; men thinking that He could not work at all in the world-machine, unless they saw the Great Hand on the crank now and then, or felt the jar of miraculous interposition when some comet swept along the sky. The objection was not just, for the manifold action of the universe is only the Infinite God's mode of operation. Newton merely showed the mode of operation, — that it was constant and wonderful, not changing and miraculous; and so described a higher mode of operation than those men could fathom, or even reverence.

These things being so, all material things that are must needs be in communion with God; their creation was their first passive act of communion; their existence, a continual act of communion. As God is infinite, nothing can be without Him, nothing without communion with Him. The stone I sit on is in communion with God; the pencil I write with; the gray field-fly reposing in the sunshine at my foot. Let God withdraw from the space occupied by the stone, the pencil, and fly, they cease to be. Let Him withdraw any quality of his nature therefrom, and they must cease to be. All must partake of Him, immanent in each and yet transcending all.

In this communion, these and all things receive

after their kind, according to their degree of being and the mode thereof. The mineral, the vegetable, and the animal represent three modes of being, three degrees of existence; and hence so many modes and degrees of dependence on God and of communion with Him. They are, they grow, they move and live, in Him, and by means of Him, and only so. But none of these are conscious of this communion. In that threefold form of being there is no consciousness of God; they know nothing of their dependence and their communion. The water-fowl, in the long pilgrimage of many a thousand miles, knows naught of Him who teaches its way

> "Along that pathless coast,
> The desert and illimitable air,
> Lone wandering, but not lost."

To the dog, man stands for God or devil. The "half-reasoning elephant" knows nobody and is conscious of nothing higher than his keeper, who rides upon his neck, pulling his ears with curved hook. All these are ignorant of God.

We come to man. Here he is, a body and a spirit. The vegetable is matter, and something more; the animal is vegetable also, and something more; man is animal likewise, and something more. So far as I am matter, a vegetable, an animal,— and I am each in part,— I have the appropriate communion of the vegetable, the mineral, the animal world. My body, this hand, for example, is subject to statical, dynamical, and vital laws. God is in this hand; without his infinite existence, its finite existence could not be. It is a hand only by its unconscious communion with Him. It wills nothing; it knows nothing; yet all day long, and all the night, each monad thereof retains all the primary statical and dynamical qualities of matter; continually the blood runs through its arteries and veins, mysteriously forming this complicated and amazing work. Should God withdraw, it were a hand no more; the blood would cease to flow in vein and artery; no monad would retain its primary dynamical and static powers; each atom would cease to be.

All these things, the stone, the pencil, and the fly and hand, are but passive and unconscious communicants of God; they are bare pipes alone into which His omnipotence flows. Yes, they are poor, brute things, which know Him not, nor cannot ever know. The stone and pencil know not themselves; this marvellous hand knows naught; and the fly never says, reasoning with itself, "Lo, here am I, an individual and a conscious thing sucking the bosom of the world." It never separates the Not-me and the Me. But I am conscious; I know myself, and through myself know God. I am a mind to think, a conscience to perceive the just and right; I am a heart to love, a soul to know of God. For communion with my God I have other faculties than what He gives to stone and pencil, hand and fly.

Put together all these things which are not body, and call them Spirit: this spirit as a whole is dependent on God, for creation first, and for existence ever since; it lives only by communion with Him. So far as I am a body, I obviously depend on God, and am no more self-created and self-sufficing than the pencil or the fly. So far as I am a spirit, I depend equally on Him. Should God withdraw Himself or any of His qualities from my mind, I could not think; from conscience, I should know nothing of the right; from the heart, there could be no love; from the soul, then there could be no holiness, no faith in Him that made it. Thus the very existence of the spirit is a dependence on God, and so far a communion with Him.

I cannot wholly separate my spirit from this communion; for that would be destruction of the spirit, annihilation, which is in no man's power. Only the Infinite can create or annihilate an atom of matter or a monad of spirit. There is a certain amount of communion of the spirit with God, which is not conscious; that lies quite beyond my control. I "break into the bloody house of life," and my spirit rushes out of the body, and while the static and dynamic laws of nature reassume their sway over my material husk, rechanging it to dust, still I am, I depend, and so involuntarily commune with God. Even the popular theology admits this truth, for it teaches that the living wicked still commune with God through pain and wandering and many a loss; and that the wicked dead commune with Him through hell against their will, as with their will the heavenly saints through heavenly joy.

I cannot end this communion with my God; but I can increase it, greaten it largely, if I will. The more I live my higher normal life, the more do I commune with God. If I live only as mere body, I have only corporeal and unconscious communion, as a mineral, a vegetable, an animal, no more. As children, we all begin as low as this. The child unborn or newly born has no self-consciousness, knows nothing of its dependence, its spontaneous communion with its God, whereon by laws it depends for being and continuance. As we outgrow our babyhood we are conscious of ourselves, distinguish the Me and the Not-me, and learn at length of God.

I live as spirit, I have spiritual communion with God. Depend on Him I must; when I become self-conscious, I feel that dependence, and know of this communion, whereby I receive from Him.

The quantity of my receipt is largely under my control. As I will, I can have less or more. I cultivate my mind, greatening its quantity; by all its growth I have so much more communion with my Father; each truth I get is a point common to Him and me. I cultivate my conscience, increasing my moral sense; each atom of justice that I get is another point common with the Deity. So I cultivate and enlarge my affections; each grain of love — philanthropic or but friendly — is a new point common to me and God. Then, too, I cultivate and magnify my soul, greatening my sense of holiness, by fidelity to all my nature; and all that I thus acquire is a new point I hold in common with the Infinite. I earnestly desire His truth, His justice, His holiness and love, and He communicates the more. Thus I have a fourfold voluntary consciousness of God through my mind and conscience, heart and soul; know Him as the absolutely true and just and amiable and holy; and thereby have a fourfold voluntary communion with my God. He gives of his infinite kind; I receive in my finite mode, taking according to my capacity to receive.

I may diminish the quantity of this voluntary communion. For it is as possible to stint the spirit of its God, as to starve the body of its food; only not to the final degree, — to destruction of the spirit.

This fact is well known. You would not say that Judas had so much and so complete communion with God as Jesus had. And if Jesus had yielded to the temptation in the story, all would declare that for the time he must diminish the income of God upon his soul. For unfaithfulness in any part lessens the quantity and mars the quality of our communion with the Infinite.

In most various ways men may enlarge the power to communicate with God; complete and normal life is the universal instrumènt thereof. Here is a geologist chipping the stones, or studying the earthquake-waves; here a metaphysian chipping the human mind, studying its curious laws, — psychology, logic, ontology; here is a merchant, a mechanic, a poet, each diligently using his intellectual gift; and as they acquire the power to think, by so much more do they hold intellectual communion with the thought of God, their finite mind communing with the Infinite. My active power of understanding, imagination, reason, is the measure of my intellectual communion with Him.

A man strives to know the everlasting right, to keep a conscience void of all offence; his inward eye is pure and single; all is true to the Eternal Right. His moral powers continually expand, and by so much more does he hold communion with his

God. As far as it can see, his finite conscience reads in the book the Eternal Right of God. A man's power of conscience is the measure of his moral communion with the Infinite.

I repress my animal self-love, I learn to be well-tempered, disinterested, benevolent, friendly to a few, and philanthropic unto all; my heart is ten times greater than ten years ago. To him that hath shall be given according to the quantity and quality of what he has, and I communicate with God so much the more. The greatness of my heart is the measure of my affectional communion with Him.

I cultivate the religious faculty within me, keeping my soul as active as my sense ; I quicken my consciousness of the dear God ; I learn to reverence and trust and love, seeking to keep his every rule of conduct for my sense and soul; I make my soul some ten times larger than it was, and just as I enhance its quantity and quality, so much the more do I religiously commune with God. The power of my religious sense is the measure of my communion with my Father. I feed on this, and all the more I take, the more I grow, and still the more I need.

In all this there is nothing miraculous, nothing mysterious, nothing strange. From his mother's breast it is the largest child that takes the most.

At first a man's spiritual communion is very little, is most exceeding small; but in normal life it becomes more and more continually. Some of you, grown men, can doubtless remember your religious experience when you were children. A very little manna was food enough for your baby-soul. But your character grew more and more, your intellectual, moral, and religious life continually became greater and greater; when you needed much, you had no lack, when little, there seemed nothing over; demand and supply are still commensurate. Nothing is more under our control than the amount of this voluntary communion with God.

> "Misfortunes, do the best we can,
> Will come to great and small."

We cannot help that, but we can progressively enlarge the amount of inspiration we receive from Heaven, spite of the disappointments and sorrows of life; nay, by means thereof.

> "Thy home is with the humble, Lord!
> The simple are Thy rest;
> Thy lodging is in childlike hearts,
> Thou makest there Thy nest."

Sometimes a man makes a conscious and serious effort to receive and enlarge this communion. He looks over his daily life; his eye runs back to childhood, and takes in all the main facts of his outward and inward history. He sees much to mend, something also to approve. Here he erred through passion, there sinned by ambition; the desire from within, leagued with opportunity from without, making temptation too strong for him. He is penitent for the sin that was voluntary, or for the heedlessness whereby he went astray, — sorrowful at his defeat. But he remembers the manly part of him, and with new resolutions braces himself for new trials. He thinks of the powers that lie unused in his own nature. He looks out at the examples of lofty men, his soul is stirred to its deeper depths. A new image of beauty rises, living from that troubled sea, and the Ideal of human loveliness is folded in his arms. "This fair Ideal," says he, "shall be mine. I also will be as whole and beautiful. Ah, me! how can I ever get such lovely life?" Then he thinks of the Eternal Wisdom, the Eternal Justice, the Eternal Love, the Eternal Holiness, which surrounds him, and now fills up his consciousness, waiting to bless. He reaches out his arms towards that Infinite Motherliness which created him at first and preserved him ever since; which surpassed when he fell short, furnishing the great plan of his life and the world's life, and is of all things perfect Cause and Providence. Then, deeply roused in every part, he communicates with the Infinite Mind and Conscience, Heart and Soul. He is made calmer by the thought of the immense tranquillity which enfolds the nervous world in its all-embracing, silent arms. He is comforted by the motherly aspect of that Infinite Eye, which never slumbers in its watch over the suffering of each great and every little thing, converting it all to good. He is elevated to confidence in himself, when he feels so strong in the never-ending love which makes, sustains, and guides the world of matter, beasts, and men; makes from perfect motives, sustains with perfect providence, and guides by perfect love to never-ending bliss. Yea, the tranquillity, pity, love, of the Infinite Mother enters into his soul, and he is tranquil, soothed, and strong, once more. He has held communion with his God, and the Divine has given of the Deity's own kind. His artistic fancy and his plastic hand have found an Apollo in that pliant human block.

That is a prayer. I paint the process out in words, — they are not my prayer itself, only the cradle of my blessed heavenly babe. I paint it not in words, — it is still my prayer, not less the aspiration of my upward-flying soul. I carry my child cradled only in my arms.

I have this experience in my common and daily life, with no unusual grief to stir, or joy to quicken, or penitence to sting me into deep emotion: then my prayer is only a border round my daily life, to keep the web from ravelling away through constant use and wear; or else a fringe of heaven, whereby I beautify my common consciousness and daily work.

But there strikes for me a greater hour; some new joy binds me to this, or puts another generation into my arms; another heart sheds its life into my own; some great sorrow sends me in upon myself and God; out of the flower of self-indulgence the bee of remorse stings me into agony. And then I rise from out my common consciousness, and take a higher, wider flight into the vast paradise of God, and come back laden from the new and honeyed fields wherein I have a newer and a fresher life and sweeter communings with loftier loveliness than I had known before. Thus does the man, that will, hold commune with his Father, face to face, and get great income from the Soul of all.

In all this there is nothing miraculous; there has been no change on God's part, but a great change on man's. We have received what He is universally giving. So in winter it is clear and cold, the winds are silent, clouds gather over the city's face, and all is still. How cold it is! In a few hours the warmth steals out from the central fire,—the earth's domestic, household hearth; the clouds confine it in, those airy walls, that it flee not off, nor spread to boundless space; the frost becomes the less intense, and men are gladdened with the milder day. So, when magnetic bars in time have lost their force, men hang them up in the line of the meridian, and the great loadstone, the earth, from her own breast, restores their faded magnetism. Thus is it that human souls communicate with the great central Fire and Light of all the world, the loadstone of the universe, and thus recruit, grow young again, and so are blessed and strong.

There may be a daily, conscious communion with God, marked by reverence, gratitude, aspiration, trust, and love; it will not be the highest prayer.

> "'T is the most difficult of tasks to keep
> Heights that the soul is competent to gain."

And the highest prayer is no common event in a man's life. Ecstasy, rapture, great delight in prayer, or great increase thereby, — they are the rarest things in the life of any man. They should be rare. The tree blossoms but once a year; blooms for a week, and then fulfils and matures its fruit in the long months of summer and of harvest-time, — fruit for a season, and seed for many an age. The sun is but a moment at meridian. Jesus had his temptation but once, but once his agony, — the two foci round which his life's beauteous ellipse was drawn. The intensest consciousness of friendship does not last long. They say men have but once the ecstasy of love; human nature could not bear such a continual strain. So all the blossomings of rapture must needs be short. The youthful ecstasy of love leads man and maid by moonlight up the steep, sheer cliffs of life, "while all below, the world in mist lies lost;" then, in the daylight of marriage they walk serenely on, along the high table-land of mortal life, and though continually greatening their connubial love and joy, it is without the early ecstasy.

Men sometimes seek to have their daily prayer high and ecstatic as their highest hour and walk with God; it cannot be; it should not be. Some shut themselves up in convents to make religion their business, — all their life; to make an act of prayer their only act. They always fail; their religion dwindles into ritual service, and no more; their act of prayer is only kneeling with the knees and talking talk with windy tongues. A Methodist, in great ecstasy of penitence or fear, becomes a member of a church. He all at once is filled with rapturous delight; religious joy blossoms in his face, and glitters in his eye. How glad is the converted man!

> "Then when he kneels to meditate,
> Sweet thoughts come o'er his soul,
> Countless, and bright, and beautiful,
> Beyond his own control."

But by and by his rapture dies away, and he is astonished that he has no such ecstasy as before. He thinks that he has "fallen from grace," has "grieved away" the Holy Ghost, and tries by artificial excitement to bring back what will not come without a new occasion. Certain religious convictions once made my heart spring in my bosom. Now it is not so. The fresh leaping of the heart will only come from a fresh conquest of new truth. The old man loves his wife a thousand times better than when, for the first time, he kissed her gracious mouth; but his heart burns no longer as when he first saw his paradise in her reciprocating eye. The tree of religious consciousness is not in perpetual blossom, — but now in leaf, now flower, now fruit.

It is a common error to take no heed of this voluntary communion with God, to live intent on business or on pleasure, careful, troubled about many things, and seldom heed the one thing needed most; to take that as it comes. If all this mortal life turned out just as we wished it, this error would be still more common; only a few faculties would get their appropriate discipline. Men walking only on a smooth and level road use the same muscles always, and march like mere machines. But disappointment comes on us. Sorrow checks our course, and we are forced to think and feel, — must march now up hill, and then down, shifting the strain from part to part. In mere prosperity most men are contented to enlarge their estate, their social rank, their daily joy, and lift their children's faces to the vulgar level of the vulgar flood whereon their fathers float. There comes some new adventure to change and mend all this. Now it is a great joy, success not looked for, — some kindred soul is made one with us, and on the pinions of instinctive connubial love we fly upwards and enlarge our intercourse with God, — the object of passion a communion angel to lead the human soul to a higher seat in the universe and a more intimate acquaintance with the Soul of all. Sometimes the birth of a new immortal into our arms does this, and on the pinions of instinctive affection men soar up to heaven and bring back healing on their wings, — the object of affection the communion angel to convey and welcome them to heaven.

Sometimes it is none of these, but sorrow, grief, and disappointment that do this. I set my heart upon a special thing; — it is not mine, or if I get the honor, the money, the social rank I sought, it was one thing in my eye and another in my grasp. The one bird which I saw in the bush was worth ten like that I hold in my hand. The things I loved are gone, — the maid, the lover, husband, wife, or child; the mortal is taken from longing arms. The heart looks up for what can never die. Then there is a marriage and a birth, not into your arms, but out of them and into heaven; and the sorrow and the loss stir you to woo and win that Object of the soul which cannot pass away. Your sorrow takes you on her wings, and you go up higher than before; higher than your success, higher than friendship's daily wing ascends; higher than your early love for married mate had ever borne you up; higher than the delight in your first-born child or latest born. You have a new communion with your Father, and get a great amount of inspiration from Him.

This is the obvious use of such vicissitudes, and seems a portion of their final cause. In the artificial, ecclesiastical life of monasteries, men aim to reproduce this part of nature's discipline, and so have times of watching, fasting, bodily torture. But in common life such discipline asks not our consent to come.

As I look over your faces and recall the personal history of those I know, I see how universal is this disappointment. But it has not made you more melancholy and less manly men; life is not thereby the less a blessing, and the more a load. With no sorrows you would be more sorrowful. For all the sorrows that man has faithfully contended with, he shall sail into port deeper fraught with manliness. The wife and mother at thirty years of age imprisoned in her chair, her hands all impotent to wipe a tear away, does not suffer for nothing. She has thereby been taught to taste the fruits of sweeter communion with her God. These disappointments are rounds in the ladder whereby we climb to heaven.

In cities there is less to help us communicate with God than in the fields. These walls of brick and stone, this artificial ground we stand on, all remind us of man; even the city horse is a machine. But in the country it is God's ground beneath our feet; God's hills on every side; his heaven, broad, blue, and boundless, overhead; and every bush and every tree, the morning song of earliest birds, the chirp of insects at mid-day, the solemn stillness of the night, and the mysterious hosts of stars that all night long climb up the sky, or silently go down, — these continually affect the soul, and cause us all to feel the Infinite Presence, and draw near to that; and earth seems less to rest in space than in the love of God. So, in cities, men build a great church, — at London, Paris, Venice, or at Rome, — seeking to compensate for lack of the natural admonitions of the woods and sky; and, to replace the music of the fields and nature's art, enlist the painter's plastic hand and the musician's sweetest skill.

All that seek religion are in search for communion with God. What is there between Him and thee? Nothing but thyself. Each can have what inspiration each will take. God is continually giving; He will not withhold from you or me. As much ability as He has given, as much as you have enlarged your talent by manly use, so much will He fill with inspiration. I hold up my little cup. He fills it full. If yours is greater, rejoice in that, and bring it faithfully to the same urn. He who fills the violet with beauty, and the sun with light,—who gave to Homer his gift of song, such reason to Aristotle, and to Jesus the manly gifts of justice and the womanly grace of love and faith in Him,—will not fail to inspire also you and me. Were your little cup to become as large as the Pacific sea, He still would fill it full.

There is such a thing as having a godly heart, a desire to conform to the ideal of man in all things, and to be true to Him that is "of all Creator and Defence." He who has that is sure of conscious spiritual communion with the Father; sure to find his character enlarging in every manly part; sure to be supplied with unexpected growth, and to hold more of the Divine; sure of the voluntary inspiration which is proper to the self-conscious man.

There are continual means of help even for men who dwell hedged up in towns. There are always living voices which can speak to us. A good book helps one; this feeds his soul for a time on the fair words of David, Paul, or John, Taylor, À Kempis, Wordsworth, Emerson; that, on the life of him who gives a name to Christendom. He who has more than I, will help me; him that has less, I shall help. Some men love certain solemn forms, as aids to their devotion; I hope that they are helped thereby, — that baptism helps the sprinkler or the wet; that circumcision aids the Jew, and sacrifice the heathen who offers it. But these are not the communion, only at most its vehicle. Communion is the meeting of the finite and the Infinite.

If a man have a truly pious soul, then his whole inward, outward life will at length become religion; for the disposition to be true to God's law will appear the same in his business as in his Sunday vow. His whole work will be an act of faith, he will grow greater, better, and more refined by common life, and hold higher communion with the Ever-Present; the Sun of righteousness will beautify his every day.

God is partial to no one, foreign to none. Did he

inspire the vast soul of Moses, — the tender hearts of lowly saints in every clime and every age? He waits to come down on you and me, a continual Pentecost of inspiration. Here in the crowded vulgar town, everywhere, is a Patmos, a Sinai, a Gethsemane; the Infinite Mother spreads wide her arms to fold us to that universal breast, ready to inspire your soul. God's world of truth is ready for your intellect; His ocean of justice waits to flow in upon your conscience; and all His heaven of love broods continually by night and day over each heart and every soul. From that dear bounty shall we be fed. The Motherly Love invites all, — as much communion as we will, as much inspiration as our gifts and faithfulness enable us to take. He is not far from any one of us. Shall we not all go home, — the prodigal rejoice with him that never went astray? Even the consciousness of sin brings some into nearness with the Father, tired of their draff and husks; and then it is a blessed sin. Sorrow also brings some, and then it is a blessed grief; joy yet others, and then it is blessed thrice. In this place is one greater than the temple, greater than all temples; for the human nature of the lowliest child transcends all human history. And we may live so that all our daily life shall be a continual approach and mounting up towards God. What is the noblest life? Not that born in the most famous place, acquiring wealth and fame and rank and power over matter and over men; but that which, faithful to itself continually, holds communion with the Infinite, and, thence receiving of God's kind, in mortal life displays the truth, the justice, holiness, and love of God.

> "O, blessed be our trials then,
> This deep in which we lie;
> And blessed be all things that teach
> God's dear Infinity."

END.

The following works of Mr. Parker may be had of Messrs. Little, Brown & Co.:—

A DISCOURSE OF MATTERS PERTAINING TO RELIGION. 3d Ed. 1847. 1 vol. 12mo. $1.25.

AN INTRODUCTION TO THE OLD TESTAMENT, FROM THE GERMAN OF DE WETTE. 2d Ed. 1850. 2 vols. 8vo. $3.75.

CRITICAL AND MISCELLANEOUS WRITINGS. 1843. 1 vol. 12mo. $1.25.

ADDRESSES AND OCCASIONAL SERMONS. 1852. 2 vols. 12mo. $2.50.

TEN SERMONS OF RELIGION. 1852. 1 vol. 12mo. $1.

SERMONS OF THEISM, ATHEISM, AND THE POPULAR THEOLOGY. 1853. 1 vol. 12mo. $1.25.

ADDITIONAL SPEECHES, ADDRESSES, AND OCCASIONAL SERMONS. 1855. 2 vols. 12mo. $2.50.

PAMPHLETS.—*Sermons on the following Subjects:—*

OF OLD AGE. 1854. 15 cents.

OF THE NEW CRIME AGAINST HUMANITY. 1854. 20 cents.

OF THE LAWS OF GOD AND THE STATUTES OF MEN. 1854. 15 cents.

OF THE DANGERS WHICH THREATEN THE RIGHTS OF MAN IN AMERICA. 1854. 20 cents.

OF THE MORAL DANGERS INCIDENT TO PROSPERITY. 1855. 15 cents.

OF THE CONSEQUENCES OF AN IMMORAL PRINCIPLE. 1855. 15 cents.

www.ingramcontent.com/pod-product-compliance
Lightning Source LLC
LaVergne TN
LVHW020110110826
845151LV00001B/119

* 9 7 8 1 4 2 5 5 4 3 8 8 4 *